ride the digital wave with

Verbum

the journal of personal computer aesthetics

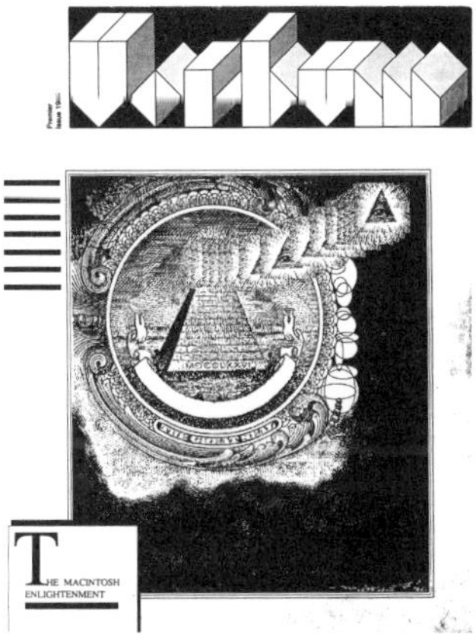

1.0 – 1986 (out of print)

1.1 – early 1987

1.2 – mid-1987

1.3 – late 1987

2.1 – Spring 1988

2.2 – Summer 1988

for graphics professionals, desktop publishers, and those interested in the new culture of pc art and creativity

to subscribe and order back issues, see reverse

MAKING ART ON THE MACINTOSH II

MAKING ART *on the* MACINTOSH II

Michael Gosney
Linnea Dayton

Scott, Foresman and Company
Glenview, Illinois London

Produced by Donovan Gosney Productions, San Diego

Book cover art and book design:
John Odam
Production:
Mark Siprut
Martha Siebert
Anthony Barnes
Production editing:
Beth Ingram
Technical consultation:
Jack Davis
Research and administrative:
Brian Duck
Jeanne Juneau
Photography, location and screen shots:
Craig McClain
Linotronic output:
Stephanie Whalen, Professional Printing Services, San Diego;
Central Graphics, San Diego; Thompson Type, San Diego

PRODUCTION NOTES: All pages were composed with *PageMaker 3.0*. Proofs were run on an AST Turbo Laser printer. Pages were output on RC paper on a Linotronic L-300 imagesetter at 1270 dpi, except for grayscale halftones, which were output as negatives at 2540 dpi and stripped in place.

Library of Congress Cataloging-in-Publication Data

Gosney, Michael.
Making art on the Macintosh II/Michael Gosney, Linnea Dayton
ISBN 0-673-38159-5
1. Macintosh II (computer) 2. Computer graphics. 3. Electronic publishing.
I. Dayton, Linnea, 1944- . II. Title. III. Title: Making art on the Macintosh 2.
IV. Title: Making art on the Macintosh Two.
QA76.8.M32G687 1989
OO6.6'765--dc19 88-26507
1 2 3 4 5 6 RRC 93 92 91 90 89 88 CIP

ISBN 0-673-38159-5

Printed in the United States of America

Scott, Foresman professional books are available for bulk sales at quantity discounts. For information, please contact Marketing Manager, Professional Books Group, Scott, Foresman and Company, 1900 East Lake Avenue, Glenview, IL 60025.

Preface

In 1984 at a small publishing house, we were producing some of the early books about the Macintosh. I took our 128 K office Mac home and swapped disks late at night, experimenting with *MacPaint* and *MacDraw*. I remembered how as a kid I had taken to the Etch-A-Sketch. And I had always enjoyed working with technical pens on black-and-white compositions. As did many, I saw this Macintosh with its icons and graphic screen effects – kind of a friendly little robot head – as a remarkable convergence of aesthetics and high technology. When the *PageMaker* program and LaserWriter were introduced, it became clear that something significant was happening. As a small-press book publisher, I was very much aware of the cost constraints of typesetting and layout for short-run books and magazines. The electronic composition and laser type looked promising. As a communications professional with a proclivity for experimental design and art (as well as writing), I also couldn't help being fascinated with the creative possibilities.

In late 1985, I developed a one-man show of Macintosh art, held at a coffehouse gallery in San Diego. The exhibit, called "Macintosh Verbum" featured about ten limited-edition laserprints, six color dot-matrix monoprints, two large photocopies, and three large serigraphs all printed on archival cotton paper, signed, and numbered. Much of the work contained written elements, an idea carried forward from my pen-and-ink work, made more appealing by the Mac's built-in type capabilities. At the Quel Fromage opening, I also had my 512 running with a Slide Show Magician piece that contained a variety of bit-mapped works, ThunderScans, and poetry. I sold this "Macintosh Verbum Slide Show" on signed and numbered floppy disks (the multicolored kind, without labels, signed on the plastic). It was all an enjoyable experiment – to see if this new kind of art had any real appeal in a fine-art context. While many were enthusiastic or at least curious, quite a number were completely baffled and even angry. The concept of "computer art" just didn't compute with some people, especially some artists. I took much of the Macintosh Verbum show to the San Francisco Macworld Expo in January 1986 where Jim Fitzsimmons mounted it with works by Australian Mac artist Malcolm Thain in a spur-of-the-moment exhibit. Passersby in the convention hall, then filled with young Mac enthusiasts in blue jeans, shook their heads and said things like "Only on the Mac," "Cool! How did you *do* that?" and (looking at the silkscreens) "Look – it's printed in *color!*"

I began using the Mac and LaserWriter in 1986 for some advertising work, but realized the real benefit initally in preparing professional proposals and reports without involved secretarialassistance. Then the publisher of *MACazine* hired us to redesign that magazine and handle their covers and editorial art on a monthly basis. This eight-month assignment provided a great opportunity to develop Mac illustrations with a variety of artists.

In the fall of 1986, we published the original *Verbum 1.0*. It contained no writing, no ads — just art: much of my Macintosh Verbum work and works from several artists, including Australian Malcolm Thain, Frenchman Jean Solé, Jack Davis, Michael Green, Nathan Weedmark, Ed Roxburgh, Jim Hance, and Jim Pollock. We received such an enthusiastic response to this 1000-copy art journal, that we launched the magazine as a formal quarterly in January of 1987. Our mission was to help facilitate the emergence of personal computer art.

Then came the Mac II introduction. When I first saw one up close at AppleWorld in Los Angeles, it was playing Peter Gabriel's "Red Rain." I began to perceive the incredible power it was going to bring to the embryonic desktop publishing and design arena, as well as other creative fields. I proposed a book to cover it all.

Linnea and I realized, a few months after we began work on the manuscript for *Making Art on the Macintosh II*, that we had a tiger by the tail. In developing the project, we depended on the talents of several individuals, without whose help it just wouldn't have happened. Sal Parascandolo reported on the programs covered in the "Making Art" section after dissecting them with surgical precision. Jack Davis, that intrepid digital experimenter, gave us his technical guidance, not to mention many excellent art samples. We also benefitted from our relationship with Jack's Macintosh graphics lab at San Diego's Platt College, with student work for samples and access to equipment. Steve Hannaford assisted us with the output section, and Bencion Calica contributed tips and material for the chapters on commmunications and mass storage. John Odam gave us his usual wit, and also just a little help on the cover and book design. Mark Siprut and Martha Siebert did a heroic job of *PageMaker* layout, offering final design touches and critical consultation during the process. Literary agent Bill Gladstone put us together with Scott, Foresman and Company. Amy Davis, our editor there, has been tremedously supportive, and patient, as we've attempted to keep pace with our subject and manifest a real book. Lastly, the *Verbum* community – our staff, local suppliers, contributing artists from around the country and world, writers, and industry people – all contributed to the development of this book. We'd like to thank everyone for their good will and hard work.

And we'd like to thank you for buying the book. Live long and prosper – making art on the Macintosh II!

— Michael Gosney

Contents

PART IV – SUPPORT TOOLS

APPENDICES

Introduction

Welcome! We hope *Making Art on the Macintosh II* will help you recognize and master the Mac II's amazing capabilities. Although the book was written specifically for Mac II users, much of the information about hardware, software, and principles of making art also applies to the Mac Plus and Mac SE.

Making Art on the Macintosh II offers comprehensive coverage of the graphic arts applications and hardware available for the Mac II. The book provides basic information, tips, sidebars (boxes), figures, and, in Part II, galleries of art for reference. We recommend that you browse the entire book, and then refer to specific sections as needed for purchasing decisions, technical guidance, and creative reference.

Part I, "Know Thy Mac," is an overview of the Mac II system. The Mac II manual, Macintosh magazines, and books on the technical aspects of the Mac II all will supplement the information presented here.

In Part II, "Making Art," we cover the leading graphics applications, grouped in the categories of "Painting," "Drawing," "PostScript Illustration," "Digitizing," "Desktop Publishing," and "Presentation Graphics." Each of the first five chapters in Part II contains a gallery of art samples, and following Chapter 8 is the color gallery, with 16 pages of sample images organized in the same sequence as the preceding chapters. The gallery material, particularly in "Desktop Publishing," shows the importance of using several applications together to achieve desired results. It's important to learn the distinction between the general application categories, to know how to use different types of applications in concert, and of course, how to use given applications well.

Part III, "Output," reviews the various processes, programs, and hardware involved in printing. As enjoyable as it is to interact with the Mac II and see your inspiration take form on the high-resolution screen, good-looking output is the goal.

Part IV surveys the "Support Tools" needed for a fully functional Mac II graphic art work-station – from fonts and desk accessories to hard disk drives. Understanding and using these tools can make a positive difference in productivity and can enhance the quality of your results.

Finally, the Appendices provide complete product listings and information on other resources for the Mac graphic artist.

The Macintosh II is the current culmination of the desktop revolution, a revolution we tend to think of as a microchip-related happening, a phenomenon of the last decade or so. But the desktop revolution has been going on for years. Lewis Waterman was part of it when he invented the fountain pen in 1884, freeing entrepreneurs from their ink wells and making it easier for them to go outside the office in search of more business. In 1874 gun manufacturer E. Remington & Sons introduced typewriters to the marketplace, greatly enhancing our ability to communicate from the desktop. And the phonograph that Thomas Edison invented in 1877 was designed to be a dictating machine.

Many improvements, some of them more revolutionary than others, have occurred over the years: electric typewriters and correcting ribbons, for example. The look of the pages generated by desktop equipment improved, too, as typewritten strove to imitate typeset.

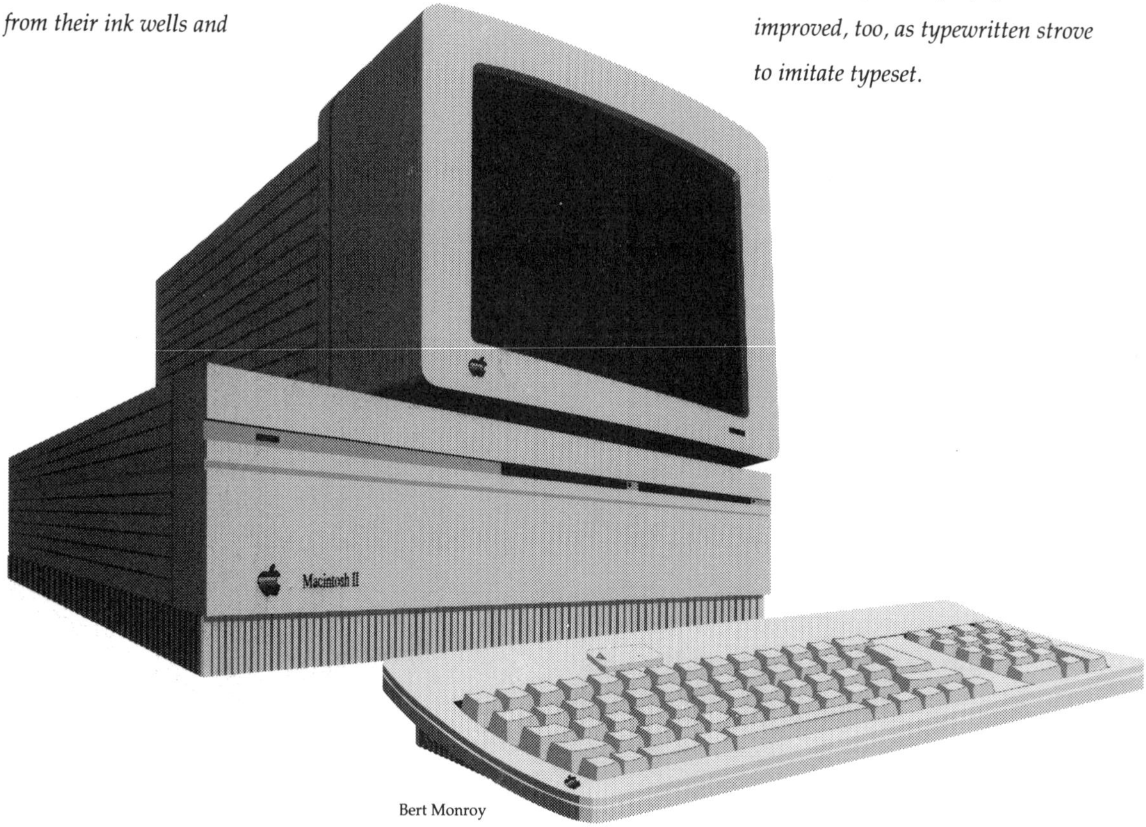

Bert Monroy

PART ONE

KNOW THY MAC

Computers came along, big ones at first. With electronic miniaturization came minicomputers, with tremendous calculating and sorting power locked into a package about the size of a small refrigerator. Used for computational purposes at first, computers became the basis for corporate word processing centers — centers that efficiently turned out machine-typed material for review and revision, and a final typed "original" good enough to send outside the corporate walls. Mini became micro, and microcomputers came forth, multiplied, and have pretty well filled the earth. Having begun as terminals, or workstations (satellite brains attached to the mainframe via nerves of cable), micros soon gained independence as personal computers, giving the user increased efficiency and control.

And where was the graphic artist during all this? Mostly elsewhere. A few artists became involved in high-end, high-tech production of animation and special effects for film and video, using expensive hardware and software especially designed for those purposes. Some played fairly primitive computerized video games on inexpensive pcs hooked up to their TV sets.

But mostly, graphic artists didn't find much use for the metal and plastic computing machines that stared up from the desktop with their alien floppies and F keys. Mostly, though they didn't know it, they were waiting for the Macintosh.

CHAPTER 1

Evolution of a Revolution

The Macintosh II is the culmination of a fascinating product evolution. Its sophisticated user interface, powerful graphics processing capabilities, and advanced software add up to a truly revolutionary art-making tool.

FROM INCEPTION TO THE MAC II

The world first experienced Macintosh in January 1984. You may remember the famous "1984" television commercial that stunned Super Bowl viewers with a vision of Macintosh as saviour in a world dominated by the "Big Brother" of centralized computers. The Mac's mouse-driven, graphical interface with icons and pull-down menus appealed immediately to artists and others who had resisted the world of A> prompts and arcane command sequences. *MacPaint*, an elegant bitmapped drawing program with electronic equivalents of many of the traditional artist's tools, came bundled with each Mac (along with the *MacWrite* word processor). The ImageWriter dot matrix printer provided graphics output that looked just like the 72 dots per linear inch (dpi) that appeared on the screen. The 128 K Mac, combined with *MacPaint* and the ImageWriter, formed the first truly friendly — and aesthetically stimulating — computer system. It piqued the interest of thousands of artists and brought many into the personal computer revolution. But it was just the beginning.

To get to the present, we have to backtrack a little further, to a time before the Macintosh machine. The Mac had a predecessor: Apple's Lisa. This was a higher-priced machine (about $10,000 with an internal 10 Mb hard disk) geared for the business market. It boasted the same user interface later used in the Mac, but with a few holdover features from command-driven systems. The use of a mouse, icons, pull-down menus, and windows introduced on the Lisa and refined on the Mac was a technology originally developed by Xerox's Palo Alto Research Center. Apple co-founder Steve Jobs, the father of the original

Macintosh, saw the potential of this "intuitive" interface and licensed the technology for use in the new Apple products. Although the Lisa was eventually discontinued, the Mac made a success of the new user interface. Within 90 days of the Mac's launch, over 50,000 had been sold and a third pc standard had been established.

In the fall of 1985, Apple introduced the LaserWriter and the AppleTalk network that could connect several Macs to the advanced new printer. The Macintosh-LaserWriter-AppleTalk combination was a dramatic step in the evolution of the revolution. The LaserWriter provided high-resolution, near-typeset-quality output. Meanwhile, software developers improved some of the features of *MacPaint* and added new ones to produce programs better suited to graphic artists. Most important, Aldus Corporation introduced a page composition program called *PageMaker*. This program, combined with the Mac's interface and the superior print quality of the LaserWriter, ignited the explosive new market known as "desktop publishing," and further stimulated artists to use these high-tech tools.

Apple responded to criticisms of the original Mac — that it had too little internal memory (either 128 or 512 K) and was too slow — by introducing the Mac Plus in early 1986. It had three key improvements: a double-sided (800 K) disk drive, a full 1 Mb of memory, and a high-speed port for connection to hard disk drives. The Plus was well received by the business community and became Apple's flagship machine.

In March 1987, Apple introduced the long-awaited new generation Macintosh. Along with the Mac SE — a completely redesigned basic Macintosh that was functionally the same as the Plus except for improved speed, a better power supply, and a single expansion slot — Apple presented the Mac II. Code-named Paris and then Cabernet, it had been talked about for two years as the "color Mac," the "open Mac," the "IBM-compatible Mac." When finally unveiled at the AppleWorld gathering of 3000 key marketers, educators, and press representatives, it was all these things and more. It sported the fast new 68020 Motorola chip, six expansion slots, and a high-resolution color monitor. The new pc introduced itself to the crowd by playing a color animation of a sun rising over a landscape to a classical music score. (Three years before, the original Mac had introduced itself at the Apple shareholders' meeting by talking to the crowd and introducing Steve Jobs as "a man who's been like a father to me.")

The Mac II, although winning instant converts from all market segments, didn't ship in quantity until the fall of 1987, and Apple's color monitors weren't readily available until January of 1988. The new platform represented by the Mac II is only now being realized, with the availability of new and updated software and advanced peripheral hardware. It's an amazing machine, encompassing the existing Macintosh world and opening a significantly expanded universe. The Mac II is an exciting computer for many applications. But one of the most exciting is its role as an advanced desktop publishing and graphic art workstation. The Macintosh II is one of the key factors in the technological revolution that's currently transforming the graphics professions.

AMAZING CAPABILITIES

What makes the Mac II different from its predecessors and so appropriate for desktop publishing and graphics? Earlier Macintosh machines were built and marketed as self-contained units — complete, optimally configured, "plug-and-play" personal computers. Not only did the folks at Apple consider it unnecessary for anyone to make additions or

Figure 1-1. A Mac II workstation optimized for graphic art: 5 Mb RAM, two 800 K floppy drives, internal 80 Mb Apple hard drive, 19" SuperMac Technology color monitor, Microtek scanner, and Summagraphics tablet.

changes to customize the machine, they purposely made it difficult for the user to make modifications. But the Macintosh II was designed to be different. Developed for the expanding range of desktop roles for which people were using the Macintosh, the Mac II is a high-performance personal collection of components (Figure 1-1). You can pick and choose from among many options to put together the system that works best for you.

The **Main Unit**, or System Unit, of the Mac II includes:

- The **central processing unit (CPU)**, which does most of the work of the computer, and a math coprocessor.
- 1 megabyte (1 million bytes, or characters; abbreviated 1 Mb) of random access **memory** (RAM), where the Mac II stores programs and data while you are using them. The motherboard that houses the 68020 and the RAM also allows you to expand memory to 8 Mb with 1 Mb chips (simple in-line memory modules, or SIMMs).

Figure 1-2. Mac II connections for peripherals, on the Main Unit.

- An **Apple Desktop Bus (ADB)** and **SCSI** and **serial ports** allow attachment of the keyboard, the mouse, external disk drives, and other peripheral components. All of these connections are on the back of the Main Unit (Figure 1-2).
- The **power supply**, which allows the computer to run on either 120 VAC or 240 VAC at 50 or 60 Hz. This makes the Mac II useful worldwide. The Mac II automatically configures itself (sets itself up internally) to run on the type of power provided.
- **NuBus**, an interface that provides six expansion slots to accept cards that add capabilities to your Mac II. ("Customizing Your Machine" in Chapter 2 tells about some of these options.) One of the six expansion slots must be used for a video output card, as described in "Video Output" later in this chapter.

- Mass data storage. You can get your Mac II with either one or two internal 800 kilobyte (abbreviated K; 1000 bytes) **floppy disk drives**. A **hard disk** (with 20, 40, or 80 Mb) can also be installed internally, or an external hard disk can be attached as a peripheral component.

Peripheral components, those not built into the Main Unit, include:

- The **mouse**, which moves the pointer around the screen and through which you interact with the Mac II. The mouse attaches via a connector on the keyboard or through one of the Apple Bus connectors.
- The **keyboard**. The standard keyboard has 81 keys, including a numeric keypad and arrow keys for moving the cursor around the screen. Apple's extended 105-key keyboard also includes 15 function keys.
- One or more external **hard disk drives** can be connected to the Mac II through the SCSI ports. Other mass storage devices (see Chapter 23, "Mass Storage") can be added to provide ready access to even more data.
- At least one **monitor**. Apple offers both a black-and-white and a color monitor, and third parties offer more of both (see "Customizing Your Machine" in Chapter 2). Apple's 12-inch high-resolution monochrome monitor has a density of 76 dots per linear inch (dpi), and the high-resolution red-green-blue (RGB) monitor provides 69 dpi.

Power, Speed, and the 68020

The real power of the Mac II hardware is in the Motorola 68020 processor. First of all, it can move data 32 bits at a time, twice as many bits at once as the 16-bit data paths of the 68000 processor used in the Mac Plus and SE. Not only does the 68020 move the data in bigger bunches, it moves the bunches twice as fast — at 16 MHz instead of 8 MHz. Doubling both the data-handling capacity and the speed quadruples the performance of the 68020 over the 68000.

The Mac II's 68881 floating point coprocessor assists the 68000 on math calculations, dramatically improving the speed of applications requiring intensive arithmetic calculations, such as 3D programs.

NuBus

The processor isn't the only part of the Mac II responsible for its speed. The NuBus is a high-speed, 32-bit industry standard bus that lets information travel between the expansion cards and main memory at the rate of 10 Mb per second. In addition, many expansion cards contain coprocessors, separate processors that can execute programs on their cards independently of the 68020 Mac II processor. For example, the optional Page Memory Management Unit card includes a 68851 coprocessor for adding memory beyond the standard maximum 8 Mb. Most expansion card coprocessors bypass the 68020 CPU and communicate directly with a designated area of the Mac II's memory. This means that the CPU doesn't have to interrupt what it's doing to receive information from peripheral devices controlled by such expansion cards. So both the CPU and the NuBus-connected peripherals work faster.

Besides improving operating speed, NuBus boards provide an advantage over the expansion cards used in other personal computer systems. The expansion capability gained from the Mac II's six slots doesn't bring a lot of configuration headaches with it, because the NuBus **configuration ROM** allows the Mac II to recognize what board is in which slot and to set up the system so the cards don't conflict with each other. That means you don't have to pore over manuals to figure out how to set DIP switches. You just plug the boards in, and the Mac II takes over from there.

NuBus plays a role in Mac II memory expansion as well. If the 8 Mb of RAM that can fit on the motherboard is not enough, through the NuBus you can add as much as 4 gigabytes of RAM.

Video Output

Apple's standard video card uses 256 K of RAM to produce both monochrome and color output signals for the monitor(s) of your choice. Apple also offers an expanded video card (described in "Gray Scale" and "Color" in this section), and other vendors provide their own video cards to operate the monitors they market. Choosing a monitor is discussed in Chapter 2.

Gray Scale

Previous Macintosh computers used only 1 bit (on/off signal) of information to define each pixel on the monitor screen, so that pixel could be only black (off) or white (on). The Mac II can use 4, 8, or 24 bits to describe each pixel. Each bit regulates a particular level of pixel light intensity, and each bit can be off or on. The effect of the bits is additive. Between all bits off (black) and all bits on (white), there are 254 other levels of brightness, providing a total of 256 possible shades of gray. Keeping track of 256 possibilities for each of the hundreds of thousands of pixels on the screen would require a lot of memory, so the Mac II equipped with the standard video card with 256 K of RAM uses only 16 shades of gray at a time. Enhanced with an expansion kit that doubles the RAM on the video card and equipped with a monitor capable of producing all the light intensity levels, the Mac II can display all 256 shades of gray at once.

Color

Supporting a color monitor, the video card can specify levels of brightness in each of the monitor's three different color signals — red, green, and blue — providing a palette of nearly 16.8 million colors altogether, 16 of which are available at a time. The video card expansion kit allows the display of 256 colors at once.

Sound

The Mac II's sound chip, housed on the motherboard, lets you play back realistic digitized sound in stereo. The sound chip handles most of the sound generation tasks so that the 68020 doesn't have to.

Software

The term ***software*** covers all the programs your Mac II uses. System software consists of the files and resources the computer uses to run itself. Application software consists of programs for manipulating information and doing work such as writing or drawing.

System Software

At the time the Mac II was introduced, Apple released updates to both the System (version 4.1) and the *Finder* (version 5.5). (The *Finder* has been Apple's application software for managing documents and "directing traffic" from your input through the Mac to disk storage, and vice versa.) Two new software introductions from Apple — *MultiFinder* and *HyperCard*, while they will run on the Mac Plus and SE, are at their best running on the Mac II. (These programs are now bundled with the Mac II; they can also be purchased separately.)

MultiFinder — *MultiFinder* is a new and improved application within the operating system that provides two-stage multitasking, allowing the Mac II to do spooling

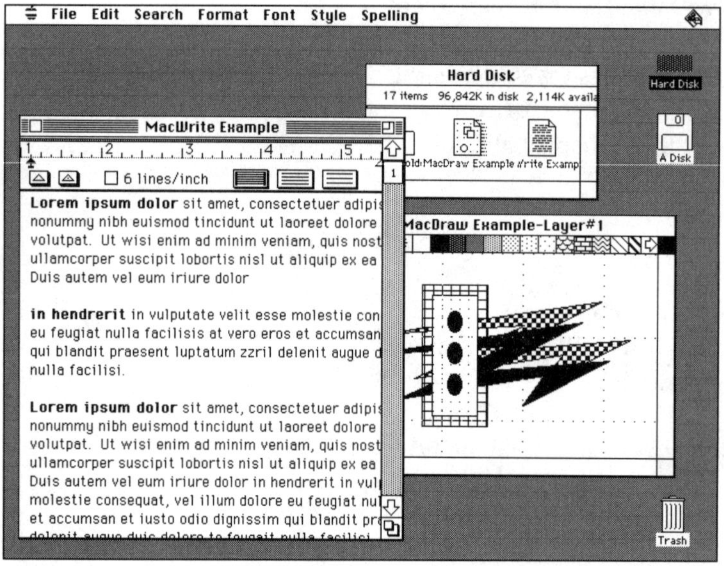

Figure 1-3. *MacDraw II* and *MacWrite* open and running on the desktop under *MultiFinder*.

(queuing up of tasks to be done in sequence), printing, hard disk backup, recalculating, or sorting in the background (unseen) while at the same time it runs the application you're working with on screen. *MultiFinder* also allows easy switching among several on-screen applications, a word processing program and drawing software, for example (Figure 1-3). To use *MultiFinder* comfortably, your Mac II will need at least 2 Mb of RAM (see "Customizing Your Machine" in Chapter 2).

HyperCard — *HyperCard* is software that lets you organize information much as you do in your mind — by linking it to other similar data or to information you associate with it. *HyperCard* provides the tools you need to create data in the form of text, graphics, or sound; store it; sort or browse through it to find what you need; or pinpoint specific information by association. Any information that can be created on the Mac II or imported into Mac II files (digitized video images or stereo sounds, for example) can be incorporated into and retrieved from the *HyperCard* software. The linking abilities of *HyperCard* can also be used to launch another Mac II program, dial a telephone number, or coordinate information stored in other media such as digitized audiotape or videotape, for example. (*HyperCard's* metaphor — a stack of index cards that can be linked by "buttons" — is described in Chapter 22.)

The HyperTalk programming language that comes with *HyperCard* is so much like standard English that it tends to make programmers of users. *HyperCard* and HyperTalk blur the distinction between program and data and provide limitless opportunities for those who make art on the Mac II.

Application Software

With the Mac II, Apple supplies a System Tools disk of useful utility programs, as well as demonstrator versions of *MacPaint*, *MacDraw*, *MacWrite*, *MacProject*, and *MacTerminal*. While you may decide to buy competitive products rather than the complete versions of these programs, the demonstrators will show you how programs for painting, drawing, word processing, project organization, and modem support, respectively, work.

Help on Paper

Along with the Mac II hardware and software comes assistance in the form of thorough, well-written, and well-illustrated manuals. If you are not familiar with the basics of operating the Mac II, familiarize yourself with them by reading and referring back to these documents. In the remainder of this book, it is assumed that you are familiar with the basics of using the Mac II.

CHAPTER 2

Doing Macintosh

THE INTUITIVE WAY

If you're a newcomer to the Macintosh world, you may not be thoroughly familiar with the metaphorical user interface that makes it so easy for Mac owners to learn to use the machine. Apple has standardized and promoted among software developers a way for the user to interact intuitively with the computer. The Mac uses on-screen icons (little pictures not unlike those in the outside world that direct us to telephones, roadside food and lodging, or restrooms of the appropriate gender) and a mouse, the device we use to move an on-screen pointer to make choices from among the icons and other items on the screen.

METAPHORS

When you turn on your Mac II, the first icon to appear on the screen is the "Where's the disk?" icon. Once the Mac has established that it has contact with a disk (hard or floppy, internal or external) with a System file on it, it shows you the "happy Mac" sign, welcomes you, and sets up the metaphorical **desktop** (Figure 2-1). The disk icons that appear on the desktop represent the storage media connected to your Mac II, and can be double-clicked open to reveal **windows** full of the **files** (individual documents) and **folders** (containers for groups of documents) stored on these media. These files and folders can be moved around the desktop, opened, and closed much as their counterparts can on a desktop outside the Mac II.

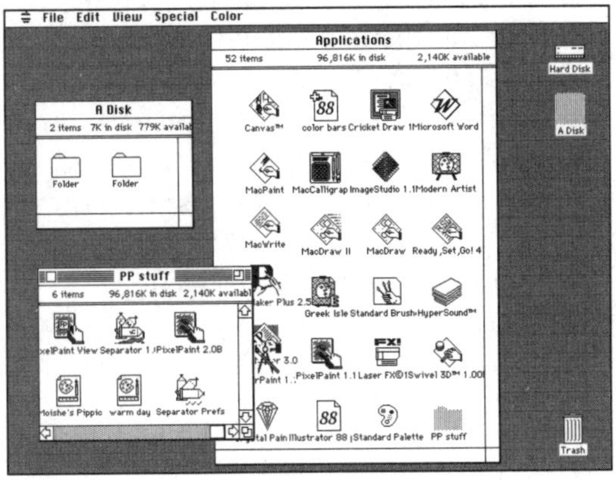

Figure 2-1. A Mac II desktop.

The words at the top of the desktop announce **menus** (lists of functions) that can be pulled down like old-fashioned window shades by holding down the mouse button. By holding down the button, dragging the **arrow pointer** to one of the **menu selections**, and then releasing the button, you choose the named function. A function name followed by an **ellipsis** (. . .) indicates that, before the function is carried out, you'll be presented with a **dialog box** requesting you to "talk to the Mac" — to make another choice or provide specific information (Figure 2-2). Like the menu selections, boxes and buttons in a dialog box have been labeled to make your range of choices as obvious to you as possible, to make your intuitive choices the right ones.

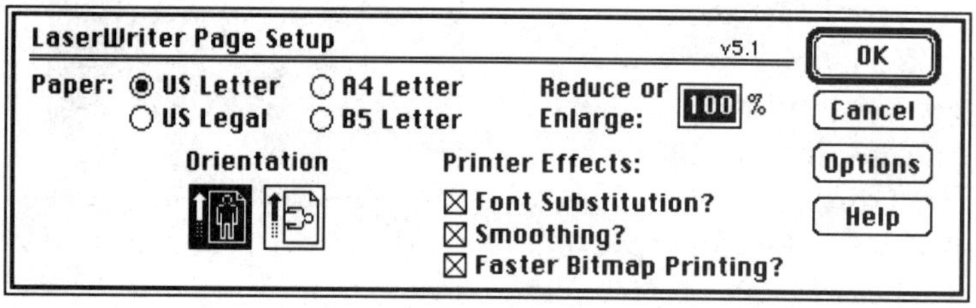

Figure 2-2. The desktop Page Setup dialog box.

Another icon prominent on the desktop is the trash can in the lower right corner. Moving document icons to the trash can is a way to rid your storage media of no-longer-wanted files and thereby make space for new ones.

More Basic Information

Typically, Macintosh users abhor reading user's manuals. But as Mac systems have become more complex, the user's manuals provided by Apple have become more welcome as a source of information about the standard functions of the machine. This book is no substitute for the Mac II manuals. Instead, its goal is to provide you with shortcuts and other information that expands the knowledge you gain from familiarity with the manuals. Even if you're experienced with the Macintosh environment, look through the manuals to get a feel for how you can find the detail you need when you need it.

CUSTOMIZING YOUR MACHINE

The amazing capabilities provided by the Mac II present a challenge — choosing the hardware, software, and other components to give you what you need and want without buying so much that the expense is overwhelming. On the one hand, you want to invest in the options that make the Mac II work best for you. But on the other hand, you don't want to spend money needlessly.

> TIP
>
> **Key Commands**
>
> When you select the Open command and you're presented with a list of files and folders to choose from, you can use the keyboard to select the file you're interested in. The up and down arrow keys of your Mac II will move you vertically through the list. The Tab key is equivalent to clicking the Drive button to switch disks, and the Return or Enter key will open the selected folder or file. You can also quickly type the first few letters of a file or folder name, and that file or folder will be selected.
>
> To make choices from the keyboard rather than with the mouse, you can use the Tab key to move around in dialog boxes and the Return key to press the selected (dark outline) button.

Hardware

To get the most from your Mac II, you'll need at least the following:

- A monitor — so you can see what you're doing.
- Storage media — so you have enough data storage to provide easy access to the files you need.
- A printer — so you can get your output on paper.
- Additional RAM — so you can have all the flexibility you need in moving among the memory-intensive applications of interest to graphic artists and desktop publishers.

Monitors

Since color is one of the primary features that distinguishes the Mac II from the rest of the Mac family, it would seem appropriate for a person in the graphic arts field to have a color monitor for the Mac II. However, color monitors are expensive, and it may make sense to look at some other possibilities. Options include black-and-white monitors, full-page (or even two-page) black-and-white monitors (which can display an 8-1/2-by-11-inch page [or two] at nearly full size), gray-scale monitors (which display the multiple levels of brightness of the Mac II gray scale), Apple's 12-inch color monitor (which can display black-and-white, gray-scale, or color images), or a 19-inch color monitor (which can display a two-page layout nearly full size and in full color). Here are some things to consider in choosing a monitor:

TIP

The New Trash Can

In the early days of the Mac, if you put a file in the trash can, it stayed there until you turned off the machine or selected Empty Trash from the Special menu. Not so today. The superefficient new trash can empties itself whenever you change applications, for instance. This can be a helpful service, clearing space on the disk and thereby speeding up operation — as long as you're not expecting to be able to open the trash can and retrieve a file. It's better not to put a file in the trash unless you're sure you don't want it anymore.

Size and Resolution — Look not only at the measured size, but at the image size, which can be much smaller. Remember that the Mac II WYSIWYG (what-you-see-is-what-you-get) screen display is at 72 dpi. A monitor that increases screen resolution to 80 to 90 dpi *will* provide a sharper-looking image but the image will also be reduced in size. Menus will be harder to read, and you won't be seeing the artwork in the same size it will appear as printed output.

Speed — Larger sometimes means slower, because the Mac II has to account for many more pixels on a large screen than on a smaller one. You may notice the slower speed when you're working at the desktop level — moving items around the whole screen area — more than you will when you're working on page layout. However, if you're working on two three-column pages on the screen, making a correction on the leftmost column can cause a bit of a wait as all six columns are adjusted to reflect the change. Some monitors have built-in microprocessors to relieve the Mac II of some of the display work, thus reducing or eliminating the slow-down.

Picture quality — For black-and-white monitors, contrast and brightness are important to producing a good picture on the screen. You'll want to be able to control them directly. Steadiness, the ability of the monitor to hold an image without flicker or other detectable movement, is also very important to avoiding eye fatigue. Distortion (curving) of the image in the corners of the screen is another element of picture quality to look at.

Multiple monitors — The Mac II can support multiple monitors. This allows you to have two application programs or two versions of an artwork open on the desktop at once under *MultiFinder*, each on its own screen, or to spread the screen display for one application over two screens. Each monitor you use with your Mac II needs its own video card. Some monitors come with their own, and some require that you buy a card separately.

Set-up — For most monitors, set-up is easy. You just have to install the video card, connect the monitor cable, and add one file to the System of your Mac II. But some take a little more work or equipment, so it's worth checking before you buy.

Compatibility — Just to make sure that the software you use will display properly on the monitor you buy, take your software with you to a monitor demonstration and try it out thoroughly.

> TIP
>
> **Your Own Startup Screens**
>
> Using *MacPaint*, *PixelPaint*, and other painting applications, you can save a graphic in the startup screen format. Label the file StartUpScreen and put it in your System folder. Shut down and start up again. In place of the "Welcome to Macintosh" greeting, you'll get to enjoy your own sunset, mandala, painting, koan, or photo of your daughter while the Mac II revs up. (You may need to adjust the position of the image. If it's in color, make sure it uses the System palette.)

Data Storage

A desktop artist should plan to start with 40 Mb of hard disk storage. In comparison to many other functions performed on computers, Macintosh graphics are "K intensive"; that is, the documents produced with graphics software require a lot of memory for data storage. One easy way to provide the hard disk storage you need is to buy your Mac II with Apple's 40 or 80 Mb drive built in. Later, you can expand your hard disk storage to up to 300 Mb. Additional data storage in removable media and other mass storage systems is discussed in Chapter 23.

Printers

A PostScript-based laser printer is virtually essential for the Mac II owner. Laser printer output can sometimes be used as camera-ready art, but more often it's used for comping or for proofing layouts to be produced in final form on a higher-resolution imagesetter. Beyond a laser printer, your printing needs will depend on what kind of final output you need and what kind of access you have to printers outside your work place. The laser printer and several other kinds of printers and printing systems are covered in Part III of this book.

Additional RAM

As delivered, the Mac II is equipped with 1 Mb of random access memory (RAM), which provides the storage space needed to run programs (applications). Graphics applications require a large amount of RAM space in order to define and

TIP

Zounds!

StartUpSound and ShutDownSound files are available in the public domain. You may even want to create your own using MacRecorder (see the Product appendix).

manipulate the information needed to produce a graphics image. To use the Mac II for graphics applications with any sort of efficiency requires 2 Mb of RAM.

The Mac II's RAM is provided in the form of "SIMMs" microchips that fit into eight slots (two sets of four slots each) within the computer. The microchips to be used in these slots come in two sizes: 256 K and 1 Mb. Either set of four slots must be either completely empty or completely full, and in a full set all slots must contain the same size chip. This allows the following configurations:

- 1 Mb (standard) = four 256 K chips in the first set of slots and none in the second set
- 2 Mb = eight 256 K chips
- 5 Mb = four 256 K chips in the first set of slots and four 1 Mb chips in the second set
- 8 Mb = eight 1 Mb chips

The 5 Mb configuration can be considered the most economical, because it provides the greatest amount of RAM possible without replacing any of the chips originally supplied with the machine.

Other Hardware

In addition to the four categories of essential hardware, you may also want to consider these possibilities:

- A digitizing system to scan in photos and other models (see Chapter 7)
- A color printer (see Part III for some possibilities)
- A film recorder for recording and outputting 35 mm slides (see Chapter 16)
- A digitizing tablet with a stylus to simulate pen or pencil drawing (see Chapter 24)
- An extended keyboard, with function keys to which you can assign **macros**, tasks that include a series of steps, such as making a menu choice or typing a string of characters.

Software

There's a smorgasbord of software available to meet all your needs as a graphic artist or desktop publisher and more software to meet your business and record-keeping needs. (There's even more software you could probably create a need for if you tried.) But if you're interested in starting with the essentials, this section provides some recommendations.

Essentials

- **Graphics programs** for creating and modifying artwork to meet your design and production requirements. Chapters 4 through 6 tell what bitmapped, object-oriented, and PostScript-based graphics programs can do in general and compare the individual programs that have established themselves as significant software.
- **Image-processing programs** for altering digitized images from scanners or video cameras. See Chapter 7 for a description of image-processing software in general as well as specific programs.
- **Word processing software** for preparing text. Word processors are discussed in the next section of this chapter.
- **Page-layout, or desktop publishing (DTP), software** for page design and production. Chapter 8 tells about established page-layout software.
- **Printer drivers** to provide an accurate, efficient link with the output hardware. Printer drivers are essential for communication between Mac and printer. Several printer drivers are supplied with the Mac II; others are provided with specific software packages or printers.

You may also want presentation software (see Chapter 9) to help you format your output for 35 mm slides and overhead transparencies and to drive some of the slide-producing hardware described in Chapter 16.

TIP

A Simple "Address Book"

If you want to keep your life relatively simple, instead of finding a Rolodex program, you can use *Word* or another word processor to keep track of phone numbers and addresses. Type in each entry with the elements separated by commas, with the last name first, then first name, address, area code and phone number, and any other notes you might want to keep track of with regard to that person. Finally, hit the Return key. Choose Sort from the Document menu to alphebetize the entries. If you forget someone's last name, you can use Find from the Search menu to locate the entry by the first name, city name, or telephone area code, for example.

> **TIP**
>
> **Shortcuts**
>
> From the outset, the Mac's software has had countless shortcuts: double-clicking, using the Option and Command keys, etc. Often, many of these shortcuts aren't even documented. Make sure to review the shortcuts in the program manuals, and keep your eye out for tips and shortcuts in magazines and books. *The Macintosh Bible* (also available in HyperCard format) is an excellent compendium of Mac shortcuts (see Resources appendix).

Word Processing Software

A word processor is a program for entering and editing text. Even if most of the work you do is graphic design, you'll need to prepare text occasionally, and a word processing program makes this process much faster and easier. It's possible to enter text in a page-layout program, but it's not practical. Experience shows that it's best to do as much of the writing, editing, and formatting as you can inside a word processing program. The two most important things to look at in a word processor are what it can do and how it will work with the other software you'll be using.

Besides accepting keyboard input and allowing editorial changes, which all word processors do, a good word processor should:

- Provide a spelling checker, preferably one that not only identifies words it doesn't recognize as being part of its extensive, accurate dictionary, but also suggests words that you might have meant when you misspelled or mistyped a word.
- Provide automatic indexing and table of contents features. This will be important only if you'll be producing long documents.
- Allow you to define, save, and apply several text styles within a file; for example, standard text, bulleted lists, numbered lists, extracts, and headlines.
- Find and change combinations of characters such as words, or single characters such as punctuation marks, within a document. (This function is especially helpful because of the differences between the typesetting capabilities provided by the computer keyboard and the way we originally learned to type on typewriters. For example, typists are used to typing two spaces after the period at the end of a sentence. In typeset material, only one space is used. Some word processors let you search for the two-space combination and replace it with one space.
- Provide several kinds of tabs (left, right, center, and decimal) and tab leaders (spaces, dotted line, or dashed line).

- Provide a character count to make copy fitting easier in the page layout software.
- Provide the ability to change elements universally throughout a document; for example, changing the leading for all body copy or changing the type style of all heads or the point size of subheads.

Perhaps the most important feature of a word processor is compatibility with your page-layout program. (Compatibility with database or spreadsheet programs will also be important if you will need to integrate business data into the documents you produce. Microsoft *Word* (Figure 2–3) and *MacWrite* provide excellent features and compatibility. *FullWrite Professional* represents a new generation of word processors with significant overlap with page-layout software.

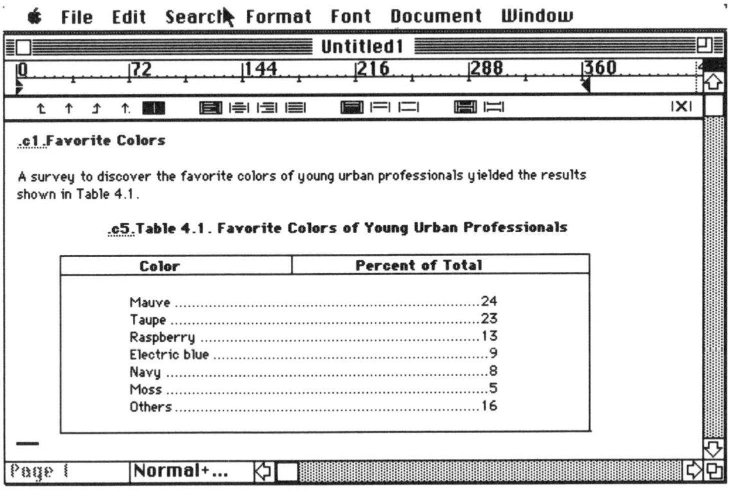

Figure 2-3. Microsoft *Word* offers many useful editing and formatting functions, including search, change, and spell-checking functions; horizontal and vertical rules; hidden text for compiling index and table of contents; and tab leaders.

TIP

Changing Between Black-and-White and Color.

Because black-and-white is faster, most people switch from black-and-white to color fairly frequently. But going to the Control Panel to make the changes back and forth can get to be a nuisance. One solution is a shareware program by Bill Steinberg called *Switch-A-Roo* that enables the user to switch between the two modes by pressing a few keys. It's available from most user groups and on-line services including Compuserve (see Chapter 3).

Another way to make switching easier is to bring the Monitors icon near the top of the Control Panel list, to avoid scrolling down to find it each time. Simply go into the system folder and rename Monitors to be Monitors with a space in front. This will cause it to sort to the top of the list under General (which is always on top). Sometimes the file is modified so that it can't be renamed. If so, just duplicate Monitors, rename the copy, and throw the original away.

TIP

Shutting Down Safely

To make sure that no information is lost when you turn off your Mac II, always turn it off by returning to the desktop and choosing Shut Down from the Special menu. This method provides you with dialog boxes to help you handle any unfinished chores, so that nothing is lost or damaged as the system is turned off.

Other Software

Other types of software you'll need are (1) **fonts** that expand the repertoire of typefaces available to your Mac II system, (2) **desk accessories** that provide many graphics and other functions without requiring that you close the program you're working in to access them, (3) electronic **clip art** images that can be used with the various kinds of graphics software, and (4) page-layout **templates** that provide predesigned formats for several kinds of projects. All these kinds of software are covered in Part IV.

In addition to these types of software, a **screen saver** program can help maintain the health of your screen. A screen saver automatically darkens your screen if you want to stop work temporarily but leave your computer turned on. After a specified time without keyboard or mouse activity, the screen saver darkens the screen (except for a small, moving display to let you know that the machine is still running) to prevent deterioration of the phosphor coating on the inside surface of the cathode ray tube. The *Pyro!* screen saver from the makers of the *Suitcase* program (see Chapter 19) provides a colorful but subtle fireworks display while saving the screen. Other screen savers are available in the public domain (see the Product appendix).

The Time Quandary

When you set up your Mac II system initially and every time you make a major hardware or software purchase thereafter, you'll face the question of timing: Should you buy a newly developed piece of hardware or software as soon as you see the need for it? What if you don't anticipate needing it again soon — should you wait for the new improved version or the competitor's product rumored to be just around the corner? Should you wait for the price to come down? In general, denying yourself some needed benefits of the existing product while waiting for a lower price or promised new developments is unproductive. Most hardware and software developers appreciate shoppers who have been willing to commit themselves and have become buyers, and so they provide updates to owners of their products at a reduced cost. If, when it comes to market, the rumored new competitive product is that much better than what you've bought, you may decide to replace what you have. In the meantime, though, you'll have got several months of good, productive use from the equipment you bought.

TIP

Screen Glare

If looking at a computer screen for long periods of time bothers your eyes, there are two simple solutions. The first is a polarizing filter. Several companies make screen-sized filters that attach by Velcro to the front of your computer screen. These are fairly expensive, so the best way to see if they're effective for you is to try looking at your screen through a good pair of polarizing sun glasses.

The no-cost solution that many people find effective, is to simply turn down the brightness control of the monitor.

CUSTOMIZING YOUR OPERATION

Customizing your operation means setting up your Mac II system to work best for you. It includes making your work place comfortable and efficient, setting up a filing system on your hard disk, adjusting the responses of keyboard, mouse, and sound systems to best suit your work habits, connecting your Mac II to your printer, and, if you'll be operating as part of a network, connecting your machine to other Macs (networking is covered in Chapter 3). And, of course, customizing your system also includes getting color onto your electronic desktop (see "Colorizing the Desktop" on page 24).

Workplace

Setting up your Mac II workplace involves the same primary considerations as setting up any work area. You need good lighting, in this case from the screen as well as for the surrounding area. Making the screen too bright will be hard on your eyes.

Monitor height can also play a role in your comfort. Set the monitor high enough off the surface of the desk so the screen is at eye level when you sit up straight. This will help you maintain good posture as you work, which should reduce fatigue.

If you'll be working from copy on paper a lot of the time (for example, typing in text or copying a drawing from an existing one on paper), use a device that holds the copy at the same distance from your eyes as the screen (for example, a standard office copy holder or a copy-holding device that attaches to the top of the monitor).

Colorizing the Desktop

Even before you fire up your first color graphics program, there are steps you can take to bring color to your Mac II. You start by choosing the Control Panel desk accessory (DA) from the apple menu, choosing the monitor from the icons that appear in the left column of the Control Panel, and then choosing Color and 256.

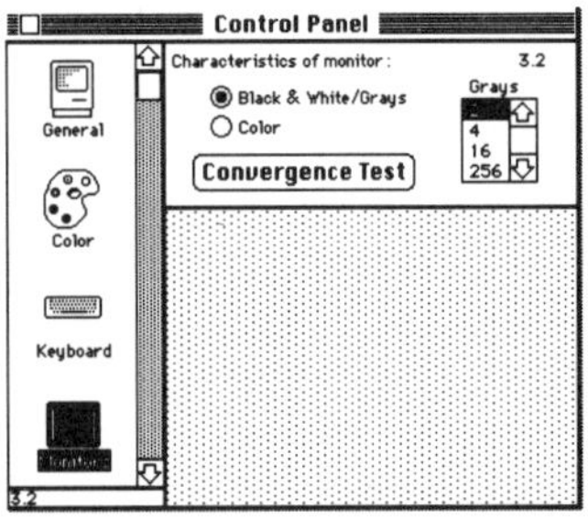

The Monitors dialog box, reached via the Control Panel desk accessory from the apple menu.

At this point you may notice a subtle change in what had been a black-and-white screen. Shades of gray appear, and the apple in the upper left corner becomes rainbow-colored. By clicking on an icon to select it, pulling down the Color menu at the right of the menu bar, and clicking on one of the colors exposed, you can turn a selected icon to the color of your choice. This method can be used to color any and all icons on the screen.

The next step in colorizing the desktop is to open the General icon in the Control Panel. By using the arrows at the top of the righthand (full desktop) icon, you can scroll through the many predesigned desktop pattern options. By clicking on the squares in the color strip and then clicking in the left (enlarged view) pattern box, you can design a pattern of your own. By double-clicking on the full desktop icon, you can assign the current pattern to your desktop.

The eight colors that appear in the color strip in the General dialog box when the standard bitmapped gray desktop pattern is in view can be classified into three groups:
(1) black- and-white, (2) red, green, and blue, the three primary colors of additive color mixing, and (3) cyan, magenta, and yellow, the three primary colors of subtractive color mixing, traditionally used in process color production. By double-clicking on one of the colors in the color strip, you open the Color Picker.

To understand what you're doing with the Color Picker, you need to know a little bit about color and color mixing. Additive color mixing is done by blending light of different colors. A blend of equal parts of the primary colors of light — red, green, and blue — produces white. If you focus three separate beams of red, green, and blue light on a spot on a blank wall, for example, the spot will appear white as the colors blend. The absence of all colors of light produces black.

The Color Picker lets you adjust the three main properties of color: hue, brightness, and saturation. These properties are primarily determined by the wavelength, amplitude, and purity of light, respectively.

Hue — Our perception of hue is determined mostly by the wave-length of light. In the Color Picker, hue changes as you move around the color wheel. Each of the

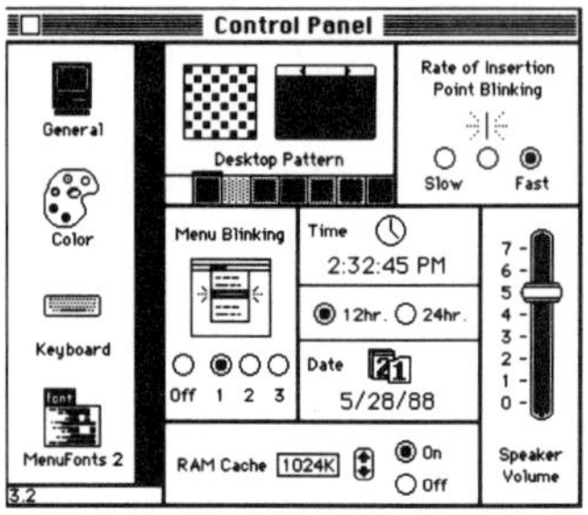

The General dialog box, reached via the Control Panel.

segments of the color wheel represents thousands of related hues. To select a hue, you place the pointer in the color segment that shows the color that most closely approximates the one you want to use, and click. Then, by using the Hue scroll box on the left, you can fine tune your color choice. The number in the Hue box represents the current color, which is displayed in the top half of the color box. The bottom half of the color box shows the color you started with. The numbers of the Color Picker dialog box provide a way of recording a description of a color you might want to match later.

Brightness — Brightness is deter-mined mainly by the amplitude of light waves. In the Color Picker, you can control brightness (or shading) by means of the scroll box to the right of the color wheel or with the Brightness scroll box at the left. The truest (unshaded) colors appear with the brightness turned all the way up. You'll notice that if you move the scroll box all the way to the bottom of the bar, all light disappears and the color wheel turns black.
(continued on next page)

Colorizing the Desktop (continued)

Saturation — Saturation is a function of the purity of light. (A pure color is light of one particular wavelength, rather than of several wavelengths mixed together.) The reddest red, for example, is pure red, with no blue or green light added to it. By choosing a color from the wheel and then increasing or decreasing its saturation with the scrolling arrows, you can make the color more intense or more pastel (closer to white), respectively. You'll notice that as you increase saturation of red, green, or blue, the numbers indicating the amounts of the two other primary colors get lower and the color in the upper color view box becomes more intense. You can accomplish the same kind of change in saturation by moving the pointer outward or inward on the color wheel, but the Saturation box gives you more precise control.

There's one more change you can make to colorize the desktop. To set the indicator color for selected text, choose the Color (palette) icon from the Control Panel, and then click Change in the dialog box that appears. This brings you back to the Color Picker and allows you to choose a screen color for selected text.

For even more control in colorizing your desktop, there are programs available that allow you to customize the menu bars, windows, scroll bars, thumbs (scroll boxes) — virtually every element of the Mac interface. Two such programs are *Kolor*, written by employees of Apple Computer, and available in the public domain; and *Colors*, part of a package of programs called *Colorizer* by Palomar Software.

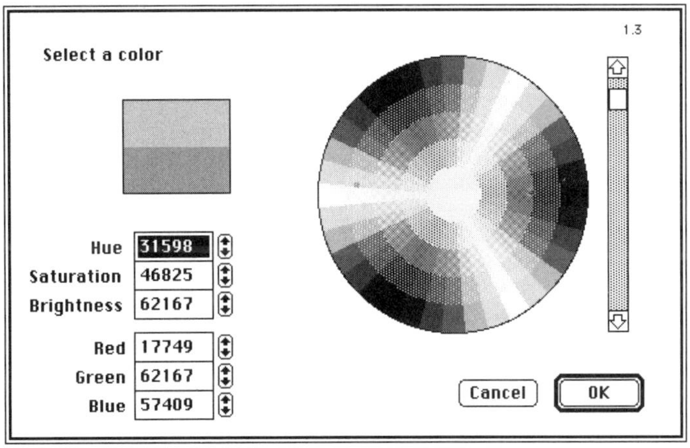

The Mac II Color Picker, reached by double-clicking a color box in the General dialog box or via the Color (palette) icon in the Control Panel. This dialog box provides access to System color in the Mac II. Color graphics programs use this dialog box or their own color-accessing systems to provide users with a choice of colors.

Files

The Mac II provides certain software devices that make it easy to use its metaphoric filing system. You can group your files within folders according to your own system of logic and then put those folders within other folders, and so on. This hierarchical filing system gives you quick access to many files without cluttering your desktop with an icon for each one. And if at some point your original logic escapes you and you can't remember where you put a particular document, Find

File, a desk accessory available through the apple menu (see Chapter 19), can search it up for you.

Some people like to view their files by icon (choose By Icon from the View menu), using a system of folders within folders to keep the desktop uncluttered (as shown in Figure 2-1) while providing access to hundreds or even thousands of files. Others like to display their files By Name, which provides an alphabetical listing of files on the screen (Figure 2-4).

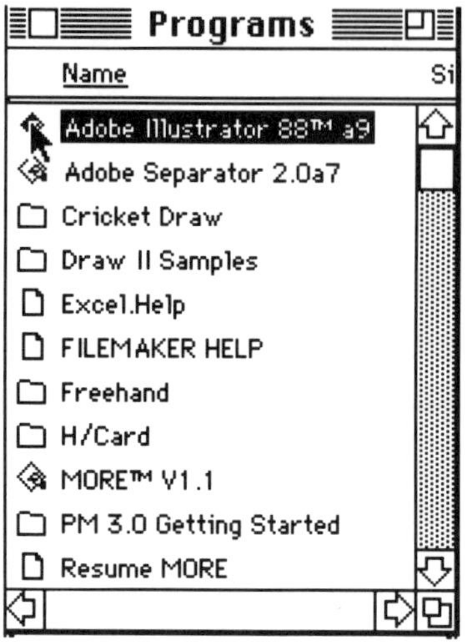

Figure 2-4. Files shown by name.

RAM Cache

The Control Panel, besides allowing you to adjust desktop color, lets you set the response characteristics of your Mac II — for example, how fast the cursor blinks, how loud the warning tones are, and how quickly and how often characters repeat if keys are held down. It's obvious what most of the choices on the Control Panel do. But the size of the RAM cache may not be so apparent. RAM cache is a special part of RAM that's set aside for the Mac II to automatically store program segments that are used often. Having these often-used bits of software so readily available speeds up program operation. Setting the size of the RAM cache is a trade-off between the desire for speed and the availability of RAM. As a rule of thumb, don't put more than one-third of your Mac II's RAM in the RAM cache.

Customizing your Mac II and the way it operates may include connecting it to other Macs, pc's of other varieties, or information sources outside your immediate workplace. Chapter 3 tells about making these connections.

TIP

Using Color for Filing

Colorizing the icons for files and folders can be a very useful way to organize. When you use the By Name option (from the View menu) for listing your files, they'll be arranged on the screen in an alphabetized list. A program you use often may have a name that's too far down the alphabet to appear on the screen without your scrolling down the list looking for it. To cut down on scrolling time, you can colorize your file folders and choose By Color from the View menu. The files in the list will be grouped by color (and within a color, alphabetically by name), and the color groups will appear in the same order you see in the Color menu. For example, you might choose to have two page-layout programs and a word processor listed at the top of your list of files. You could choose red for the folders that contain the two page-layout programs and blue for the word processor. The page-layout programs would appear at the top of the list, followed immediately by the word processor and then by the alphabetical list of noncolored files. These color choices would give you the option of colorizing other types of files later to appear before (orange), between (magenta and cyan), or after (green and brown) your two existing color groups.

CHAPTER 3

Making Connections

The connections you can make with your Mac II range from easily moving and sharing files among many people in the same office or studio, to the electronic equivalent of Federal Express to get a file halfway across the country in the least possible time. Making connections takes quite a bit of time and effort compared to other aspects of using the Mac II, but the time it can save you is likely to be worth it.

TYPES OF COMMUNICATIONS

The two basic categories of connections you can make with your Mac are telephone communications and network communications. **Telephone communications** can, in turn, be divided into Mac-to-Mac communications (sending of files from one machine to another over local or long distance phone lines) and Mac-to-Service (a method of getting information from other computer users whom you may never have met). Still other Mac-to-Service communications include mail and public domain exchanges.

Network communication is primarily the transfer and translation of files between computers in the same office. For example, several Macintoshes can share the same set of files. Or files can be transferred from other computers (such as MS-DOS-based pc's to Macintoshes) and translated to Macintosh file formats. Desktop publishers often use networking to bring text from an IBM PC over to the Mac to do final layout.

TELEPHONE

The common requirements for all types of telephone communications (or telecommunications) are a piece of hardware called a **modem** and specific **communications software**. Modems vary in price based primarily on maximum speed of transmission. The most

TIP

Why a Modem?

More people are using Macs in the graphics business all the time, including your associates, clients, and suppliers. You'll find increasing uses for telecommunications, including:

- Sending and receiving files. For example, a writer may send you copy for an ad layout, thereby saving time and travel expense.
- Sending files to a service bureau for imagesetting. Many service bureaus have dedicated lines to receive files at all hours.
- Getting information from one of the on-line services such as CompuServe. You can also communicate with others who are participating in special interest "forums" at specified times (usually evenings).

common speeds are 300, 1200, and 2400 baud. Baud refers to the speed of transmission. Here are a few things you should know when you're going to buy a modem:

- The speed refers to the maximum speed. This means that a 2400–baud modem can also be used at 1200 and 300 baud.
- The modem should be "Hayes compatible." The Hayes programming commands have become the standard for running modems. You may successfully go through your life without ever directly using these commands, but your communications software will have to use them.
- Of the cascade of features that most modems will claim to have, auto answer is the most important. It allows the modem to automatically answer the phone if you instruct it to do so.
- Finally, speed of transmission between two computers is limited by the maximum speed of the slower of the two modems. So if you'll be working with one person exclusively and he or she has a 1200-baud modem, you may want to think twice before spending the extra money on a 2400-baud modem.

Mac-to-Mac by Telephone

Mac-to-Mac communications consist almost exclusively of the transfer of files from one location to another. Most graphic files on the Macintosh are relatively large, so realize that this process can tie up your computer for some time. The best way to reduce this time is by using compression software, which can reduce the size of the file you need to send by up to 60 percent. (The person you're sending the file to will also need the same compression software to return the file to its original state.) Since a good bit of this type of communication seems to take place at 5:01 on Friday afternoon, that time savings can mean a lot.

Here's an overview of some good communications software for the Macintosh:

Red Ryder started out as one of the best public domain programs ever seen for the Macintosh. *Red Ryder* was updated over 10 times, each time with new features added in response to user suggestions. In 1987, version 10.0 changed from being shareware (you send money to the programmer if you find the program useful after trying it) to being a commercial product. The program has a full macro language for the stout of heart, and is extremely powerful.

Microphone is another powerful program with public domain origins. It is very intuitive and easy to use. Both *Microphone* and *Red Ryder* have enthusiastic supporters.

Smartcom II was created by Hayes, the makers of the industry-standard modems. Hayes modems tend to be a bit more expensive, but they usually come with *Smartcom II.* This is an easy program to use. If you don't get *Smartcom II* with your modem, it may be a bit too expensive to justify buying it instead of *Red Ryder.*

MCS, unlike the others, serves only one function: direct Mac-to-Mac communications (see Figure 3-1). *MCS* stands for *multichannel communications software.* This shareware program will dial a preprogrammed number, look to see if there's a copy of *MCS* up and running at the number dialed, and when it finds that other copy, lock with it, and start

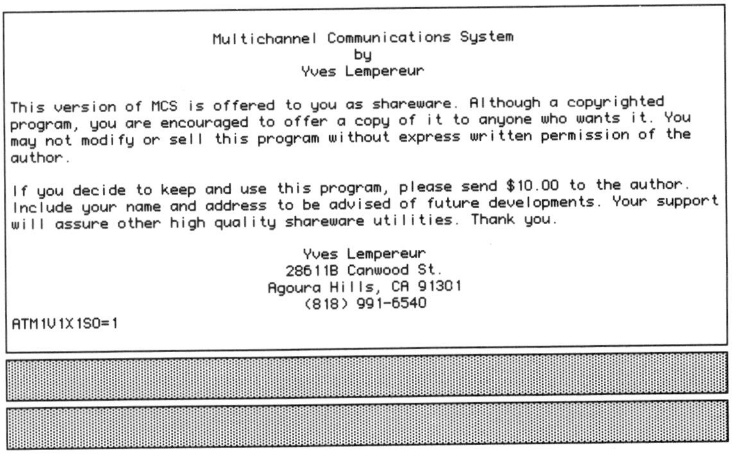

Figure 3-1. An *MCS* window, used to communicate with this relatively new service for Macintoshes.

sending the file(s) you've selected. If the other person has selected files to be sent to you, *MCS* will send both sets of files *at the same time.* As an added bonus, you can type messages back and forth to each other while it's sending the information. The hardest part of *MCS* is getting the phone number in the program in the first place. Once it's set, it's truly the easiest and most reliable software for Mac-to-Mac file transfer on the market.

Stuffit is a commonly used compression program. It allows you to compress a single or many files into one smaller file. It often adds the suffix **.pit** to the end of the file name. If you receive a file with this in the name that won't open as you think it should, the person sending it to you has probably compressed it (packed it) with something like *Stuffit. Stuffit* is also shareware and is a must in the frequent telecommunicators tool kit.

Mac-to-Service

On-line services are usually based on minicomputers somewhere out in the world that you can access using your communications software. They serve three basic functions. First, they provide a forum for computer users to exchange ideas and answer questions. Second, they're a source of exchange of public domain and shareware software. Third, they serve as electronic mailboxes. Most of these services charge by the hour for their use. To cut down on the long distance charges added to this fee, most of the services have local numbers across the country that connect you with the main computer. Most services let you try them out by buying a starter pack at a computer dealer. A service's pack usually includes free connect time along with information about what the service offers and how to use it.

Compuserve is the most popular of the on-line services. It plays host to MAUG (Micronetted Apple Users Group) and is one of the best sources in the country for getting a technical question answered. It's one of the more expensive services, at $6/hour for 300-baud access and $12/hour for 1200/2400 access. This makes 2400 baud the best deal when you're copying (downloading) programs from MAUG. The way to access MAUG is to type GO MAUG when you get onto Compuserve. Compuserve also has probably the most up-to-date collection of public domain and shareware software of any of the services. Spending some time browsing among these programs can reveal a treasure trove of utilities and graphic enhancements for very little money.

Probably the biggest help in using MAUG is a piece of Compuserve-specific software called ***Navigator*** (Figure 3-2). This program is sold by Compuserve and puts a much less intimidating cover over MAUG. This software can save you quite a bit of money by letting you collect your mail, log off, and then read and answer messages. This way the time you spend on line isn't extended by your typing or reading.

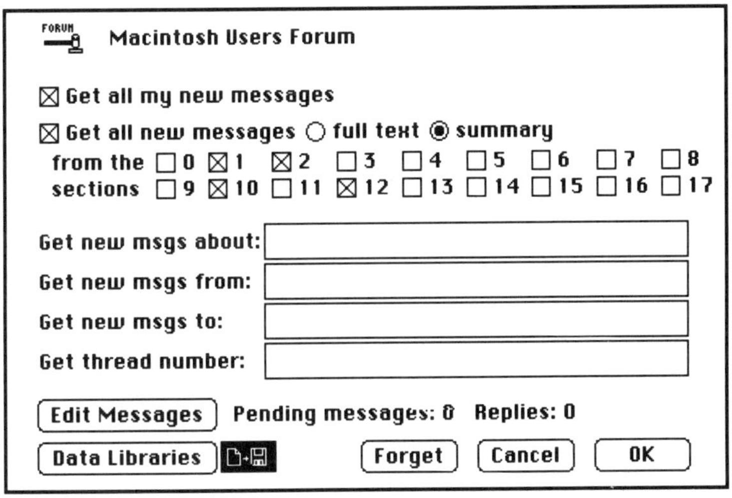

Figure 3-2. A dialog box for the *Navigator* software used with the Compuserve service.

Delphi has many of the same features as Compuserve, but at less cost. It's not quite as active and doesn't have an equivalent to the *Navigator*, but if you're going to spend a lot of time on a service, it's well worth looking into.

MacNet is a relatively new service that started out dedicated to the Macintosh. It's main strengths are low price and an excellent program that's used to access the service. The public domain and shareware libraries are rarely up to date, but the mail facility is probably the best of all the services, and *MacNet* is worth getting just for that.

MCI Mail is a very frequently used electronic mail service. If you communicate often with many different people who use computers, you'll find that many have MCI Mail accounts. The primary advantage of MCI Mail is that a message is automatically sent in the U.S. mail if the electronic mail isn't picked up by a certain time; but the service is expensive. ***Desktop Express*** is software specifically designed to make MCI Mail easier to check and use (see Figure 3-3). If you open an MCI mail account, you should look into purchasing this program.

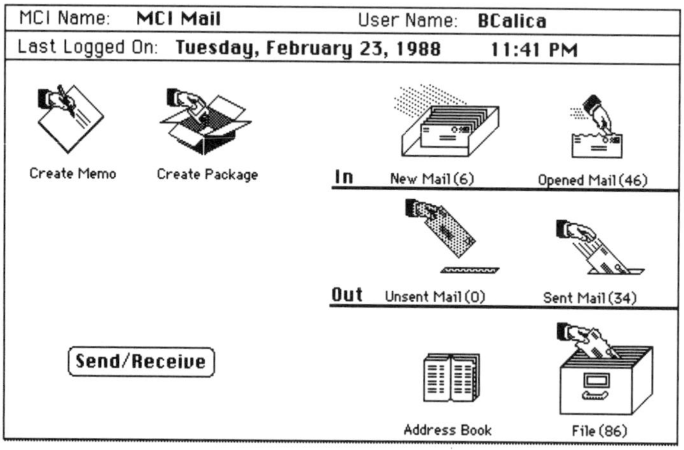

Figure 3-3. *Desktop Express* software for checking and using the MCI Mail electronic mail service.

NETWORKS

Network communications are the interactions between computers on what's called a **LAN**. LAN stands for **local area network**, and that simply means computers that are in the same studio, office building, or equivalent and are directly connected by wires. If you have a computer and a LaserWriter, for example, you have the simplest version of such a network. LANs require (1) the hardware to make the physical connections and (2) network software.

Mac-to-Mac LANs

Mac-to-Mac networks are the simplest networks on any computers. This is because most of the networking hardware was built into every Mac. The hardware is the easy part. It's taken a bit longer to iron out the bugs in the software. The three functions used most often in Mac-to-Mac networking are the transfer of files from one machine to another; the sharing of hard disks, printers, and modems; and the sending and receiving of local electronic mail.

Wiring

The wiring used to connect Macintoshes is basically twisted—pair cable — two wires like the ones that are usually left over when a phone is installed. The generic name for this kind of wiring between Macs is **AppleTalk.** Apple makes a version called **LocalTalk,** and a company called Farallon makes another version called **PhoneNet.**

Network Software

With the wires in place between Macs, the next task is to install the software to make the network operate.

Tops is network software that allows users to make sections of their personal hard disks available for other users on the network. It provides simple password protection and slightly slows down the machines it's running from. The software has gone through many versions and is currently solid and reliable. It's an excellent solution for small networks.

AppleShare is Apple's networking software. It's expensive and requires a Macintosh and a hard disk to be **dedicated** to being a **server** to the network. This means that the machine can't be used by anyone directly — its sole purpose is to maintain the shared files and to handle traffic within the network. The advantages of using *AppleShare* are that it's much faster than a nondedicated system when many people are using it and it provides many levels of passwords and security. An *AppleShare* server can be used also as an electronic mail server.

Mac-to-PC LANs

Communication between a Mac and another type of computer is a bit more complicated than a Mac-to-Mac LAN. Not only does the information have to be transferred from one machine to the next, but the files often need to be translated into something the other machine can use.

One of the advantages of ***Tops,*** the software discussed in "Mac-to-Mac LANs" earlier in the chapter is its ability to include other types of machines on an AppleTalk network. *Tops* for the PC, for example, is more expensive than the Mac version because it includes a hardware card that fits into the PC to give it an AppleTalk connection. *Tops* for the PC works much like *Tops* for the Mac except that it includes the ***Mac Link*** software. *Mac Link* is the best software for translating files from PC formats to Mac formats and vice versa. For example, it will convert from *Wordstar* on the PC to *MacWrite* on the Macintosh, and from there the file can easily be translated into *Word* format if you like. The program includes software for both machines and will work over a network, over phone lines with modems, or via a cable directly connecting a Mac to a PC. You can buy such a cable with the software, if you so choose. If you need to do this type of conversion, the *Tops–Mac Link* combination is the way to go. *Mac Link* is also available for Mac-to-Wang and other connections.

Electronic Mail

The last valuable use of a network is electronic mail. This is simple mail that is sent between the machines. The most often used mail programs are *Inbox* by Think Technologies, Microsoft *Mail,* and *Quickmail,* by CE Software. Electronic mail reduces the amount of time people spend wandering around in a network trying to find each other.

Part II explores the most important categories of Macintosh II applications for graphic art: "Paint" (bitmapped) graphics, "Draw" (object-oriented, or vector) graphics, "PostScript" graphics, "Image Processing" (photo retouching), "Desktop Publishing" (page layout), and "Presentation" graphics (output on media other than paper). Each chapter in Part II describes the general characteristics and capabilities of one of these six types of software and then provides brief reviews of the character and special features of several of the best and most popular programs of that type. At the end of each chapter is a gallery of artwork produced with those programs. More artwork created with the graphics applications covered here can be found in the Color Gallery following Chapter 8.

As a graphic artist becomes proficient with Mac II graphics software, the possibilities for

Dominique de Bardonneche Berglund

producing artwork by using the programs in combination seem limitless. Some of the artwork in the end-of-chapter galleries demonstrates what can be achieved with these interactions.

Mac II Artwork in General

Before we begin to define the six types of software covered in this section and to explore how they differ from each other, it's worthwhile to review the way the Mac II handles artwork of any type. The image the Mac II sends to the monitor screen is made up of dots — 72 dots per linear inch (dpi). Each dot is a picture element, *or* pixel. *A screen image is simply a collection of these dots, each with its own attributes of color and brightness. The basic Mac II system provides 256 colors or shades of gray, including black and white. If a screen pixel is turned off, it appears black; if it's fully on, it's white. Intermediate shades and tones of color or gray result from different levels of pixel brightness. You can think of each pixel as having the capacity to work like a three-way light bulb, but with many more than three possible wattages.*

The Macintosh II's display architecture has a very powerful color capability: the instant substitution of one color for another in one part of an artwork or throughout an entire piece. With this, the artist can fine-tune the mood of a finished illustration, with subtle variations in hue, or with color choices from across the spectrum. Not tied to the Mac's standard System palette (see Chapter 2), some graphic arts applications provide their own color palettes.

Although screen resolution is limited to 72 dpi, printed output from the Mac II can be at much higher resolution, as described in Part 3 of this book. Some, but not all, graphic arts application software can take advantage of the highest resolution an output device can produce, even though the image on the screen remains at 72 dpi.

Painting

Painting with Mac II applications closely mimics traditional painting. Using metaphoric tools, such as paintbrush, eraser, and airbrush, the artist spreads electronic color on an electronic canvas. Instead of a continuous flow of paint, Mac II painting tools deposit discrete dots along the paths traced by their painting strokes. Visually, the pixels blend, and painting programs give the artist a free hand to cover the electronic canvas with paint. But daVinci couldn't have lifted the painted smile off the Mona Lisa, *modified it, and put it back without disturbing a bit of cheek or chin; and the electronic artist using a paint program is under similar constraints. Paint programs are ignorant of what all their pixels represent — that knowledge is exclusively in the mind of the artist. Despite its sophistication, the software can't recognize an enigmatic smile, or tell whether a particular pixel is part of a lip, an eye, the nose, or the background landscape.*

Drawing

Whereas paint software employs the tools of the fine artist, drawing software provides tools more reminiscent of those of the traditional draftsman: straightedge; compass, ruler, and protractor for measuring; and templates for geometric forms. Drawing software produces object-oriented drawings, *or* vector graphics, *formed of "intelligent" objects — intelligent in that they "know" and can retain their basic forms. A circle remains a circle, for example, even when it's enlarged or filled with a new pattern. This "memory" that's built into object-oriented graphics, comes from the drawing software's use of Apple's built-in QuickDraw routines for creating basic geometric shapes, line weights, colors, and patterns. The graphic artist never has to deal directly with the QuickDraw language, because the metaphoric tools of the graphics programs call the drawing routines. As a draftsman might use several openings in a template to create ellipses of the same shape but different sizes, drawing software can produce an object that can then be duplicated, resized, distorted, defined by a thicker outline, or filled with one of any number of patterns.*

Draw objects, besides knowing their shape, size, and visual texture, also know where they stop and the rest of the world begins. It's as if each object were drawn on its own sheet of clear acetate, so that it can be moved around independently of the other objects in a drawing and can even be slid over or under those objects to form a collage.

Draw software is good for drawing plans or for artwork that makes use of geometric shapes or requires high-resolution output. Compared to the "frozen" world of bit maps, object-oriented software gives the artist more room to experiment and rearrange to arrive at a final product. A modern-day L'Enfant might use a draw program to design Washington, D.C., for example, or Mondrian might use it to plan his Lozenge Composition in a Square.

Painting and Drawing Together

Some Mac II graphics applications combine the best features of paint and draw software in one program. Elements of an artwork can be created in both paint and draw media and then combined. The painting and drawing features of these applications are discussed separately, in Chapter 4, "Paint," and Chapter 5, "Draw," respectively.

PostScript Illustration

QuickDraw graphics, though flexible and powerful, are more limited than PostScript graphics. While vector graphics use geometric primitives *(preprogrammed shapes), a range of dot screens, and basic drawing routines, PostScript graphics are generated by code written in the PostScript programming language, the page description language that drives most of the Apple laser printers and most high-resolution imagesetting systems, as described in Part III.*

PostScript graphics programs provide many of the same tools and use many of the same vector graphics screen routines as do object-oriented programs, for assembling illustrations from independent objects and for indicating fill patterns, line widths, and so on. But they also do analytic geometry for you, constructing equations from the lines you draw and encapsulating the equations in a file. They translate your on-screen efforts into the code necessary for creating highly customized illustrations. In addition, they allow a wide range of halftone and special-effects screens, curves, and visual effects. The screen pixels in a PostScript-based page are the best representations your monitor can provide of the complex illustrative elements defined by the PostScript code.

What artist from the past might use PostScript-based graphics software if he were alive today? Perhaps M. C. Escher, with his carefully calculated transformations.

Digitizing

Image-processing software is designed to modify scanned images. Scanners produce halftones either by recording "live" via video camera or by copying continuous-tone originals. Image-processing software provides tools specifically designed to manipulate these halftone images, perhaps allowing the electronic artist to imitate the darkroom wizardry of a Man Ray.

Desktop Publishing

Melding words and artworks into effective page layouts is the work of desktop publishing (DTP) software. Transforming word-processed text into typeset columns, establishing type as a design element, and sizing and placing graphics — perhaps all elements supplied from different applications — DTP software allows the desktop designer to produce posters, newsletters, tabloids, manuals, and books.

While the other types of programs for graphic artists can be viewed as timesavers or ways of avoiding physically messy processes, DTP software, more than the other types, is what gives the artist new control of the processes that stand between the creative idea and the final published product. Not since the days of the hand-illuminated manuscripts that graced so many of the world's cultures before the advent of the printing press has the artist had such direct control.

Presentation

Presentation graphics software is designed to produce output mainly in a form other than print on paper. Somewhat limited in the artist's tools and techniques it provides, presentation graphics software formats illustrations as 35 mm slides, overhead transparencies, or hand-outs to accompany an oral presentation. Presentation software also drives the output devices that produce these final products. The graphics produced by these programs may be bitmapped, Color QuickDraw–based, or even PostScript-defined.

Chapter 4

Painting

Electronic painting programs produce bitmapped images in Paint format (see "File Format #1: Paint" on page 45). As with conventional painting, you can paint, erase, and overpaint. Macintosh painting applications offer more than traditional media, though, simply because they're not bound by the physical limitations of pigment, brush, and canvas. These applications expertly assist the artist in placing and modifying pixels, individually or by the thousands.

TOOLS

With the typical Macintosh paint application, you command a set of functions that are the electronic counterparts of artist's implements. Their basic functions are essentially the same in each paint program, although some applications offer additional tools and unique special effects tool modes that range from slightly enhanced to spectacular.

The **paintbrush** is a basic tool for making strokes of variable size, shape, pattern, and color. Brush attributes are generally editable — that is, the user can change the size and shape of a brush's "footprint."

The **spray can** or **airbrush** sprays pixel patterns of a size and density that, in some applications, can be controlled by setting preferences such as pattern width and "air pressure." Airbrush effects are usually time dependent. The longer the spray stream lingers on an area, the denser the finished stroke.

The single-pixel **pencil** is another free-form drawing tool. It performs much like the smallest paintbrush, but it also provides a scratchboard effect, automatically drawing in white on a black background. The pencil can also turn individual pixels on and off, in both normal and enlarged (FatBits) views of the painting.

TIP

Paintbrush Erasers

For erasing jobs that require a cleaning tool finer than the square eraser but not as precise as the pencil in FatBits, use a paintbrush tip of appropriate size and white paint.

TIP

Large Rectangular Erasers

Another precision erasing technique is drawing a white rectangle with no border. Drag the rectangle from the far corner of the area that you want to erase and release it when the area is covered exactly. This allows the erasing of a large rectangular area with incredible accuracy, because if you overshoot the area you want to erase, you can just pull back, as long as you haven't released the rectangle.

Paint applications all provide a basic **line tool** that draws a line from one click-point to another. Some have a dedicated vertical/horizontal line tool to speed straight-line construction by keeping the line from straying off the straight up-and-down or side-to-side path.

The **polygon tool** is as universal as the pencil or paintbrush. Its function is to render a multisided free-form shape. You click where you want vertices, and the application connects these points with straight lines.

The tool palette's basic geometric shapes include the **rectangle/square** and **oval/circle**. Perfect circles or squares are rendered by holding down the Shift key while dragging the shape. The width and pattern of lines can be set from a fairly varied pre-established set, or in some cases they can be numerically specified.

The **paint bucket** is used to fill any size enclosed area with a specified paint "color" and pattern. For noncolor applications you choose only a fill pattern. The fill patterns appear in one or more palettes of their own, and are generally user-editable, either by modifying an existing pattern or by defining a completely new one.

The basic **eraser** is a small square that removes all paint from whatever path it travels. Some applications provide options such as erasing to black (versus white), or to a specific color, or to a prior version of the image.

Selecting areas of a painting for subsequent editing action can be done with the **marquee** (a rectangular selection tool), or with the **lasso** (a free-form selection tool). The basic set of **editing features** used on selections includes cutting, pasting, resizing, duplication, stepped rotation, and controlled distortion, including stretching and shrinking. Whether it's a rectangle, circle, free-form line, or elaborate pattern, a painted graphic is nothing more than adjoining dots. So when a section of a painted graphic is stretched to, say, four times its area (with an editing tool) its component dots are also stretched (one pixel becomes four pixels). The painting application can't help enlarging *everything* in the area; it has no idea what the stretched object is. An object with a thin border will stretch into an object with a *thick* border. Enlarged diagonal lines become grossly jagged. If a detailed graphic is reduced and then at a later time enlarged, it won't return to its original appearance. During reduction, some pixels are literally squeezed out of existence, and they aren't re-created when the image is enlarged.

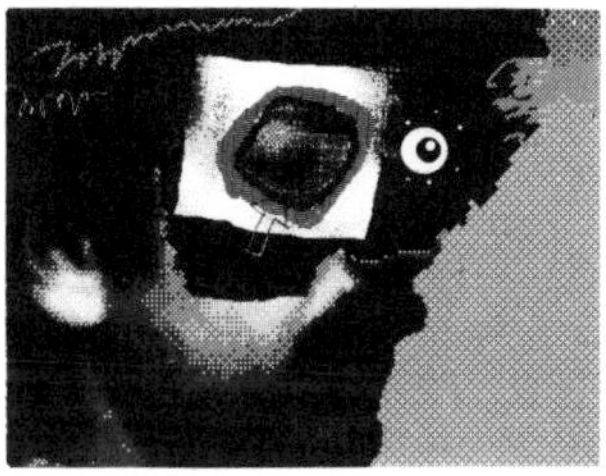

Joseph Bellacera

Most applications also allow the user to **undo** any editing operation, so you can make "what-if" changes or recover from a mistake.

Each application supplies a number of unique methods for applying **special effects**. Some effects, such as transitions from one color to another, are nearly infinitely variable and can be customized by menu selections, typed-in values, sliding scales, or special key combinations.

LAYERING

Although, in general, painting software can't identify which pixels are part of which images, some paint applications support **layering**, allowing you to paint images on two or more overlapping transparent canvases. You can use one layer as a background, for example, and other layers to hold foreground images. You can paint and edit on any layer without affecting the pixels of other layers. This "collaging" capability can help a great deal when you want to rearrange the elements of a painting, or change one element without disturbing the others. Within any one layer, however, the difficulties of shifting pixels remain the same.

TIP

Black-and-White for Speed

Most graphics programs operate significantly faster if you set your Macintosh II to black-and-white two-color mode. The difference in speed is especially noticeable during scrolling.

PRECISION

Paint applications are generally used for free-form rather than precision work. However, most such applications offer vertical and horizontal rulers, sometimes combined with a numeric indication of the x and y coordinates of the position of the tool you're using. In some cases, you can customize the ruler units to be picas, pixels, inches, or centimeters. You may also be able to reposition the zero point of one or both rulers anywhere on the canvas. These aids can help position and size images. Once you've created or placed an image, you have the opportunity to undo that action, but only if you hit the Undo command before making further changes.

Besides these alignment tools, paint programs provide an underlying grid pattern with a basic unit, or step (typically 8 pixels square), that can be used to keep patterns intact as areas are stretched or shrunk, and to help the user align corners and edges of adjacent painted shapes.

RESOLUTION

The standard Macintosh screen resolution is 72 dpi. All painting applications support this resolution, and most can also support higher resolutions from 300 to 2540 dpi. Images produced by document scanners and other digitizing devices can produce 300-dpi image files that can be edited by 300-dpi paint applications. With high-resolution painting, you normally work at several levels of magnification within an enlarged view of a small area.

High-resolution bitmapped documents use a large amount of disk space, easily hundreds of kilobytes. Working with such large files requires enough RAM to hold all the image dots, plus the elbow room to support cutting, pasting, and undoing.

Paintings (bit maps) print at the resolution at which they were painted, regardless of the resolution of the output device. For example, each screen pixel of a 72-dpi painting will be rendered as the same size printed dot by every type of printer.

The ImageWriter II strikes the paper with one relatively large pin to form that pixel. The 300-dpi LaserWriter will render it with a clump of 16 closely spaced dots. A 2540-dpi Linotronic will create the same image with nearly 1200 of its very fine dots. The LaserWriter can be instructed to smooth out jagged contours of low-resolution paintings, which significantly improves their quality, but smoothing is no substitute for true 300-dpi graphics.

File Format #1: Paint

Paint programs produce files that store on/off (for black-and-white), brightness (for gray-scale images), or full color information for each pixel on the screen. These are called bit-map or Paint files. The information they send to the screen and to the printer (whether dot matrix, laser, or even higher-resolution) is a collection of dots at 72 dpi. Some paint programs can also produce files in other formats (see the "File Format" boxes in Chapters 5, 6, and 7 for descriptions of these other file types.)

PAINT PROGRAMS

MacPaint (2.0)

MacPaint 2.0 (Figure 4-1) is the direct descendant of the original *MacPaint* program that set the standard for painting interfaces. It's simple to use, and its rather basic tools work quickly and intuitively. Three of its features stand out: a fully operational reduced view, tear-off palettes for tools and fill patterns, and its "Take Snapshot" capability, which is a way to save the current image without changing the officially named and saved version of the file.

Figure 4-1. The *MacPaint* window, with tear-off menus.

TIP

Custom Brush Tips

MacPaint's brush tips are not user editable, but you can make your own brush tip by constructing its "footprint" with painting tools, selecting it with the marquee or lasso, setting the line width to the narrowest setting, and holding down the Command and Option keys as you drag your new brush to paint.

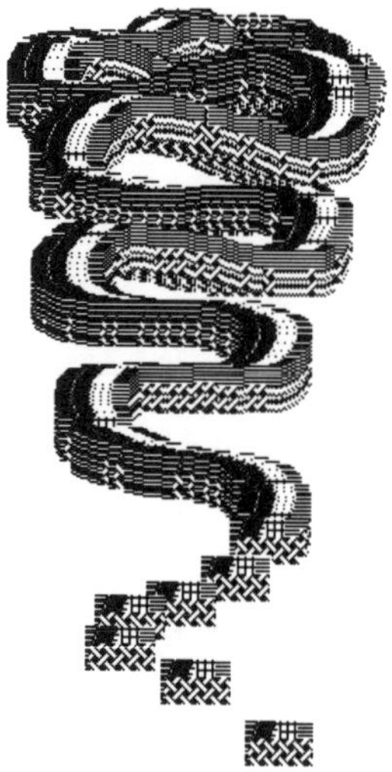

Unfortunately, *MacPaint* works only in black-and-white, a document can span only one 8-1/2-by-11-inch page, and rotation of a selected area can only be in 90-degree steps.

MacPaint Features

Multiple documents: Up to nine documents can be open simultaneously; the actual number is limited by available memory.

Tear-off menus: The painting tool and fill pattern menus can be "torn" from the menu bar in their fully open state, and can act as palettes that can be dragged anywhere on the work surface. *MacPaint 2.0* can be instructed to remember where you want the tear-off menus to appear, so that when you close and then reopen, they'll appear where you want them.

Numerical size scaling: A selected area can be sized. The contents of a selection marquee can be sized by hand, or proportionally scaled by specifying a percentage.

Magnification and reduction: There are three levels of working magnification (200, 400, and 800 percent) and one level of reduction (50 percent). All tools are fully operational in both enlarged and reduced views.

"Snapshot" and "magic eraser": The current picture can be preserved without affecting the last saved version. You can revert to this snapshot at any time. In conjunction with the snapshot feature, the magic eraser can erase down to the level of the last snapshot without disturbing the snapshot itself. This feature is excellent as a high-powered selective "undo."

User-set preference of image overlay effects: The user can specify that overlapping images be transparent or opaque, or that they show other interactive characteristics.

Three text overlay modes: The user can choose opaque white background and black text, clear background and black text, or clear background and black text that reverses to white when laid over black pixels.

Variable grid steps: Grids steps may be specified as 2, 4, 8, 16, or 32 pixels.

Line thicknesses: Vertical and horizontal line widths can be varied independently of each other.

Geometric shapes: Shapes can be drawn from their center or from a corner (for a rectangle) or a point on the circumference (for an ellipse).

Brush mirrors: This selection creates a kaleidoscopic effect, producing up to eight symmetrical curves from one brush stroke. Mirrors can be independently activated along the 90-degree (vertical and horizontal) and 45-degree (diagonal) planes.

Trace Edges: Trace Edges surrounds selected, enclosed images with one or more outlines of specified width.

Start-up screens: Paintings can be saved as start-up screens, to appear when the Mac II is turned on.

Stationery: Paintings can be saved as stationery sheets that remember your working preferences (for example grid size and overlay mode) and contain often-used backgrounds.

"Paintings" Gallery Figures 1, 3, 4, 6, and 16 were produced using *MacPaint*, as was Color Gallery Figure 29.

Canvas (2.0) (Paint Mode)

Canvas (Figure 4-2) is one of several two-part (paint and draw) applications. It can work simultaneously in two worlds: bitmapped and object-oriented. This section focuses on the bitmapped mode and points out the advantages of painting with access to an object-oriented environment. *Canvas*'s draw mode is discussed in Chapter 5.

Figure 4-2. The *Canvas* window showing painting and drawing tools as well as the application's organization by layers.

Canvas's user interface is well designed and responds with good speed. It offers traditional painting tools with a number of significant extensions. Two areas worthy of immediate note are its potentially vast canvas size and its ability to manage paintings on "floating" easels of any shape. These features provide great flexibility in composition even though you're working in a bitmapped environment. One feature of the interface that seems a little awkward is the system of double-clicking and dialog boxes used to make the transition (or to *avoid* making it accidentally) from the paint layer to the draw layer and vice versa. Tripping over dialog boxes that appear unexpectedly can interrupt the "creative flow."

Canvas's special effects include free rotation as well as rotation in 90-degree increments, 1- and 2-point perspective distortion, skewing (shearing), and free-form distortion. *Canvas* operates in color, but unfortunately colors are limited to black, white, red, green, blue, cyan, magenta, and yellow.

Canvas also comes as a desk acessory (DA) with 70 percent of its full application power. Missing from the DA are special effects like rotation, smoothing, and distortion. The advantages of painting with a DA are discused in Chapter 19.

Canvas Features

Painting easels: Easels can be made from any shape drawn in the program's object-oriented mode. Paint tools are active only within the bounds of an easel. Painted easels become free-floating objects in the layout and can be freely mixed with objects in the draw layer.

Bit-map resolution: *Canvas* can paint at a resolution of 72, 150, 300, 635, 1270, or 2540 dpi.

Size: The painting surface can be as large as 10 pages by 13 pages.

Magnification and reduction: Painted images can be enlarged from 2 to more than 32 times and reduced from 1/2 to 1/32.

User-set preference of image overlay effects: The user can specify that overlapping images be transparent or opaque, or that they show other characteristics.

Color: Painted easels can be colorized or recolorized in any of eight colors in the object layer.

Single and bidirectional arrows: The line tool can draw lines with arrowheads at the ends.

Line thicknesses: Vertical and horizontal line widths can be varied independently of each other in 1-pixel increments up to 10 pixels wide.

Airbrush patterns: The airbrush "footprint" is editable, and the user can specify the flow rate of the spray.

Macro-objects: Paint images (as well as draw objects) can be named and saved as "macro-objects" in "libraries." Any library can be opened and its objects made accessible as menu selections in the Macro menu. A thumbnail view appears next to each object name in the menu. When you select a menu object and click on the canvas, a copy of the object appears.

Several of the Gallery figures in Chapter 5 were produced with *Canvas*.

PixelPaint (2.0)

PixelPaint is a full-color painting application that lets you use up to 256 colors simultaneously and supports 24-bit color. Colors can be selected from the standard Color Picker wheel as well as Pantone, Process Color (CMYK), RGB (Red, Green, Blue) and HSV (Hue, Saturation, Value). It has a two-mode interface: the Normal mode offers conventional painting tools, solid-color fills, and a few special options and effects. The Special Effects mode amplifies just about every tool with a rich set of customizable options.

Its ability to import gray-scale images saved as TIFF or PICT2 files (see "File Format #2: PICT" in Chapter 5) makes it useful as a photo-retouching tool, although it's not nearly as powerful as applications like *ImageStudio* and *Digital Darkroom*, which are dedicated to that task (see Chapter 7). As well as having capabilities of gray-scale editors, *PixelPaint* includes features of PostScript illustrating programs (covered in Chapter 6), but since its interface is most like that of paint programs, it's discussed here. Check Chapters 7 and 6, respectively, for more information about gray-scale and PostScript features in general.

PixelPaint's tools and windows are well laid out and predictable in function, and its interface is smooth, responsive, and conducive to producing art in a nearly limitless variety of styles. Special consideration has obviously been given to convenience and easy access to the many features of this application.

For all the features it provides, *PixelPaint* requires a lot of memory. Memory limitations will determine the maximum size of the canvas, and 2 megabytes of RAM is the lower limit for using this program.

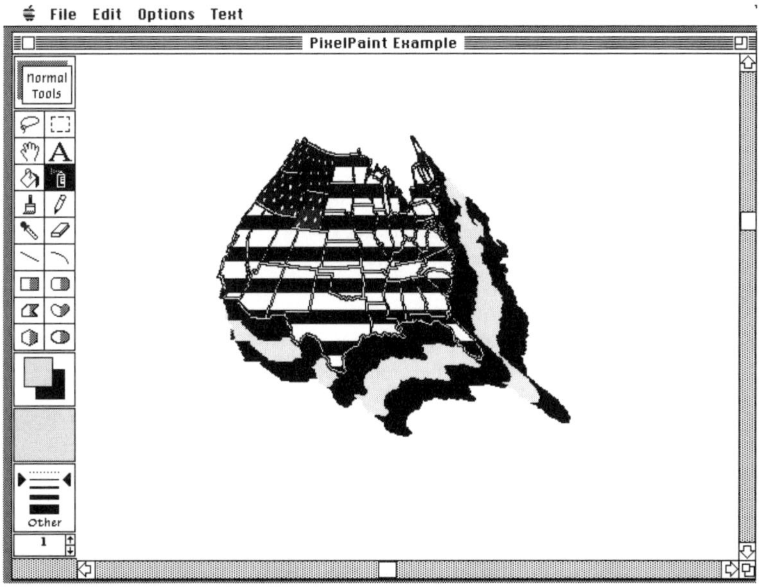

Figure 4-3. The *PixelPaint* window showing tiling, shadows, and distortion.

PixelPaint Features

Import formats: *PixelPaint* can import Paint, PICT, PICT2, TIFF, and EPSF format files, and color start-up screens.

Canvas: There are six preset sizes, from 512 x 512 to 1024 x 1024, plus U.S. letter and other standard sheet sizes, and NTSC and PAL monitor standards.

Halftone control: This enables the control of dot shape, screen angle, and resolution (dpi).

Special Effects mode: This mode provides options for customizing the working enviroment. Each tool type can be customized individually, or the same effects can be applied to all tools.

Ready-made palettes: Palettes include Rainbow, System, Earthtones, Fleshtones, Pastels, Vivid, Metallic, Grayscale, Single Hue, and 8, 16, or 32 hues, each with varied intensities.

Editable palettes: Palettes can be saved as named color sets that can later be recalled and used in other paintings. Colors can be copied and pasted from spot to spot on a palette. Buttons in the Color dialog box can modify a selected color by warming, cooling, darkening, or lightening it, or by changing it to its contrasting color. The Color Wheel provides finer precision for modifying color.

Pop-up palettes and menus: Color palette and special effects menus appear under the cursor when the Command and Option keys are held down while clicking.

Three active colors: Three colors are active at any time — Background and Foreground (for obvious purposes) and Blend (which allows you to choose a color to ramp to). (*Ramping* is making a smooth transition over space from one color to another.)

Automatic blending of palette colors: If you select a color palette item and assign it a color, and then select another item some distance away and assign it another color, *PixelPaint* will blend the entire range of palette entries between the first and last items so that they form a smooth color transition between the two end colors.

Optional remapping of colors: Colors can be remapped to closely matching colors in a new color palette. That is, colors from the old and new palettes are paired by color attributes rather than by position in the palette. With this option turned off, all existing image colors will be replaced with the colors that reside in the corresponding positions in the new palette.

Fill effects: Closed shapes can be filled with a uniform hue, or with a range in color from the Foreground color to the Blend color. The shape of the fill pattern and its ramping direction can be specified from a wide set of choices: directional, sunburst, "shapeburst," and others. The ramping effect transitions through all the colors of the current palette that are between the Foreground and the Blend color.

Gray-scale brush effects: Smooth, Smear, Lighten, Darken, and Charcoal effects are available. In Minimum mode, when the brush passes over other pixels, the least luminant color prevails. In Maximum mode, when the brush passes over other pixels, the most luminant color prevails.

Smooth and Smear: These techniques use the brush to blend adjoining colors and to push a small amount of one color into another.

Other brush effects: Whatever is in the **clipboard** can be used as the brush. You can push pixels gradually in any direction by **nudging** them with a brush. **Double-dipped** mode will paint in both the Foreground and the Blend color. **Shadow mode** follows the brush stroke with a shadow that falls at a specified distance behind it.

Tiling: A section of a clipboard picture can be used as a repetitive pattern, which can then be used to fill closed objects. The repeating unit of the pattern can be 16, 32, 64, or 128 pixels.

Spray can (airbrush): The spray can sprays with a pixel-dot pattern that can be numerically specified. The degree of coverage is time dependent: if you continue to spray in one place, more and more color will be built up. **Spatter** mode makes larger drops of varying sizes. The paint effect of the spray can transitions from the Foreground color to the Blend color.

Pencil: The pencil can act as a fine airbrush, or it can be used as a fine detailer or draggable magnifying lens. Its stroke can be graduated from Foreground to Blend color.

Eraser: The eraser can remove pixels down to the Background, Foreground, Fill, or Shadow color, or erase to white or black.

Eyedropper: The eyedropper copies whatever color it's clicked on, and makes it the Foreground color. This proves very useful for resuming work in an area without fishing for its precise color in the palette.

Shadows: Shadows can be drawn automatically as the image is drawn or added to an existing image. Specifications for shadows are set in a dialog box, with visual feedback. The variables you can manipulate are angle, distance from the object, color, and intensity. Shadow types are Drop (normal), or Blend (a 3D extension of the object, with a shadow that transitions through the Foreground and Blend colors).

Line thickness: Lines can be from 1 to 100 pixels wide. Height and width can be set independently.

Line types: Multiple radial lines can be drawn from a common point by clicking on each intended endpoint. **Fractal lines** allow user-variable random bending between start and endpoint. **"Neon"** mode simulates a fluorescent light that is brighter along the centerline and darkens outward to the Foreground color. **"Tube"** mode simulates a tube with the Foreground color along the centerline, darkening outward to black. **Special lines** available as variations of the arc tool are **arcs** (plain) as 90-degree elliptical sections, **multipoint Bezier curve** (see Chapter 6 for more on Bezier curves), and **multipoint spline** (a smooth curve fitted through any number of points).

Regular polygons: Polygons with three to eight sides can be formed.

Patterns: Patterns affect the pixel layout of the current color. Patterns are formed of a single color only (in other words, they're not dithered). Patterns can be selected from a ready-made group, and any pattern can be edited.

Text effects: *PixelPaint* provides the standard styles and alignments, plus a custom "other" font size up to 255 points.

Text block handling: Only one font, style, and size is allowed per block. Text takes on the current Foreground color. It can be solid, patterned, or inverted, with a solid or patterned background of the same color (that is, solid letters on a patterned background, or vice versa).

Bert Monroy describes the artistic process he used to produce *Street Scene*, Color Gallery Figure 13.

MacWorld Expo in San Francisco was to start in another week and I found myself in a dark corner of a factory in an industrial section of the city. In this dark corner, however, was a Macintosh II with a SuperMac 19-inch monitor and the release version of *PixelPaint*. It was about 3:30 in the morning when my host finally got off the computer and went to sleep. Then *I* sat down to play! Back home in New York, they were getting blanketed with snow. I felt a little homesick, so the inspiration was that of some street scene typical of New York City.

The first problem with any panorama is the perspective. Since I was not using any reference material and just creating as I went along, I had to make my own vanishing points. Vanishing points are essential to give a scene its three dimensional quality. I like to give scenes the feeling of depth, as if you could enter the space. So I use angled streets with hidden corners and turns to achieve this sensation.

Using the thumb on the scroll bar as the vanishing point, I drew lines that would serve as the outlines for the various buildings, windows, sidewalks, and other shapes that characterize this particular street. To ensure the accuracy and consistency of the perspective lines, all the lines for the windows ran straight across all the buildings. Once the windows had been shaped by the vertical lines, the extra horizontal line segments could be erased using the eraser tool.

Next I added the vertical lines to delineate the individual structures, windows, doors, and so on. Now I was ready for the fun part — details. If you're familiar with city streets, you know that they're a fountain of different objects, colors, and shapes. Plants, garbage cans, even laundry, all add life to a street. Since this particular street was of my own invention, I had no limitations.

First, each window had to have an activity of some kind. It was at this juncture that I had to tackle the problem of color — 256 colors may sometimes seem like a lot, but not in a situation like this. Optimal use of the palette was necessary if the street was to be awake with life.

The buildings were the first consideration. Brownstones and bricks are the most common types in the City, but different shades are needed for variety. Even brownstones differ in color from one to the next. So I created wide blend ranges of browns and warm reds. The thought of the New York sky on the night of a snowfall with its rich orange cast into black gave these brown and red color ranges a twofold purpose. Next a gray range was developed for the concrete sidewalks. A yellow blend was needed for the lights in windows. Also, since the time of day in the scene was evening, I needed a blue range to give some of the windows the feeling that a television was being watched within. Finally, what street scene is complete without an occasional plant in the window. One narrow band of green was all that was needed for this purpose. These six color ranges provided enough colors to give the illusion that more than 256 colors were available.

Before adding the colors, however, I had to establish the light sources. The small clapboard structure in the center would house a storefront. This, like all late-night stores, would serve as a beacon and thus the principal source of light. A street lamp would offset it to the right, and between the two would be the light spilling from the lobby of the apartment building. The bucket tool was used in the Special Effects mode with a brick-red blend. With the "sunburst" effect, the fill pattern was directed from the base just below the store's awning, with a gradation going from light at the center to dark on the outer edges. This gave the effect of light coming from under the awning. This same procedure was then applied to the sidewalk from the center out using a white-to-black gradation.

The apartment building was now in need of the brick texture to finalize its facade. Using the brick fill pattern with the spray can tool in Normal Tools mode, I lightly sprayed the walls, leaving behind just faint sections of brick. I switched shades of brick color to give the feeling of aging.

Fill patterns were also used with the bucket tool to create the

(continued on next page)

venetian blinds in the windows and the metal work beneath the store window. The graduated metal effect on the store's base was done by first cutting a straight line through the fill effect of vertical slats in order to allow the bucket to fill with an even tone. Once the gradation was complete, the slats were closed off again.

The use of gradations throughout gives the scene its richness. Even the door lamps by the store have a sunburst effect to give them their glow.

All minute details were done in FatBits. The garbage cans are simply clones of one original with little details like the lid handles changed to give the feeling that each is different.

The 1955 Chieftain 870 Custom Safari wagon in the foreground was the only element in the scene that was taken from reference material. Knowing car buffs would scoff at some invented design, I decided to look one up. The shape was created in *Adobe Illustrator*. A screen dump was then made to be ported over into *PixelPaint* and colorized.

The street needed to look well travelled. The spray can tool in Special Effects mode is a versatile airbrush. Employing a cycle airbrush with a gray blend, I swept the street. With a finer spray and black, I coated the middle of the street for that exhaust build-up look.

Similar sprays were added to the brownstone facades, and then using the brush tool in the Smear mode, I blended the colors to give the brownstone texture effect. The concrete side of the apartment building was achieved by first adding a graduated blend and then airbrushing. The cracks were done with the line tool in the fractal mode, which lets you determine the amount of fractality a line will have. (It's a great tool for lightning also.)

In all, the best feature of *PixelPaint* is the fact that it's easy — it lends itself to a spontaneity in the creative process. And no brushes to clean!

— *Bert Monroy*

Visual effects: Visual effects act on regions selected with the lasso or marquee. Standard effects are available, as well as some especially notable and valuable ones. **Smooth** blends the edges of two different color regions to help remove "jaggies," or stair-step appearance. This effect is especially useful for gray-scale images. **Diffuse** dithers the edge pixels of two adjoining color regions to create a coarse blend, which can then be smoothed. (Dithering is a speckling technique that mixes a few colors and creates the illusion of more.) Other effects include Sharpen, Wash, Increase, and Decrease.

Dynamic effects: A selected rectangular area can be cropped, distorted, free-rotated, put into perspective, and slanted.

Export formats: Export formats include Paint, PICT, PICT2, TIFF, and EPSF/ *Adobe Illustrator* (see Chapter 6) format files, and color start-up screens.

PixelPaint was used to produce "Paintings" Gallery Figure 13 and Color Gallery Figures 1 through 14, 16, 22, 27, 30, and 34.

Modern Artist

Modern Artist provides a richly featured painting environment with some unique tools. Its user interface is fairly intuitive, but compared with other Macintosh painting applications, it breaks some new ground. Its unique features involve special shading effects that create perfect 3D shading on spheres, simulate transparent refractive globes, and provides a flat shading for the rectangular solids it also helps to create.

Figure 4-4. *Modern Artist* offers a unique "Sunglasses" feature.

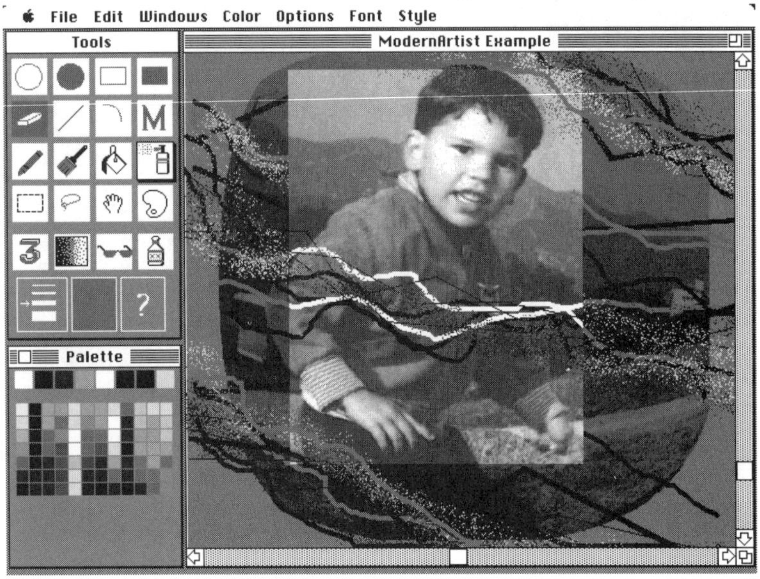

A significant feature of *Modern Artist* is its ability to create colors by dithering appropriate System palette colors, or by the normal way of rendering a single pixel the precise color selected from a custom palette. Paintings produced with dithered colors stand a better chance of retaining their original appearance when exported to other applications that use only the System color palette.

Modern Artist Features

Movable and hidable palettes: Palettes can be placed to provide the maximum possible visible working area.

Editable grid: You can specify separate *x*- and *y*-axis grid steps.

Color memory: Each tool and mode remembers the color it used most recently. A tool or mode is activated with the last color used with that tool.

Custom colors: You can produce custom color palettes that can be saved as named items and reused in other paintings.

Color transitions: Dithering (a speckling technique that mixes a few colors to create the illusion of more) allows *Modern Artist* to display many more colors than are normally available. The standard Mac II System color table is used for dithering, and this allows files to be exported to other applications without loss of fidelity.

Directional fills: Two types of shading can be used for directional fills of closed objects — transition through the rainbow from one color to the other, and direct color-to-color transition through gray.

3D shading effects for spheres: Shaded, clear, and refractive spheres can be produced. The position of an imaginary light source is specified by clicking somewhere on the screen.

Sunglasses: This tool applies an additive color wash over a selected area, a capability unusual among paint programs.

Stain tool: With this tool you can substitute any one color for another in a selected area. It's very precise about substituting for the designated color only, so it can be used to save time in recoloring painted objects, especially if they're discontinuous or intermixed with others.

Smoothing: You can smooth freehand curves if you like.

Plotted curves: If you click the brush or crayon at a series of points on the canvas, they'll be automatically connected with a fitted curve drawn with the selected brush shape and color.

Brushes: Brush tips are editable, in multicolor or single-color patterns. Brush sets can be saved as named entities and reused.

Wet Canvas: In Wet Canvas mode the brush runs out of paint as the stroke proceeds. Paint responds to the Wet Canvas option by blending with overlaid colors. This is a very realistic effect.

Erasing: Pixels can be changed to any palette color as they're erased.

Text: Text can be any color, with a clear background. A new text block is resizable and movable. Text automatically wraps inside its rectangle during entry and resizing. Any portion of text in the block is freely editable until you click outside the text block.

Online help: When you select a tool and click on the "?" icon, a Help window pops up to explain the tool's function.

Modern Artist was used to create Color Gallery Figure 29.

Draw It Again, Sam (2.01)

Draw It Again, Sam offers coexisting drawing and painting environments. Its 10-layer drawing surface can simplify the construction of highly populated paintings by keeping picture elements on separate layers so they can be edited without disturbing other elements. The program lets you construct and visually access libraries of predrawn items.

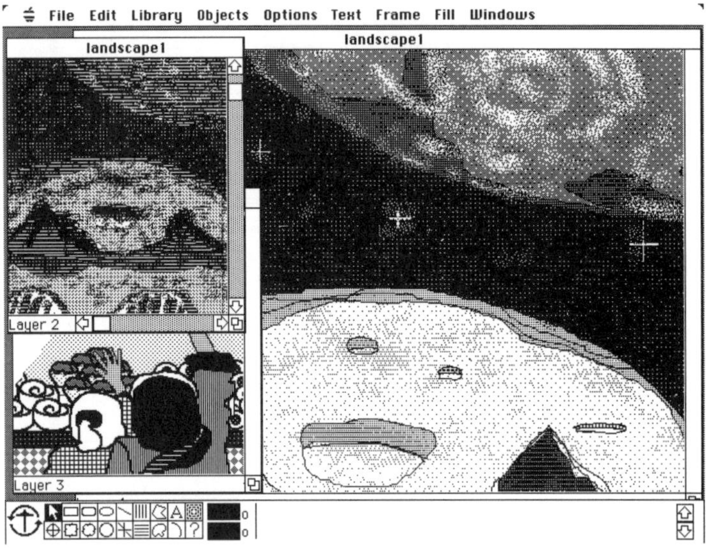

Figure 4-5. With *Draw It Again, Sam,* an artist can use several layers in one painting.

An especially good feature of *Sam* is that painting can be done anywhere on the working surface, and the easel (layer) for the bit map is created automatically and extends as far as the farthest laid paint stroke. However, shrinking a paint easel to crop its contents results in *permanent* cropping — if the easel is later enlarged, only white space appears.

Its user interface, with its hierarchical menus feels more labor intensive than other graphics applications in its paint-draw class, but its smoothness and generally quick response redeem it.

Draw It Again, Sam Features

Layers: The program provides up to 10 layers, each with its own display attributes, which include visible, grayed, framed, and invisible. Layers can also be printed individually.

Drawing and painting modes: (The draw mode is covered in Chapter 5). The painting mode lets you freely draw, edit, and rearrange bit maps. (Rotation is available in 90-degree steps only.)

Color: *Sam* uses eight basic colors, including black and white. No dithering is supported, but two or more colored objects with different fill patterns can be overlapped to produce a kind of dithering. Strangely, choosing a color for text also sets the color for future shapes. *Sam* has no true gray-scale shades.

Dedicated painting tools: Equilateral four-sided shapes, perfect circles, perfect vertical, horizontal, and 45-degree lines are provided. (There's a noticeable lag in response with the pencil, eraser, and brush. The eraser is especially sluggish in reduced view.)

Parallel line tool: This tool draws a user-specified number (1–999) of evenly spaced parallel lines, horizontally or vertically.

Graphic overlay effects: Overlays can be opaque or clear, and can invert or erase pixels of the image underneath.

Object libraries: Objects can be predrawn, named, assigned an icon, and stored in reusable object libraries. Library-object icons appear in a selection palette below the workspace, or they can be selected by name from a menu.

Spray can: This feature is excellent, one of the best. Three speeds, variable shape patterns (not just round), and several angles of graduated spray swaths are provided.

"Drawings" Gallery Figure 10 in Chapter 5 was produced using both paint and draw functions of *Draw It Again, Sam.*

DeskPaint (2.0) (Application and Desk Accessory)

DeskPaint is a full-featured paint program in an incredibly small package. It can create, open, and modify both low- and high-resolution bit maps with a standard set of painting and transformation tools. It has features absent from most of its bulkier counterparts.

It can serve as a valuable enhancer for object-oriented or desktop publishing applications that lack painting tools for creating or modifying bitmapped graphics. (See Chapters 5 and 8, respectively, for more information on object-oriented and desktop publishing applications.)

Figure 4-6. A *DeskPaint* window showing some of the many patterns available.

DeskPaint Features

Desk accessory: Many of the program's features are available via the desk accessory, which is available through the apple menu while other applications are running.

Clipboard: If you clip an image and then open *DeskPaint*, the contents of the clipboard automatically (without pasting) appear in the *DeskPaint* window.

Scanning: *DeskPaint* can scan the Scrapbook automatically or manually prompted, or can scan the contents of a folder, presenting timed or user-controlled slide shows.

Resolution: You can paint at your choice of resolutions — 1 to 2540 dpi.

Drawing size: Size is limited only by available memory.

Auto-scrolling: The painting scrolls automatically and with excellent speed when the cursor reaches the edge of the window.

Magnification and reduction: Several magnifications and reductions are available, and tools work in all views.

Autotracing: Automatic tracing of bit maps produces draw objects that can be copied and pasted into object-oriented applications. The trace feature can be customized.

Excellent tool palette: The palette is small with a very easy-to-use layout. Shapes in the palette reflect current fill pattern and line thickness. The palette can be hidden to allow a larger drawing area. (For some reason, the palette flickers after most choices.)

Airbrush: Spray size and pattern are adjustable.

Pen sizing: Vertical and horizontal stroke widths can be set independently.

Patterns: Several menus of patterns are available.

Lasso: The lasso is fully functional. (It does not automatically scroll when you reach the edge of the window, but you can use reduced view to cover a large area.) However, if something is lassoed, cut, and then pasted, it acts as if the marquee had been used, and white space is no longer transparent.

Text-mode palette: You can fully control font, size, and style through this palette.

Text-entry window: The window is fully resizable, editable, and movable while active.

Special effects: Effects include 90-degree and free rotation, perspective distortion, skewing (shearing), and free-form distortion.

Laser-scaling: Bit maps for laser printing are scaled to prevent interference patterns.

Export formats: *DeskPaint* can save files in Paint (*DeskPaint*), TIFF, and TIFF Compressed formats.

SuperPaint (2.0) (Paint Mode)

SuperPaint can work in two modes: bitmapped and object-oriented. This section focuses on the bitmapped mode. *SuperPaint* handles these modes somewhat differently than *Canvas* and *Draw It Again, Sam*. *SuperPaint* has a drawing layer and a painting layer. When one layer is active, its tools cannot affect graphics residing in the other.

Items from one layer can be transferred to the other layer by selecting them and using a single command. This feature allows graphics to be partially constructed as easily editable objects in the draw layer, and then transferred to the paint layer for bit-map editing. Similarly, finished bit maps can be transferred to the draw layer for simplified positioning and stacking.

One of *SuperPaint*'s outstanding features is its ability to use "plug-in" tools. These are custom effects that can be programmed outside of *SuperPaint* and then placed in a specially named folder. Their presence is recognized at start-up and their icons are automatically placed in *SuperPaint*'s scrolling tool box section. Some special tools include: spiral, limited paint brush, and 3D rectangular solid.

Another feature of note is its ability to automatically trace the edges of a bit map, producing object-oriented or Bezier curve outlines that can be exported to other applications.

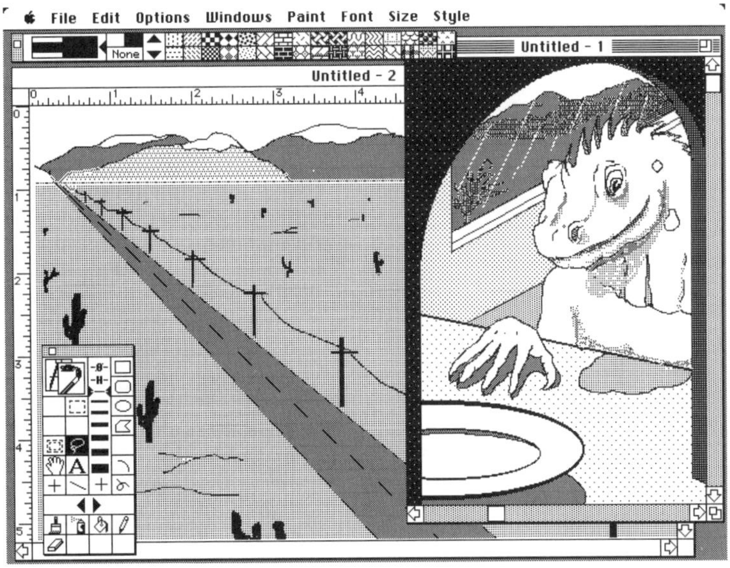

Figure 4-7. *SuperPaint* allows for the addition of custom tools.

SuperPaint Features

Hidden layer: The draw layer can be hidden during painting operations.

LaserBits: An area of a painting can be designated as a high-resolution bit map that can be edited with normal tools. This area will print at 300 dpi on a printer that supports that resolution.

Magnification and reduction: View changes are both key driven and menu driven. Tools are functional in all views.

Floating palettes: Tool and shading palettes float, appearing where and when needed.

Measurement units: Units for grid and ruler include inches, centimeters, picas/points, and screen dots. Rulers don't have an adjustable zero point.

Auto-scrolling: When the drawing tool touches the edge of the window, the window scrolls automatically. This feature can be turned off.

Colors: Colors can be applied and previewed, but not viewed while you're working.

Brush mirrors: Vertical, horizontal, and 45-degree mirrors reflect brush strokes.

Autotrace: Bitmapped graphics can be automatically traced to produce Bezier-curve outlines.

Radial brush symmetry: This feature draws from two to eight radially symmetrical copies of brush strokes. Unlike its action in the mirrors feature, when the brush moves left, its symmetrical partner moves right.

Dynamically variable airbrush: The spray pattern is random, and the size can be altered, even during spraying.

Horizontal and vertical line widths: Horizontal and vertical width are independently variable from 0 to 8 pixels. **Zero line width** can be specified for horizontal or vertical lines of a shape.

Arrowheads: A wide variety of arrowheads and other types of end-points, filled and hollow, are available. Each can be edited and saved as a reusable item through the Edit Arrows dialog box. Straight lines can have no arrowheads, arrowheads at the start, at the end, or at both ends.

Dashed lines: A wide variety of dashed line patterns can be applied to lines. Each can be edited and saved as a reusable item via the Edit Dashes dialog box. Only single lines can be dashed or have arrowheads.

Multiple images: Paint Multiple mode allows you to draw multiple images. For example, as a rectangle is drawn, it leaves behind a series of smaller rectangles, marking its growth path. Used with the Draw from Center mode, it produces a series of concentric copies of a shape.

Paint effects: Paint effects are opaque (normal), transparent (additive), paint on black (which leaves white space untouched), and invert paint (which, in addition to applying the selected shade, turns black image pixels white whenever a black drawing stroke passes over them). With the brush, invert paint produces a random mottled effect; with line-based tools, the effect is a predictable inversion of black and white.

Fill patterns and shades: Any existing pattern can be edited, and up to 32 new patterns can be added to the existing set of 96.

Multigon: This tool draws an equal-sided object with any number of sides. Polygons of 3, 4, 5, 6, and 8 sides are predefined for convenience.

Draw from corner or center: You can begin a geometric shape at its perimeter or its center.

Text: Text can be filled with any of the fill patterns. Fonts, sizes, and styles can be mixed in one block. Maximum type size is 127 points.

Text block handling: As text is entered beyond the user's view, the document automatically scrolls. Just-typed text remains selected and active during scrolling.

Selection tools: Oval and freehand selection tools are available.

Select All: This command selects the entire painting layer.

Special effects: Effects include 90-degree and free rotation, 1- and 2-point perspective distortion, skewing (shearing), and free-form distortion.

Nudge: This feature lets you shove a selected area one pixel at a time in any direction.

Special lasso modes: If you double-click on an object with the lasso, the object will be entirely lassoed. If you add the Option key, only the connected nonwhite pixels will be selected. Anything contained within the lassoed outline will not be selected.

Scaling: An area selected with the lasso or marquee can be symmetrically scaled by specifying a percentage (25, 50, 200, or 400 percent, or other) or can be asymmetrically scaled by manually dragging an edge.

Export formats: Bit maps can be exported as TIFF or *ThunderScan* files.

"Paintings"Gallery Figures 2, 5, 8 through 12, 14, and 15 were produced using *SuperPaint*, as were Color Gallery Figures 7 and 9.

GraphicWorks (1.1)

GraphicWorks can adequately be described as an object-oriented painting application (see Chapter 5 for an explanation of features of object-oriented graphics programs). Its work surface consists of panels, which can contain bit-map easels, object primitives, other panels, and text balloons. (The last reflects *GraphicWorks*' original incarnation as *ComicWorks*.)

Any item (panel, easel, object, or balloon) drawn inside a panel is automatically grouped with the panel, and will remain so until it's somehow removed. When a panel is moved, all of its contents move with it. This hierarchical management can simplify composition and expedite the production of layouts.

The *GraphicWorks* painting tools operate in a standard fashion with the exception of its smooth and versatile airbrush, which is a work of art in itself. Its object-oriented environment is workable, but it doesn't supply smoothing, open polygons, free rotation, alignment tools, or grouping, which means it lacks the depth for creating serious object-based graphics. But, as a flexible paint and text application, *GraphicWorks* offers some unique creative opportunities.

Figure 4-8. *GraphicWorks* has several different kinds of panels.

GraphicWorks Features

Import formats: Paint and TIFF (but not gray-scale TIFF) files can be imported directly.In addition, any graphic format that can travel through the clipboard, including *CricketDraw* graphics with full PostScript attributes, can be imported.

Layered working environment: Layering is achieved through panels containing other panels. Each panel can be considered a layer that can be shuffled among the rest.

One-click navigation: You can navigate through the layout by using a tool that selects each panel in turn.

Multipage drawing area: Pages are created to the right of existing pages.

Custom grids: Grids with custom divisions are easily constructed by dragging a grid cell to the desired size with the mouse. The grid can be displayed and snapped to.

Bit maps: Bit maps can be produced at resolutions of 72 through 2540 dpi.

Palettes: A true gray-scale palette provides 32 intensities plus black and white. Three other (editable) pattern palettes are also provided. The tool and pattern palettes can be accidentally obscured by stretching the document window over them.

Airbrush: The airbrush has fine controls for very thin to very broad spray, and the width can be changed while spraying. However, in 256-color mode, the airbrush effect is visible only after you release the mouse button. During spraying, eight small color versions of the airbrush path appear on the top edge of the screen.

Custom line widths: Lines can be as wide as 72 points.

Text balloons: Ballons can be basic shapes, comic type, custom-shaped, or unframed, essentially serving as invisible column guides. The size and location of the actual text block inside a balloon can be modified.

Text effects: Text can be sized to 127 points; typical styles are available, plus condensed and extended. Fonts and styles can be mixed in one text block. But text can't be fully justified.

Selection: Lasso and marquee are available. In color, a freshly a selected area (with lasso or marquee) will take on the foreground and background colors while selected, but revert to black and white after deselection. Selection handles are overpowering. They are thick, dark, and disturbing.

Simplified cropping and clipping: Panels (including oval panels) can be reshaped, without actually deleting any portions of the graphics they contain.

Option to clip or to show: Individual objects can extend beyond the borders of a panel, to produce the illusion of graphics reaching out beyond the confines of the page. This is a priceless time-saver for framing and composition.

Reshaping: Objects you create can be reshaped; vertices can be added or deleted.

Special effects: Effects include skewing, free rotation, perspective, and distortion.

Overlap effects: Effects include opaque, transparent, additive, subtractive, and more.

Mixed automatic resolution change: The Laserbits tool expands a high-resolution bit map for editing at 72 dpi, and then automatically reduces it when the bit map is deselected.

Nudge: Using control keys, you can nudge panels in 1-pixel increments in any of four directions.

Export formats: Files can be exported as Paint or PICT.

"Paintings" Gallery Figures 17 and 18 were produced with *GraphicWorks.*

MacCalligraphy (2.0)

MacCalligraphy simulates oriental ink painting. Its icons look and act like their real-world counterparts. The feel of long-bristled brushes is so authentic that an entirely new mousing technique is required. For example, with some brush-and-ink-flow combinations, releasing the mouse button doesn't end the

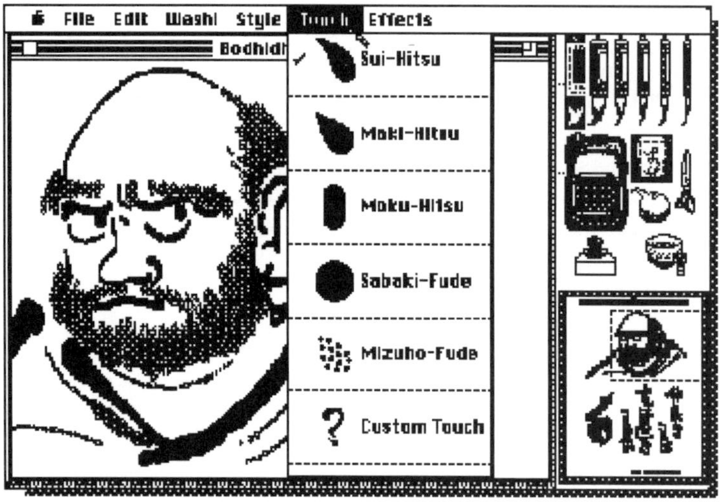

Figure 4-9. *MacCalligraphy* provides a unique painting environment.

stroke immediately. Painting continues until the stoke narrows to a point.

With *MacCalligraphy,* your own touch and strokes are the key sources of variations. Although the art involves shades of gray, this application uses various densities of black and white pixels to simulate gray tones.

Designed to imitate a strictly black-and-white medium, in the multicolor mode the program is extremely sluggish, and some tools don't work. To use *MacCalligraphy,* set up the Macintosh II for black-and-white, two-color mode. And use the Control Panel under the apple menu to set a slow mouse speed so that you don't overdrive the brushes.

MacCalligraphy Features

Bristle brushes: Brushes are available in six widths and five predefined brush shapes. And you can design your own as well.

Ink metaphors: Black pigment and water metaphors are used to produce the paint shades. Add pigment to the mix to darken the shade, add water to lighten it.

Ink penetration: Penetration of ink into the paper can be adjusted to one of four degrees, each selectable from a pictorial menu.

Stroke persistence: You can set the delay between the time you lift the brush and the end of the paint flow; four degrees of persistence are available.

Stamp design: You can design a stamp to serve as your personal seal, for signing your creations.

Scissors tool: This is basically a selection rectangle for selecting, moving, inverting, or deleting blocks of the painting.

Dry canvas: The dry canvas effect overlays the most recent shade onto the painting, regardless of any existing paint.

Underlay: This effect leaves darker pixels unchanged when a lighter shade is applied over them.

"Paintings" Gallery Figures 7 and 9 were created with *MacCalligraphy.*

CrystalPaint (1.02)

CrystalPaint is essentially a pattern-creation tool. It acts as a house of mirrors while its drawing tool traces a path, or **trail**. It supplies a wide variety of reflective modes that can turn a simple pen stroke into intricate snowflake patterns, arabesques, spirals, exotic weaves, simple repetitions, and many more kinds of output. Some paint applications provide simple mirrors, but *CrystalPaint*'s reflective talents extend well beyond central symmetry. It provides fine control over the kind of reflection it produces, as well as the distance between repetitions.

With *CrystalPaint* it's possible to randomly or intentionally create effects that are essentially impossible to achieve with other applications. A finished document can be saved or printed, or a part of it can be copied and pasted into another application that accepts bitmapped art. After pasting, the pattern may be trimmed, drawn upon, and otherwise modified as a bit map in the receiving application.

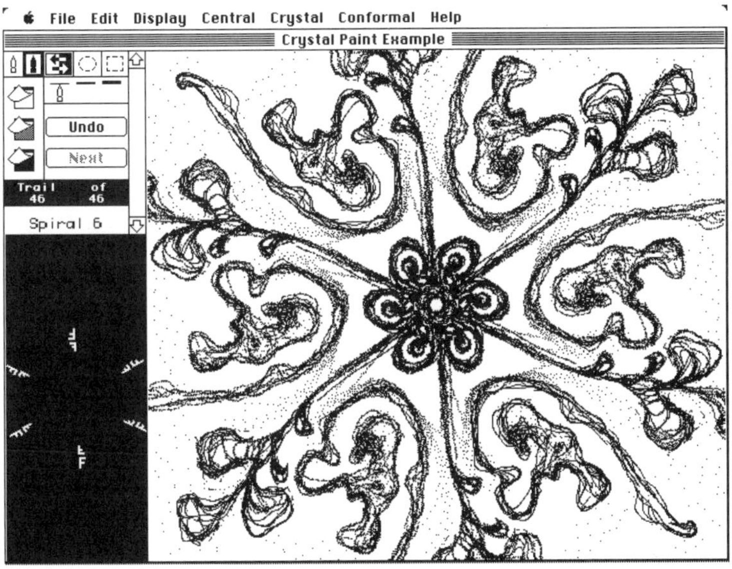

Figure 4-10. *CrystalPaint* makes great mandalas.

As a stand-alone tool, *CrystalPaint* has its limitations. Its one and only tool is the pen, and its one and only effect is reflection. And it works only in black-and-white mode. It's far from a complete painting program, although it's possible to produce some rather spectacular works by using it alone. Its Autopilot mode can provide capturable screens, allow pleasant and inspiring diversion, or serve as a most fascinating screen saver.

CrystalPaint Features

Paste into *CrystalPaint*: Bit maps from other applications can be pasted in and then made to repeat according to the selected pattern. Optionally, reflection of the pasted image can be suppressed.

***MultiFinder* compatibility:** *CrystalPaint* works with *MultiFinder*, which makes it efficient to use in conjunction with another application.

Window size: The drawing window will size itself to fill any screen, but it can't be resized.

Backgrounds: Backgrounds can be White, Black, or dithered 50 percent gray.

Drawing modes: The four modes are Black-on-White, Black-on-Black, White-on-Black, and White-on-White.

Trails: Trails are individual entities that can be edited, duplicated, or removed from the overall drawing. The most recently drawn trail can be moved. Existing trails can be redrawn using a different repetition pattern.

Pen widths: Pen widths can be set from 1 to 3 pixels.

Scaling tool: This tool controls the distance between repeated patterns.

Recycling redraw: This process repeats the entire drawing session continuously, trail by trail.

Patterned frames: Patterned frames can be produced by using an inner and an outer selection rectangle.

Custom pattern names: Names can be assigned for a more comfortable or easy-to-remember tool set.

Selection tools: Selection tools are marquee and oval.

Selection preview: You can temporarily eliminate the rest of the drawing so that a selected area can be seen alone.

Autopilot mode: Full-screen images can be captured as screen dumps and used in other drawings.

Help: On-line assistance is available to help you remember how the unique features of this program work.

CrystalPaint was used to produce "Paintings" Gallery Figure 15.

1

2

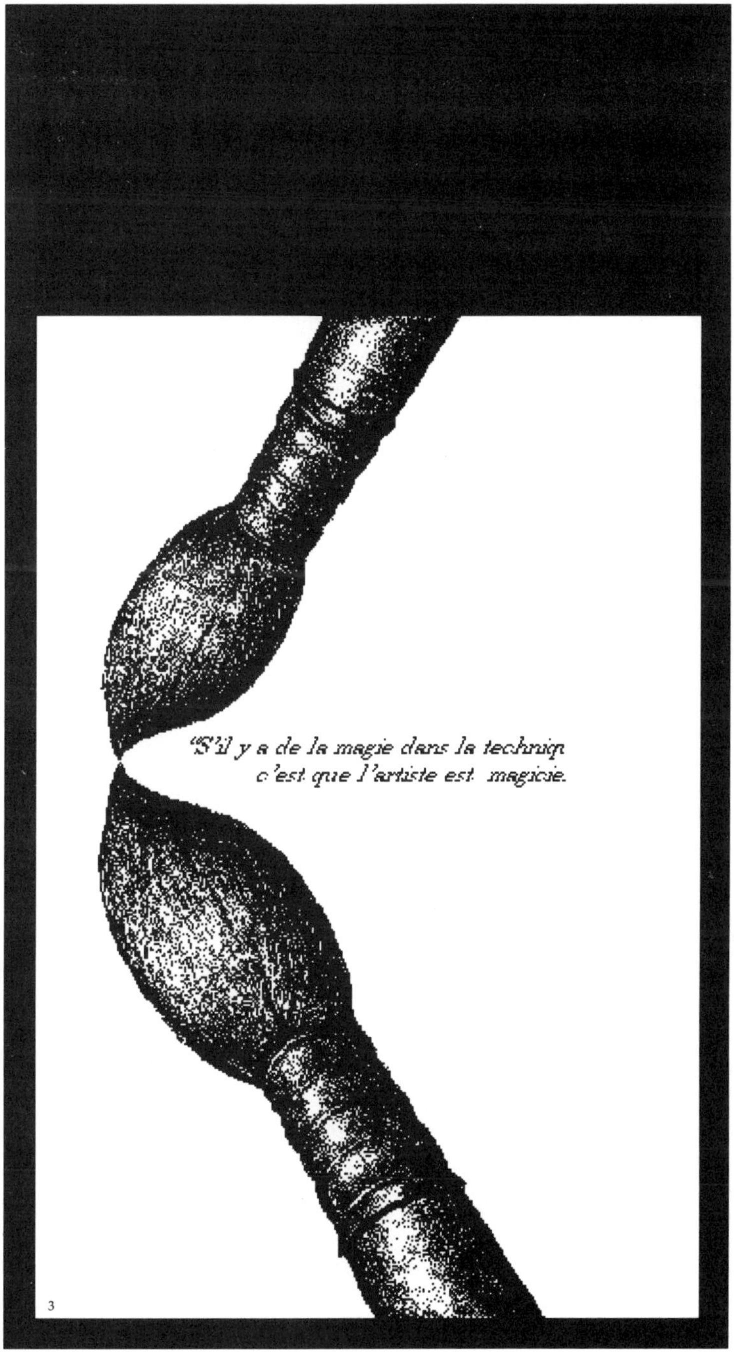

PAINTINGS

1 **David at the Beach** by Jack Davis. Revised with *MacPaint*. The artist used the painting tools to make this clip art original over in the image of a Southern California native.

2 **Autoportrait Series** by Dominique de Bardonneche-Berglund. From a series of 50 images, all hand drawn with *SuperPaint*. The artist began with the straight self-portrait and modified it in various ways, using special effects such as distort and skew, and adding new illustration elements by copying and pasting.

3 **Brush** by Dominique de Bardonneche-Berglund. Hand drawn with the mouse in *MacPaint*.

4

5

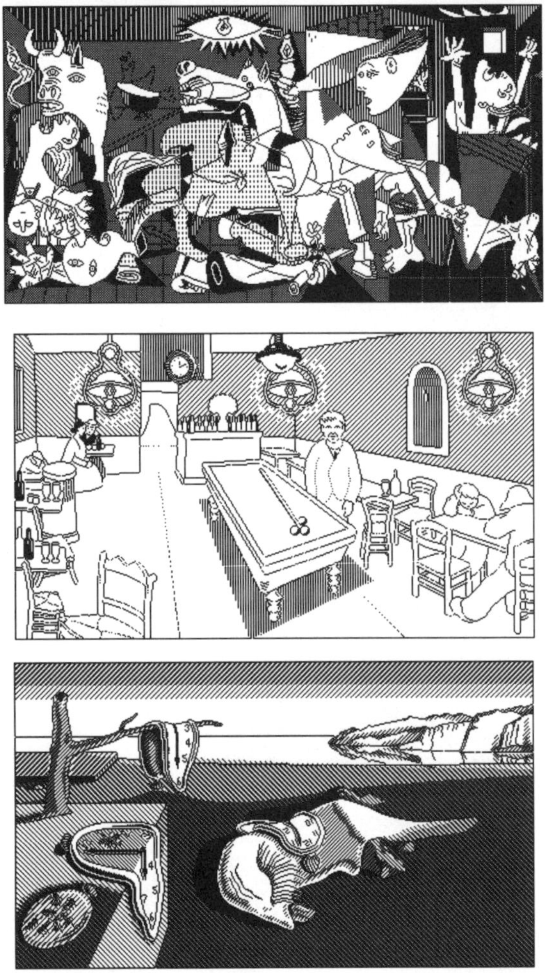

6

7

8

4 **A Door Somewhere** by Bert Monroy. An original illustration, drawn freehand with *MacPaint*. Note lighting and highlights acheived through the use of patterns and the spray can.

5 **La Maison Monod** by Dominique de Bardonneche-Berglund. Hand drawn in *SuperPaint*. The foreground tree image was brought in through the clipboard from a separate document.

6 **Masters Series** by Martin Speed. Interpretations of the originals, drawn freehand with *MacPaint*. The colors and textures of the original paintings are effectively translated into simplified bitmapped images through well-chosen screens and patterns.

7 **Calligraphic Mac** by Jack Davis. Produced with the Japanese *MacCalligraphy* program. The program emulates traditional Japanese ink brush painting, which uses ground ink mixed with water and brushed onto Washi rice paper. Flow and absorption of ink are based on how long the mouse button is held down and how quickly the mouse is moved in making "strokes."

8 **Easter Island 5** by David Brunn. Achieved through the artist's "digital photography" technique. This image was made by projecting a 35 mm slide, videodigitizing the projected image with *MacVision* (see Chapter 7), and then modifying and combining the scanned bit maps using *SuperPaint*.

9

10

11

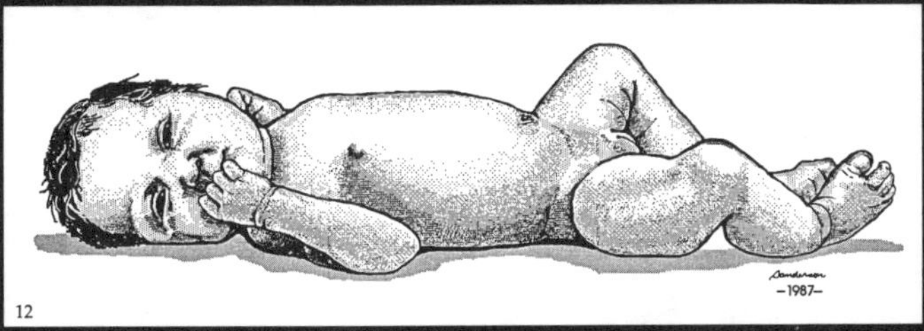

12

13

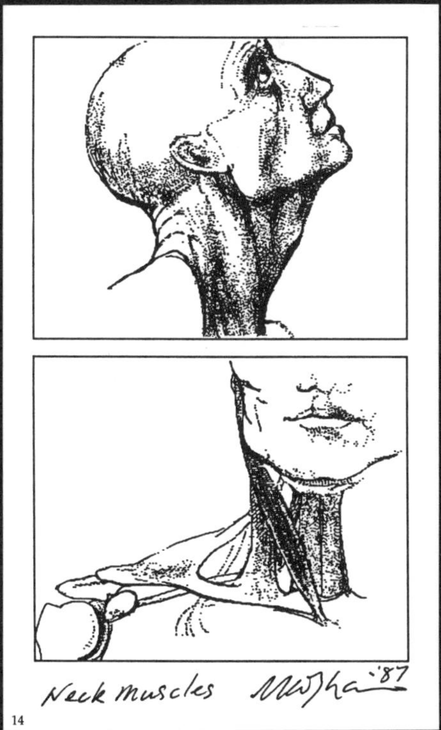

14

9 **East Portrait** by Jack Davis. A self portrait executed with *MacCalligraphy*. Several shades of "ink" were used. The enlarged swashes in the background were added in *SuperPaint*.

10 **Sleeping Lady** by Malcolm Thain. Drawn freehand in *SuperPaint*. Custom patterns were used, and the work was printed at 50 percent. (Reproduced from a LaserWriter print).

11 **George Observed Contemplating Truth** by Lawrence Kaplan. Created in *SuperPaint*, using the *MacVision* videodigitizing system. The pyramid was created by scanning Washington's face from a dollar bill using a kaleidoscope lens attached to a video camera. The image was distorted using the perspective tool, then copied to the draw layer and reduced. The cherries were made by videodigitizing real cherries, and the tree was digitized from a photograph. The sky effects were created in the paint layer by drawing various patterns using the spray can and then reducing the patterns to 25 percent in the draw layer. The section of Mount Rushmore was scanned and then softened around the edges using the spray can with white. The caption, added in the draw layer, is an integral part of the piece.

12 **Newborn** by Kathleen Sanderson. Drawn freehand using *SuperPaint*. The detail in this lifelike illustration was achieved by drawing three LaserBits objects and combining them to create the final image.

13 **Exposition** by Dominique de Bardonneche Berglund. Created in *PixelPaint*, this composition illustrates effective use of the program's graduated fills on both geometric and freehand shapes. The color original features grays on the frames and root structures, with bright red human figures. (Reproduced from a 35 mm transparency shot off a SuperMac 19" monitor).

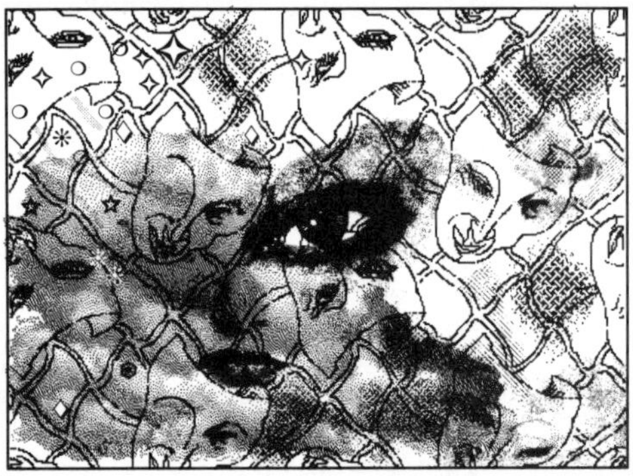

15

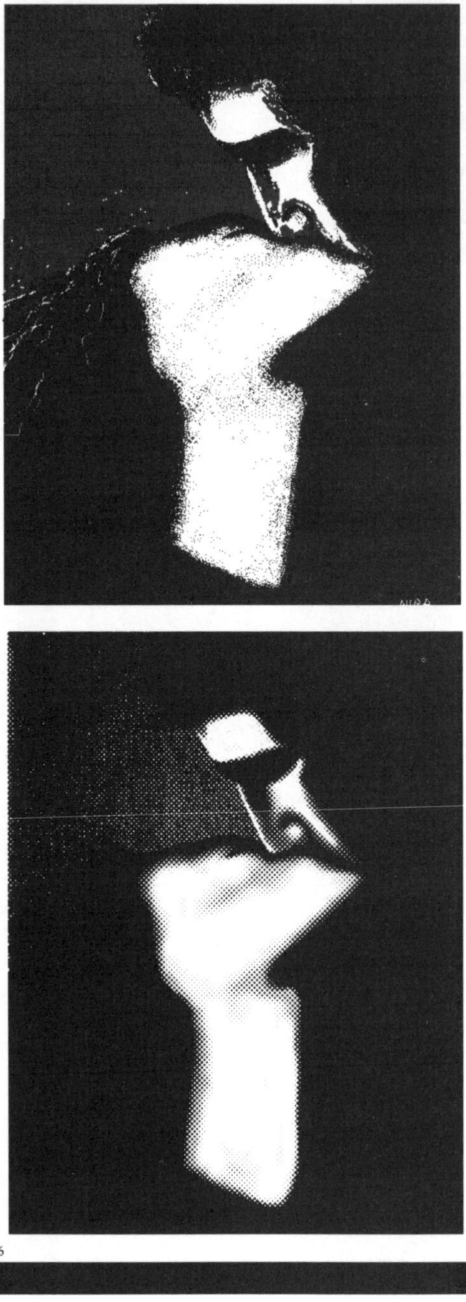

16

17

18

14 **Neck Muscles** by Malcolm Thain. Hand drawn in *SuperPaint*. The original was output at 50 percent. (Reproduced from a 50-percent LaserWriter print).

15 **Masks** by Lawrence Kaplan. Created in *CrystalPaint*, the masks and the net were then opened in *SuperPaint*, where the artist added the textures and the central face features. The type and the various jewellike shapes (from the Zapf Dingbats typeface) were added in the draw layer.

16 **Kiss** by Nira. Created in *MacPaint* and modified with *ImageStudio*. The first image was drawn freehand in *MacPaint*. The high-resolution version was created by importing the bitmapped image into *ImageStudio* and repainting it with gray scale screens using the paintbrush, charcoal, and paint bucket tools. (Reproduced from a Linotronic print).

17 **Escape 2** by Mike Swartzbeck. Built in *GraphicWorks* from several scanned images superimposed using the program's different ink modes (Xor, Matte, and so on).

18 **Siren 5** by Mike Swartzbeck. Created entirely in *GraphicWorks*, combining found images scanned with *ThunderScan*. The Trace Edges feature was used on the top image, and the airbrush was used for the background atmosphere.

CHAPTER 5

Drawing

Object-oriented graphics (drawings) offer significant advantages over bit maps (paintings). Each object you draw retains its identity as a separate item. New objects don't permanently obliterate any existing objects "below" them. As you draw an item, the application records its basic type (oval, rectangle, polygon, or freehand, for example), its location, its corner points, and other data *about* the object. When you make changes to an object, such as stretching or moving it, the program updates the stored data accordingly.

This chapter discusses the general attributes of draw programs, as well as the fine points of a number of particular draw applications. It also covers 3D programs, which have many features in common with two-dimensional draw applications as well as some rather spectacular abilities to present the third dimension.

DISCRETE OBJECTS

When you work with object-oriented (draw) programs, you typically *select* an object, and then *do* something to it. As you edit, with mouse and keys, the application carefully erases the old image of the object from the screen and draws a new one based on your actions. It doesn't matter that the changed object is half buried in a stack of 50 objects you've created; the draw application keeps track of what's visible to you and correctly presents the final view on screen. If you resize an item, its fill pattern will cover a greater area, but the dots that make it up will not be magnified. In most bit-map applications, all stacking and shuffling are out of the question, and re-sizing also magnifies the bits, increasing the jaggedness of the subject.

Martha Siebert

"ELASTIC FILM"

From a user's perspective, working with draw programs feels as if the parts of your work were drawn on their own strips of elastic film. You can freely move objects around the work surface; you can overlap, restack, resize, refill, and reshape them. If you move an object, whatever is uncovered will be displayed. Most object-oriented applications also let you import (but not necessarily edit) bit maps and manipulate them as objects. For example, you can paste in all the bit maps you need to depict a landscaped lot, and arrange them freely, without the limitations of paint-only environments. This freedom to painlessly fine-tune a composition and the ability to create resolution-independent images are the key benefits of object-oriented applications.

TOOLS

Along with freedom of motion, draw applications provide alignment and precision tools with which to manage that motion. Among these tools are a **visual grid** on the drawing surface; vertical and horizontal **rulers**; an invisible **snap-to fine-mesh grid** along which drawn objects align; **numerical display** of dimensions, area, and rotation; and lines that are automatically labeled with their precise length. A **line** tool, a **constrained line** tool (for drawing vertical and horizontal lines), and a **text** tool are typical entries from the palette of the draw programs. Draw applications provide basic **text effects** like style change, justification, and 90-degree rotation. The functions of the lasso and marquee of paint programs have been replaced by the **selection tool**, which tends to be an arrow that grabs and moves an object, combined with the **grouping** function, which lets you grab and modify several objects together. Grouping makes it easy to draw several parts and thereafter group them into a finished assembly that can be treated as a unit. Groups of objects can be grouped with others ad infinitum. All applications support progressive ungrouping, ultimately down to single objects.

QUICKDRAW DESCRIPTIONS

Object-oriented images are saved as PICT files — not as assemblages of dots, but as the **specifications** for drawing the images. (See "File Format #2: PICT.") Unlike their bit-mapped counterparts, large-area QuickDraw documents containing hundreds of objects take up little disk space, simply because the **description** of an object takes up a handful of bytes regardless of its size or location.

Most draw applications display images on screen by sending instructions to the Macintosh built-in graphics generator in the **QuickDraw** language. Object-oriented applications can produce special effects within the capabilities of the QuickDraw environment. These include free rotation, pattern fills, and smoothing of hand-drawn paths.

Because QuickDraw graphics are based on mathematical descriptions and not dots, they're rendered at the resolution of whatever output device you use. Because QuickDraw is screen oriented, applications that use it offer **line widths no smaller than 1 point** (1/72 inch).

File Format #2: PICT

Draw programs produce PICT files that store information as QuickDraw formulas — outlines of lines, geometric shapes, and other objects. These objects can be expanded, contracted, or otherwise reshaped by changing the formulas. These formulas (mostly numbers) include **vectors** (lines of a specific size at a specific angle), fill-pattern number, and stacking-order number. QuickDraw also stores information about how to fill in the outline with solid or patterned color. The object-oriented application can interpret the PICT file and redraw its components one at a time — very quickly — to reconstruct the image. QuickDraw (and thus PICT file format) is very versatile. It can be printed on the ImageWriter or a QuickDraw-based laser printer, or interpreted to PostScript by a PostScript-based printer or imagesetter. In each case, the file can be printed at the highest resolution the output device is capable of. The newer PICT2 format is used as a universal format for storing color bit maps.

TIP

Shift-Clicking to Change Selections

One of the simplest, but most useful tricks in working with a drawing program, is adding to, or removing from, a selected group of objects by Shift-clicking on one of the objects. While you hold the Shift key down and select an object, that object toggles between being selected and unselected without affecting the rest of the selected objects.

TIP

Cleaning Up a Freehand Drawing

Another draw trick is to clean up a freehand drawing by first using the Unsmooth option and then using the Smooth option. This technique cleans out all the irregularities, and it can be very helpful if that's the effect you want.

DRAW APPLICATIONS

The basic interface of each draw program includes an always visible **tool box** (palette), and an easily accessible **fill pattern palette** or **color palette**. Most editing operations and special effects are invoked with combinations of menu selections and keystrokes. Some frequently used options can be activated by clicking an icon.

When an object is selected (for some pending operation) it is given **handles**, which are small black squares attached to the two end-points of a line or the eight sides and corners of a plane figure. (In the case of circles and ovals, four of the handles appear outside the perimeter, but the resizing and reshaping functions are essentially the same.) Moving a handle will resize or reshape the object. Moving any other part of the selected object will shift the object and leave its size unchanged. You can also choose a new fill pattern or border width for the selected object.

Draw programs typically provide a very **large drawing area** — a working surface can range from 8-1/2 by 11 inches to 100 by 100 inches or more. The document width and height can be set and changed at any time.

MacDraw II

MacDraw II (Figure 5-1) is the offspring of *MacDraw,* which was one of the first Macintosh applications and whose features have influenced the interface of virtually every other object-oriented Macintosh program. It's a high-end precision drawing program with an uncluttered and intuitive visual interface. You can open several documents at once, but unfortunately there's no Windows menu to help navigate through multiple open documents.

Mac Draw II Features

Unlimited layers: *MacDraw II* lets you create layers that behave like transparent overlays in which sets of objects reside. Layers provide some of the handy features of grouping without some of its associated

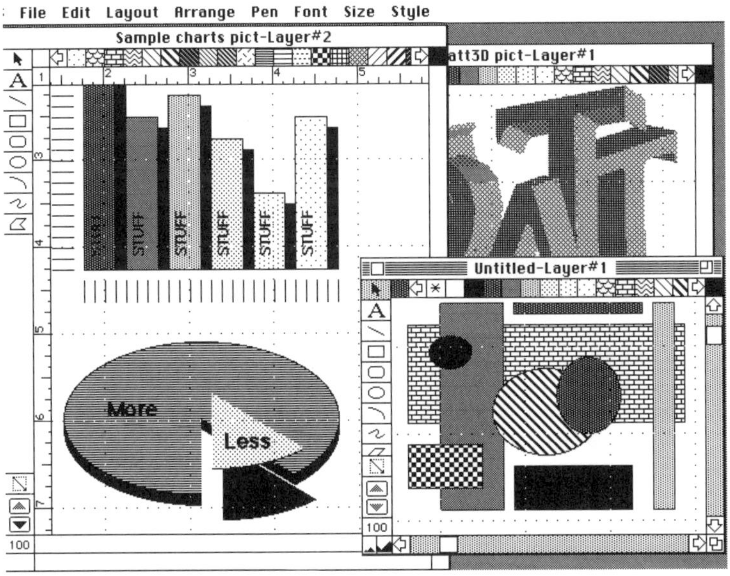

Figure 5-1. *MacDraw II* with several documents open. Its layers operate like transparent overlays.

TIP

Text Formatting in *MacDraw*

It's possible to do crude text formatting in *MacDraw* in terms of column size and position. First draw a box a little wider than the width of the column you wish to create. Next, start typing without selecting the typing tool. The words will appear inside the box. When you've finished typing, just select the box from underneath the words and delete it. You can also set the type style and the justification while the box is selected but before you start typing.

constraints. It's an important feature for complex drawings because it lets you package details in meaningful levels, and it protects existing objects from accidental editing or shifting. Selected layers can be made invisible to reduce visual clutter while you add new details. Within a layer, you can work on individual objects without going through the ungrouping-regrouping process.

Enlarged and reduced views: Drawings can be enlarged to 200, 400, 800, 1600, and 3200 percent, and reduced to 50, 25, 12.5, 6.25, and 3.125 percent. No key-driven zooming means a trip to the icon bar every time, but instant return to 100-percent view is provided.

Drawing scale: 1 inch or 1 centimeter can equal 1 inch, foot, mile, centimeter, meter, or kilometer. Six fully editable rulers are available, each with its own scaling factor. Imported objects drawn under a different scale can be scaled to match the current drawing or left the same size they were drawn.

Named views: Any spot in the document at a particular enlargement or reduction can be given a name. This helps you navigate quickly to points of interest without scrolling or using a reduced view for reference.

Shape libraries: Libraries can be built from predrawn parts. Each part is assigned a name, and you can then import parts from libraries into other documents without cutting and pasting.

Line thickness: A wide range of thicknesses is available — from hundreds of points to hundredths of a point.

Dimension lines: Lines can display their length during and after drawing. The number of decimal places for size display is fixed at four places, which could be restrictive for a very large-scale drawing.

Flexible fill patterns: Patterns can be edited, colored, and rearranged on the palette, which can hold up to 65,000 patterns altogether.
Arrowheads: Arrowheads come in two types. The width and angularity of the head can be edited on screen.
Auto-smoothing: Freehand lines are automatically smoothed (modified to eliminate small irregularities). This automatic feature saves steps and time.
Full text management: You can mix fonts and styles in one block. All justification options (left, right, center, and fully justified) are available.
Eight colors: Eight basic colors are directly available through the color palette. These can be manually combined, by dithering, into a much larger number of virtual colors.
Rotation: You can fully rotate all objects and text in 1-degree increments.
Smoothing: Polygons can be smoothed to transform segmented lines into smooth curves.
Reshaping polygons: Reshape mode can be used for selecting, moving, and reshaping objects. To create a new vertex in a line, you click anywhere on the line away from an existing handle.
Nudging: Using cursor keys to "nudge" allows fine adjustments in both vertical and horizontal directions, by one pixel or by one grid step.
Proportional resizing: Objects can be toggled to new sizes with the Caps-Lock key.
Stationery: Documents can be created to store your preferences, such as special patterns, colors, grid settings, named views, layer names, and so on. Once set up, they can be saved as stationery for yourself and others to use. Stationery is protected from accidental modification.
Color separations: *Mac Draw II* can print four-color separations with registration marks but is limited to eight colors.

"Drawings" Gallery Figures 1 through 6 and Color Gallery Figures 1 and 2 in the center of the book were drawn with *MacDraw*.

MacDraft (1.2a)

MacDraft (Figure 5-2) has a history of being a cut above the rest of the draw applications. Its features are polished and have the ease and depth to cater to the casual user and also to meet the needs of the professional designer. Its magnification powers, rulers, scaling, grid, and auto-dimensioning displays can support a high level of accuracy. Unfortunately, *MacDraft 1.2a* operates in black-and-white only. And it has just a few slightly clumsy characteristics: when a change is made, it redraws more than it has to, which somehow interrupts the working flow; it also places an inordinately large number of reshaping handles on freehand objects.

MacDraft Features

Import formats: Objects from other *MacDraft* documents are resized to fit the scale of the receiving document. *MacDraft* can work with PICT files and with objects pasted from *MacDraw*. Imported bit maps can be filled with any *MacDraft* pattern, including None.

Working scale: You can work at scales from .25x to 10x actual size. Map-type scales can range from 1.5 inches = 1 foot, through 1 inch = 100 feet.

Key-controlled zooms: You can zoom up to 8x magnification and down to 1/16 reduction with keys and mouse.

Flexible expression of size units: You can choose metric or English units, and within English units, you can choose fractional or decimal divisions. Dimensions can be displayed at from 1 to 4 decimal places.

Area display: You can numerically display the area of any closed object, including irregular shapes.

Auto-sizing: Lines show their size during and after drawing. The size value is centered along the line but it can be moved elsewhere in the drawing. The size value will change to reflect the current size if the line is stretched or shrunk.

Circles: Circles can be drawn by radius (from an anchored center point) or by diameter (from an anchored edge point).

Circular arcs: Arcs can be drawn by radius or by three-point fit. Unfortunately, you can't draw elliptical arcs.

Cross-hair cursor: This cursor shape helps with alignment even of distantly spaced objects. It saves repositioning steps and unnecessary guidelines. The traditional arrow cursor shape is also available.

Variable perimeter positions: Perimeter lines of objects can be positioned in three modes relative to the true boundary: inside, centered on it, or outside.

Fill patterns: Patterns are editable, but limited in number.

Round corners: The corner radius of rounded-corner rectangles can be hand modified. Depending on the drawing mode the corner radius can change proportionally to the size change of the rectangle, or it can remain constant.

Reshaping polygons: Ungrouped polygons are always in the reshape mode. They can be changed by grabbing a vertex

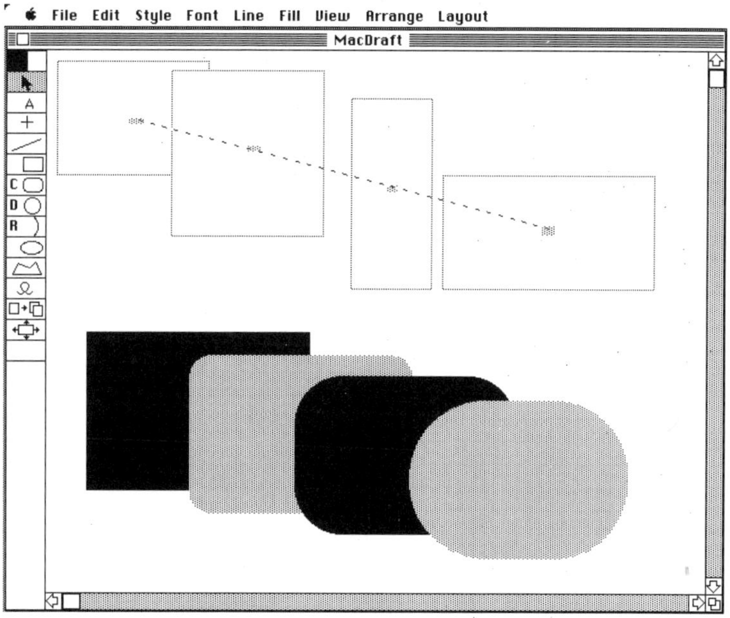

Figure 5-2. A *MacDraft* window, showing the program's ability to distribute objects evenly along a line (top) and to customize rounded corners (bottom).

handle and moving a single corner point or by grabbing an edge handle and moving an entire side without resizing it or changing its slope.

Splitting vertices: New vertices (and thus new sides) can be added to existing polygons by splitting one vertex into two.

Free rotation: Objects can be freely rotated in 1- or 5-degree increments. You can unrotate an object back to 0 degrees in one step, no matter how many steps you took to get it there. Imported bit maps can be rotated in 90-degree increments.

Even distribution: The Distribute Objects feature evenly spaces and centers objects along any line of any length.

Resizing: Single objects and bit maps can be resized disproportionately (stretched more horizontally than vertically, for example), but grouped objects can be resized only proportionally.

Color Gallery Figure 20 in the center of the book was prepared with *MacDraft*.

Canvas (2.0) (Draw Mode)

You can find a general description of *Canvas* (Figure 5-3) in Chapter 4, along with particulars on its paint features. Described here are its draw characteristics, as well as some even more powerful features.

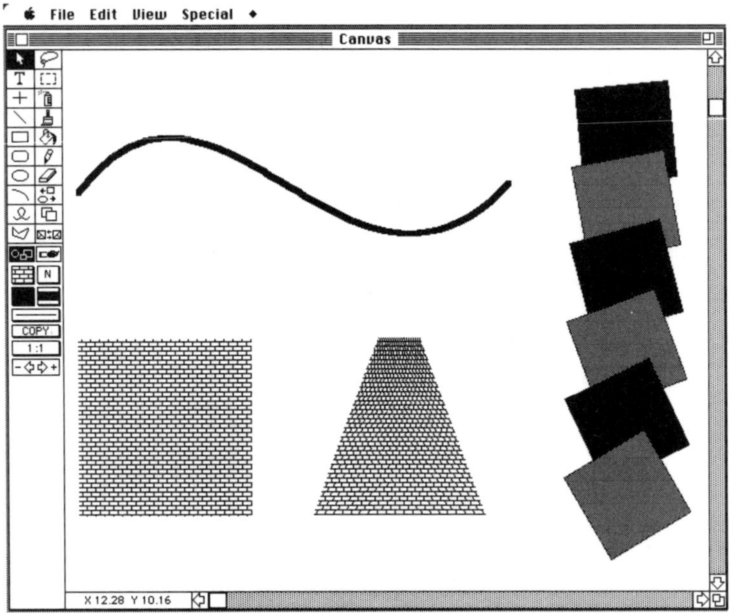

Figure 5-3. A *Canvas* window showing a multipoint Bezier curve, perspective distortion, and duplication of an object with alternation between patterns.

Canvas Features

Desk accessory version: The desk accessory version (see Chapter 19) has 70 percent of the capabilities of the full program. The one-menu DA interface is somewhat different from that of the main application.

Import formats: PICT, PICT2, TIFF (including IBM) (see Chapter 7), Paint, and *MacDraw 1.9.x* format files can be imported. In addition, *Canvas* accepts, via clipboard, graphics from a wide variety of applications, including *ImageStudio, PixelPaint*, and others, which it labels "Picture objects." Imported color images are displayed in full color.

Unlimited layers: Layers can be bulk-colored, grayed (screened back to be used as templates or guides), made invisible, individually printed and saved, and reordered in the stacking sequence. You can access any layer instantly.

Autotrace: *Canvas* automatically outlines bitmapped graphics with Bezier curves.

Precision: Drawings can be accurate to 1/64,000 of an inch.

Size calculations: Area and perimeter are automatically calculated and displayed.

Named views: Any spot in the document at a particular enlargement or reduction can be given a name. This helps you quickly navigate to points of interest without scrolling or using a reduced view for reference.

Reusable objects: You can draw and save objects as named Macrobjects. Their names along with thumbnail views will appear in the macro menu. Macrobjects can then be selected from the menu and used many times.

Object specification: The working window displays numerical and other characteristics of a selected object. These can be modified with keyboard entries and by making selections from the attributes presented in the window.

Magnification and reduction: Magnification goes from 2x to 32x and beyond. Reduction goes from 1/2x to 1/32x. *Canvas* provides one-step access to any view, and all tools remain fully functional at any level.

Multiple rulers: Horizontal and vertical rulers can be copied and dragged anywhere on the work space. Rulers with different scales can be created and dragged onto the document. Up to eight ruler settings can be saved with each document. Dragged rulers behave like objects — they can be moved, cut, copied, pasted, or deleted — but they can't be printed.

Adjustable zero points: The zero points for both *x* and *y* axes can be moved around the work space.

Scales and measurement units: The user can specify the scale and units of measure. Units include inches, centimeters, points, picas, and engineering units.

Guidelines: Nonprinting guidelines (both vertical and horizontal) can be placed as needed.

Grids: Grid units may be set independently of ruler units. Independent *x* and *y* grid snap is provided.

Aligning objects: Objects can be aligned along the slope of a line, or relative to each other.

Multipoint Bezier curves: Bezier curves can be exported to PostScript programs such as *Illustrator* and *FreeHand*.

Line thicknesses: Thicknesses of vertical and horizontal lines are independently variable, from a 1/300-inch hairline on up.

Automatic dimensioning: Lines show their numeric size during and after drawing. Arc dimensions include the angle.

Arrowheads and other terminators: Six types of line terminators are provided. These can be edited and assigned to lines or arcs.

Overlay effects: Overlapping images can be transparent, opaque, additive, subtractive, and otherwise, as specified by the user.

Text block handling: Standard styles and alignments, plus color or gray level, can be assigned on a character-by-character basis. Blocks and the text they contain can be scaled, stretched, and distorted, like any object, and can still print at high resolution.

256 colors: A palette provides 256 colors, selected from the 16.7 million available. *Canvas* supports the full 16.7 million when a 24-bit color graphics controller board is used.

PostScript gray screens: True PostScript gray screens in 1-percent increments can be used for lines and area fills.

Special effects: Effects include 90-degree and free rotation, 1- and 2-point perspective distortion, skewing (shearing), and free-form distortion of objects, bit maps, and text.

Duplication options: Any object, including text, can be duplicated a specified number of times, with options to perform the following transformations on each successive copy: rotation in 1-degree increments based on the object's center or any of the corners of its bounding rectangle, resizing along the object's x axis and y axis, disproportionally or proportionally, shifting independently along the x or y axis by specified distances, transition from a specified gray level or color to another gray level or color, and transition between two specified patterns.

Scaling: A selected object or text block can be symmetrically or asymmetrically scaled by specifying a percentage in the Object Specs window, or by manually dragging a handle.

Reshaping polygons: Holding the Option key while dragging a vertex will create a new one. Holding Option-Shift when clicking on a vertex will delete it.

Multiple-window management: Option-clicking on the current window's top bar will reveal a menu from which you can choose another open document.

Selective saving: Selected objects or selected layers can be saved as separate files.

Print and printer features: Both PostScript and QuickDraw printers are supported. Printing features include optional ImageWriter print spooling, user-definable printing order of pages of a large document, and user-controlled overlap between pages of large drawings.

Export formats: Files can be saved as PICT, PICT2, TIFF (including IBM), Paint, and Startup Screen.

"Drawings" Gallery Figures 7 through 9 were drawn with *Canvas.*

Draw It Again, Sam (2.0)

Draw It Again, Sam (Figure 5-4) offers coexisting drawing and painting environments. Its general and paint features are covered in Chapter 4, and its draw features are covered here. The program has a history of being somewhat buggy, and the *2.0* series of releases seems to be no exception. For example, it's difficult to select objects that lie behind unfilled objects; duplication of an object can often send its double off the screen, making it appear that the operation has failed, and setting the duplication offset parameters doesn't seem to help; repeated resizing, moving, and zooming of an object group gradually introduces inaccurate registration and "slippage"; sometimes duplicates of circles and rounded rectangles are slightly larger than the originals; and stray handles are sometimes left behind.

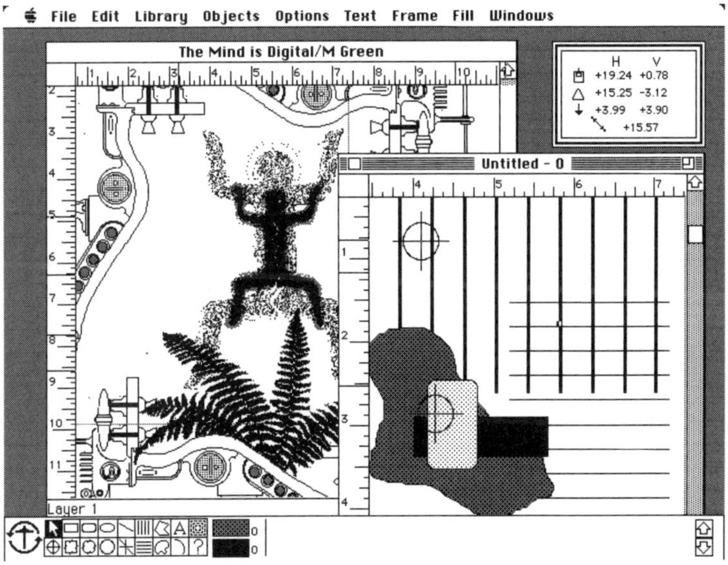

Figure 5-4. Among its other features, *Draw It Again, Sam* provides an object information window and parallel line tool.

Draw It Again, Sam Features

Drawing and painting modes (paint mode covered in Chapter 4): Freely painted or edited bit maps are sized automatically to hold your outermost strokes and can then be freely rearranged on the working surface.

Layers: You can create up to 10 layers, each with its own display attributes. Layers can also be printed individually. But there seems to be no way to delete a layer.

Object libraries: Objects can be drawn, named, assigned an icon, and stored in reusable object libraries. Library-object icons appear in a selection palette below the work space, or they can be selected by name from a menu.

Object info window: This window displays an object's attributes and lets you edit most of them, including position and size.

Grid: The Grid tool is provided for alignment. However, it's the *only* alignment tool, and the redraw of background grid lines is extremely slow. Turning them off greatly improves scrolling or zooming speed.

Dedicated tools: Drawing tools include equilateral four-sided shapes, perfect circles, and perfectly vertical, horizontal, and 45-degree lines.

Parallel line tool: This tool draws a user-specified number (1 to 999) of evenly spaced parallel lines, horizontally or vertically.

Tool switch: You have the option of retaining the drawing tool or switching to the selection tool after finishing each object.

Overlay effects: Effects include opaque, clear, invert, and erase.

Complementary fill patterns: The complementary patterns feature (the same pattern offset by one pixel) allows a two-color uniform dither of overlapping patterns.

Rotating elliptical arcs: You can grab the handle at the center of the curve, and turn the curve around its radial center.

Color: Eight basic colors are provided, including black and white. No dithering is supported, but two or more colored objects with different patterns can be overlapped to produce the illusion of more colors.

Reshaping: It's difficult to reshape a smoothed polygon. *Sam* crams in too many handles. It's best to unsmooth, reshape, and then resmooth.

Rotation: Rotation is in 90-degree steps. There is no free rotation.

"Drawings" Gallery Figure 10 was created with *Draw It Again, Sam.*

SuperPaint 2.0

SuperPaint (Figure 5-5) can work in two modes: bitmapped, and object-oriented. The bitmapped mode is covered in Chapter 4. This section focuses on the object-oriented mode. *SuperPaint* handles these two modes a little differently than *Canvas* and *Draw it Again, Sam. SuperPaint* has a drawing *layer* and a painting *layer.* When one layer is active, its tools cannot affect graphics residing in the other layer.

Items from one layer can be transferred to the other layer by selecting them and then using a single command. This feature allows graphics to be partially constructed as easily editable objects in the drawing layer, and then to be transferred to the paint layer for bit-map editing. Similarly, finished bit maps can be transferred to the drawing layer for simplified positioning and stacking.

A high degree of accuracy in rendering, editing, and positioning objects can be achieved with the aid of a custom grid, rulers, object alignment modes, numerically driven scaling, the cursor position indicator, and the object info window. Unfortunately, *SuperPaint* allows no smoothing of freehand or polygon objects, and rulers don't have an adjustable zero point.

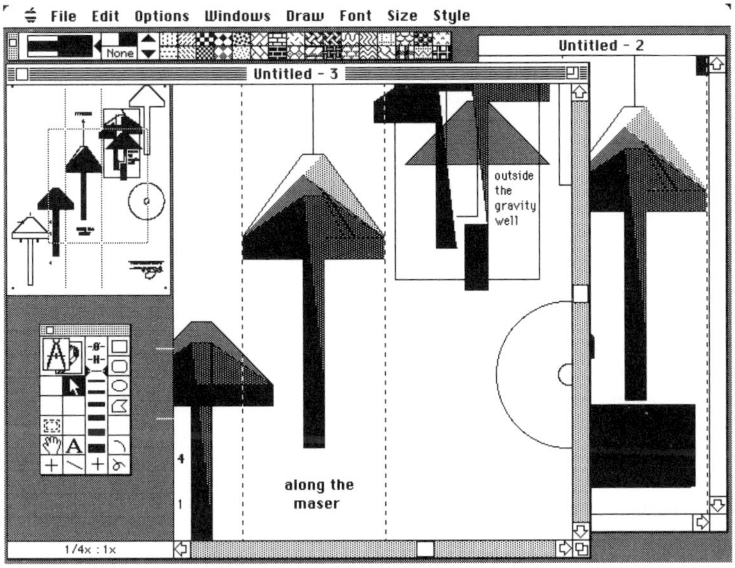

Figure 5-5. Several open windows in *SuperPaint*. The compass icon in the upper left corner indicates that the program is operating in the object-oriented (Draw) mode.

SuperPaint Features

Import formats: TIFF and ThunderScan images can be imported into the draw layer.
Hidden layers: The painting layer can be hidden while you're drawing, and vice versa.
Document size: Documents may be as large as memory allows. But size can't be changed after it's established.
Magnification and reduction: Both key-driven and menu-driven magnification and reduction are provided. The drawing tools are functional in all views.
Auto-scrolling: When the drawing tool touches the edge of the window, the page scrolls automatically. This feature can be turned off.
Superbits: Bit maps placed in the draw layer can be assigned an arbitrary resolution and can be edited.
Floating tool and shading palettes: Tool palettes can be moved around the window.
Autptrace: See *SuperPaint*'s paint features in Chapter 4.

Object info: The Object Info window displays the numerical characteristics of a selected object. These can be modified with keyboard entries.

Bezier curves: Bezier curves (see Chapter 6) can either be drawn freehand or developed with the tracing tool.

Corner or center starting points: A drawing of a geometric shape can be started (positioned) from the center or from a corner.

Completion: Filled open polygons get a forced last line connecting the start and end points.

Multigon: The multigon tool draws an equal-sided object with any number of sides from three up. Polygons of three, four, six, and eight sides are predefined for convenience.

Line width: Horizontal and vertical line widths are independently variable from 0 to 8 pixels, including a 1/300-inch hairline.

Arrowheads: *SuperPaint* provides a wide variety of arrowheads and other types of end-points, filled and hollow. Each can be edited and saved as a reusable item from the Edit Arrows dialog box. Straight lines can have no arrowheads or can have arrowheads at the start, at the end, or at both ends. Only single lines can have arrowheads.

Dashed lines: A wide variety of dashed line patterns can be applied to lines. Each can be edited and saved as a reusable item from the Edit Dashes dialog box. Only single lines can be dashed.

Text block handling: As text is entered beyond the user's view, the document automatically scrolls.

Text features: Any of the fill patterns can be used as the ink for text. Fonts, sizes, and styles can be mixed in one block. The maximum type size is 127 points.

Ink effects: Inks (text colors) can be opaque (normal) or transparent (additive).

Fill patterns and shades: Any existing pattern can be edited, and up to 32 new patterns can be added to the existing set of 96.

Colors: Colors can be applied and previewed, but not viewed while you're working on the drawing.

One-step copy: Images can be copied from one layer to the other in one easy step.

Special effects: Effects include 90-degree and free rotation, 1- and 2-point perspective distortion, skewing (shearing), and free-form distortion.

Scaling: A selected object can be symmetrically scaled by specifying a percentage (25, 50, 200, or 400 percent, or other), or it can be asymmetrically scaled by manually dragging a handle.

Nudge: The nudge feature moves a selected object by one pixel in any direction.

Replicate: The Replicate features works as a duplicator, except that any changes in position, orientation, or size will be progressively applied to successive copies. If the first copy of an object is 50 percent of the size of the original and rotated 45 degrees, then the second copy will be 25 percent of the size and rotated 90 degrees relative to the original.

Export formats: Bezier curves can be saved in *Illustrator* or *FreeHand* formats.

Color Gallery Figures 7 and 9 in the center of the book were prepared using the drawing layer of *SuperPaint.*

3D APPLICATIONS

3D applications usher the artist into that enticing third dimension — a universe in which illusionary solid objects can be **created, reshaped, rotated, joined, colored,** and **illuminated**. They combine considerable power and ease of use. Sweeping changes to the appearance of an entire 3D universe can be made with minimal effort. In one respect they provide the power and freedom to sculpt and construct, using matter without mass in a world without gravity.

3D applications are object oriented. The occasional need for a 3D illusion can sometimes be filled by a 2D rendering with perspective and shading added manually. In other cases, bypassing a 3D application can have you spending hours manually working out different views, positions, and shading. Even if used only occasionally, 3D applications generally pay for themselves. You can even supplement traditional art techniques by using a 3D program to help visualize perspective, lighting, and shading. You can make a tracing of the print onto your art surface, and rerender it by hand with another medium.

You can use a 3D application to produce finished art or to render images for export to other applications. Those 3D programs that support shading and PostScript (see Chapter 6) can print gray-scale images on a laser printer.

More than with most classes of applications, each 3D program possesses some exclusive strengths or features that have been masterfully bestowed. For any serious 3D venture, knowledge of those key features is crucial for avoiding mid-project surprises. Because no single 3D application simplifies or excels at all tasks, it's best to own several and to use the best one for each specific job.

Space and Time

The representation of three-dimensional objects on screen is mathematically intensive, and perceptibly slow, but the Macintosh II, with its fast CPU, provides reasonable response speed. The Mac II's numeric coprocessor 68081 chip gives a further boost to any 3D application that uses it. This processing power provides an ideal environment for lag-free 3D work, and it invites software developers to consider otherwise prohibitive capabilities, such as ray tracing and animation.

Designing the user interface for operating in a 3D space is an art in itself, and each application has its own approach to the task. Each interface works well within its context, and can be easily mastered, given time.

Basic 3D Capabilities

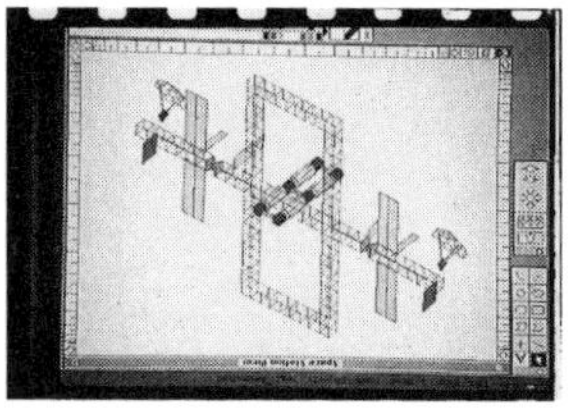

Courtesy Silicon Beach Software

All the 3D programs discussed here provide the basic functions that let you create and freely orient objects in space. To help with the shaping and arranging of objects, four **views**, one along each axis plus a "user's" view, are usually provided.

Shapes can be rendered as **wire frames**, **unshaded solids**, and **fully shaded objects** under user-variable lighting. They can be combined into temporary or stable groups and can easily be duplicated or deleted.

Objects are manipulated by clicking on them, and then performing some editing action. Separate controls allow **translation** (shift) and **rotation** of selected object(s) along one or more of the three axes. Objects can be positioned by dragging with the **mouse** or by precise **numerical specifications**. Provisions are made for rotating a selected object, the entire world, or just the user's viewpoint.

File Formats

All 3D applications offer several formats in which to save their images. When saved in a 3D application's native format, a document retains its three-dimensional nature. That same document can be reread by its creator program and edited in every way, in all three dimensions. Such a document is usually not readable by other 3D programs, or by most other applications.

The PICT or PICT2 format is generally supported as an output option. A document saved in PICT/PICT2 form is a generic object-oriented image file that can be imported by many applications, including word processors, paint, draw, and path-oriented programs. Such a file is a frozen view of the three-dimensional space — a snapshot. Its objects can no longer be manipulated in all three planes, although other forms of image editing can be performed. For example, objects can be relocated on the background, their stacking order can be modified, their shade or color can be altered, they can be resized, cut, duplicated, and more, but only as images on a flat background.

Super 3D (1.0)

Technically, *Super 3D* (Figure 5-6) is a **surface-framing tool**, as opposed to a solid-modeling tool. To create 3D objects, the user draws an outline which is then spun, given depth, or "swept" through space with a combination of rotation, relocation, and resizing along any or all of the three axes. This last method allows *Super 3D* to easily render forms like **spirals, helixes,** and **tapers**. Shapes can be grouped together to form more complex objects.

Once rendered in 3D, objects become groups of polygons oriented in a 3D space, and electronically glued together to form a contiguous surface. It's possible to reposition one or more vertices, and, with some patience, to alter or remove individual polygons from an object, forming holes.

Super 3D's user interface feels comfortable, and its results are quite predictable. Several individual tool windows can be independently displayed, relocated, or hidden. Menu selections that are used frequently are placed topmost for quick clicking. Unfortunately, only one document can be open at a time.

A Few Limitations

The version of *Super 3D* reviewed here does not support color, although it runs with no problems in the Mac II's color mode.

Its gray shading is done by **dithering** black and white dots in various proportions. This version also makes no use of the math coprocessor chip, and so the solid-view modes operate substantially slower than one would like. Subsequent versions of *Super 3D* will support full color, and will use the math coprocessor for increased operating speed. These two enhancements should nicely eliminate the two major shortcomings of the initial release.

A Useful Mac Art Tool

Super 3D's unique modeling strengths definitely outweigh its few weaknesses, which are, for the most part, only temporary. It also possesses powerful **animation capabilities**, which can be driven manually, with a dedicated dialog box, or by a textual command language. Even if half its features go unused, this program can be considered a basic tool in a Macintosh artist's studio.

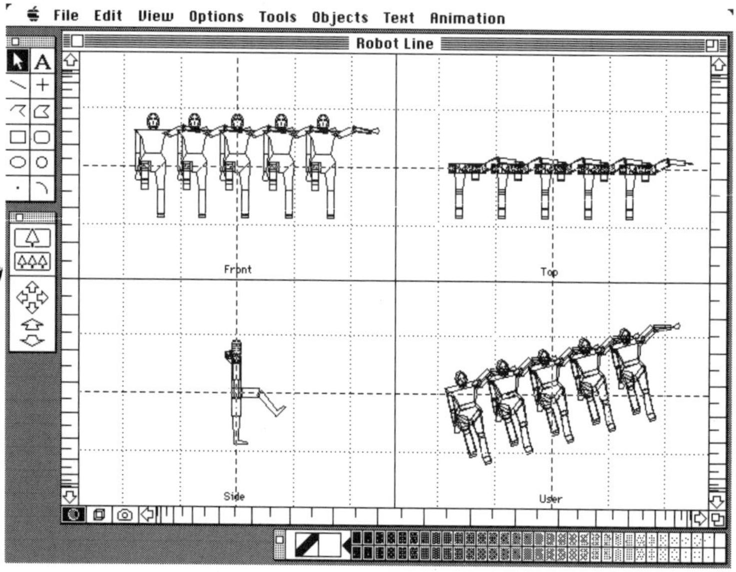

Figure 5-6. A super 3D window, showing several working views of the same scene. (The finished artwork is shown in Figure 19 of the Color Gallery). Grid lines provide cues for visual alignment. Tool and pattern palettes float.

Super 3D Features

Import formats: *Super 3D* imports images in its own native format and in Text form. A text file can be prepared by any program that writes ASCII characters, including custom applications for generating shapes by using mathematical calculations.

Imported background: A background picture can be imported by pasting from the clipboard. While the picture can't be manipulated, it can be centered in the 3D space, scaled to the current window, or aligned, with its upper left corner made flush with the upper left corner of the 3D window. Imported backgrounds can be used for decoration, clarification, or as tracing templates to guide the shaping of 3D objects.

Integration: Creation and viewing modes are integrated in a single window.

Unlimited 3D space: Space is limited only by the amount of RAM available.

Linking: The only linking capability is provided by Group, which is generally inflexible.

Multiple views: Several views of the same 3D scene are available using several windows. These views can be independently zoomed, positioned, and oriented. One view, for example, can be a wire-frame view of the overall scene, while another can zoom in on a specific object which is then fully lit and shaded.

Four light sources: Each light source has its own independent on/off switch, position, and brightness. Lights can be point-source or diffuse, and can travel with the camera or remain stationary.

Display modes: Modes include **wire frame**, which allows rapid refresh of the screen image as well as providing access to normally hidden edges and vertices, and three qualities of solid rendering.

Perspective or orthogonal views. The degree of perspective is variable.

Stored objects: Objects can be drawn and stored as named shapes and used in many other drawings. When duplicates of these objects are used, they retain their connection to the master shape. If the master shape is subsequently changed, the duplicates will also change automatically. Each named shape can have a textual description or note associated with it. Before inserting a named shape into the 3D world, the user can examine it in a preview window.

Direct access to object descriptions: In Display List mode the user can modify an object by respecifying its numerical attributes.

Visibility control: Specific objects can be made visible or invisible. This feature can reduce visual clutter and help refresh the screen much more quickly during the development stages of a 3D document.

Precision: Precision to 1/1000 of a screen pixel is achievable with numeric inputs and displays.

Grid: A grid that divides the work space into 50-pixel squares can be used for visual alignment.

Floating tool palettes: These are particularly handy for large work, with large monitors, or in work that requires frequent tool changes.

Contour tools: Tools include polygon, polyline, rectangle, rounded rectangle, free line, constrained line, oval, circle, arc, and point. Oval and circle can be rendered at various degrees of smoothness based on the number of sides the user specifies. The radius of corners of rounded rectangles can be numerically specified.

Snap to vertices: This option helps draw gap-free objects composed of multiple primitives. When new primitives are drawn very close to existing ones, their respective closest vertices are joined (overlapped), appearing as one.

Animation: Animation controls are available in a dedicated menu. *Super 3D* can save gradually changing screen images as animation frames. The saved frame sequence can be played from within *Super 3D*, or played back later, using a Projector program. Animation controls permit numeric specification of how an object will move through space, in terms of changes in distance and rotation along three axes. Smoothness of the action can be controlled by varying the number of frames between the current state and the modified state. Animations can be made very smooth, but they use a great deal of disk space.

2D-to-3D conversion tools: Tools include **Revolve** (spins an outline on a lathe using the vertical, horizontal, or near/far axis as a center; by specifying the degrees of total revolution, and the number of steps, it's possible to produce very smooth or very coarse shapes), **Extrude** (extends an outline along an axis), **Connect Cross-Sections** (produces bent asymmetrical shapes like arms and tree limbs), **Sweep Surface** (creates a solid by connecting outlines that can be simultaneously spun along any or all axes, resized, and moved in space; helixes, spirals, and screw-threads are easily rendered).

Text: Text can be placed in the 3D world, but it's not treated as a 3D object. It can be moved through the absolute space, but it can't be rotated or given depth. In every view, it always faces the viewer exactly as it was originally typed. Standard styles, plus extended and condensed, are available.

Independent grays: Surface and edge gray shades can be set independently.

Selection tools: Tools include Select All and the marquee, which selects all objects within its boundaries.

Rotation: The world, object, or viewpoint can be rotated with spin wheels, which are located around the borders of the 3D window where scroll bars are typically found. Each axis has its own spin wheel.

Editable surface segments: Segments are editable when ungrouped from their parent object. They can be reshaded, resized, deleted, relocated, and rotated.

Editable vertices: Vertices can be edited by dragging them to new locations. Several vertices of the same object can be selected and moved in unison. This effectively provides the ability to reposition object edges.

Resizing: 3D objects can be sized uniformly (using the Shift key), or disproportionally, by stretching or compressing objects along any of the three axes or at some combined orientation.

Export formats: Images can be exported as PICT, EPSF, and Text (*Super 3D*'s own graphics language). The text form can be edited with any word processor or spreadsheet program.

"Drawings" Gallery Figure 13 and Color Gallery Figures 18 and 19 were created with *Super 3D*.

Swivel 3D

Fundamentally, *Swivel* (Figure 5-7) is a **solid-modeling tool**. The user draws the contours of an object from three views, and *Swivel* converts those views into an appropriately shaped solid. From first impression onward, *Swivel 3D* feels like an artist's tool. It makes it easy to create fantastic worlds and exotic objects, by design or by pure cosmic coincidence. Its interface is elegant: a simple tool palette, few menus, excellent options, and just enough dialog boxes to receive the user's precise wishes.

The program allows **free-form contour editing** of 3D objects in a world of 16.7 million colors. Its outstanding qualities are speed and rendering accuracy. To rotate an object on a given axis, the axis tool can be selected from the tool palette. But the most powerful object-orientation mechanism works through mouse movement in conjunction with the Shift, Option, and Command keys. With these, it's possible to spin an object in space on multiple axes, examining it, resizing it, and positioning it as easily as if it were clay held in the hand.

Swivel 3D allows objects to be linked in various modes that permit, for example, the parts of an assembly to pivot or slide independently, but still move together when the assembly is moved. All aspects of an object are editable at any time. Even while linked, the elements may be reshaped, resized, colored, and repositioned.

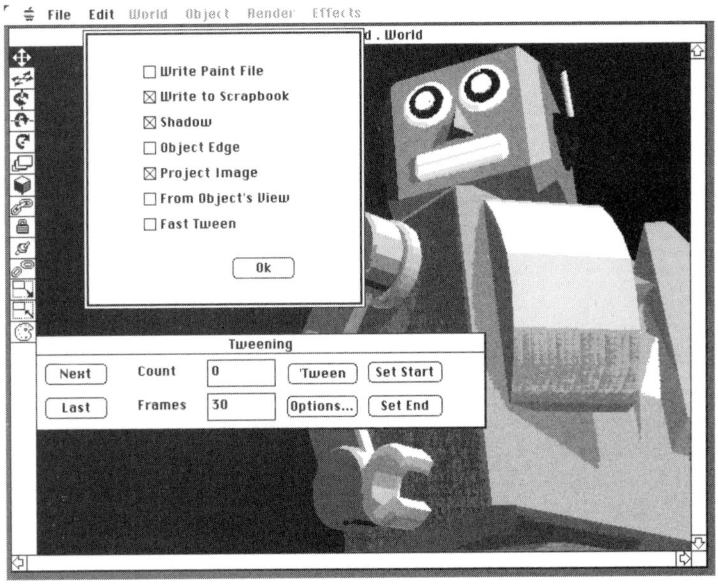

Figure 5-7. A *Swivel* project in progress, showing dialog boxes for tweening animation, shadows, and image projection.

Besides its impressive standard features, *Swivel 3D* provides **tweening animation** (see "*Swivel 3D* Features," next), **shadows**, and the ability to project bitmapped graphics onto the surfaces of 3D objects.

Swivel 3D Features

Multiple documents: Four documents can be open at once. Opening more than one document requires considerable working RAM. Although four documents can be open simultaneously, on a Mac II with 2 Mb, only one full-screen document and a second smaller document may be open at the same time.

Resizable work space: The work space can be resized from 48 x 64 pixels to 768 x 1024 pixels. Resizing the work space of one document resizes the space for all open documents.

Variable-angle light source: The light source can be repositioned at any time. Its angle affects Shadow and Project Image results. Only a single light direction is definable (through opposing strong and soft light sources) and light can be white only.

Three views: Contours may be altered in top, side, and cross-section views. Each view can be increased to full screen size for rendering large objects.

Perspective and orthographic views: Perspective and orthographic views of the work space are available.

Object views: Selecting an object and requesting a specific view of that object rotates the entire 3D world to show the specified face of the selected object.

World views: Requesting a specific view of the world rotates the entire 3D world to put the viewer squarely in line with that side of the work space.

Rendering modes: Rendering modes include wire frame, unshaded solid, shaded with outlined edges, shaded only, and contour-mapped. Each object in a 3D world can be rendered in any one of those modes.

Linking: Object-linking modes permit various forms of relative positioning for linked objects: Free link, joint, ball-joint, locked (glued) joint, and rotating joint. This is a giant leap from normal grouping. Links can be applied, changed, or removed at any time. Linked objects can be separately reshaped and colored without unlinking them. This kind of binding allows exceptional flexibility in constructing and managing complex forms.

Naming: Objects can be named and sought by name using a Find command, which causes them to be selected for editing. This is especially useful if an object disappears inside another or leaves the 3D space.

Alignment: Object alignment is aided by using attitude and position grids and world, object, and zoomed views, and by manipulating the degrees of freedom.

Grids: The **positioning grid** can be set to any degree of coarseness to constrain positioning and to aid in alignment of objects. The **attitude grid** can be set to 5, 10, 12, 15, or 45 degrees to constrain the rotation of objects to discrete steps. The **drawing grid** can be used to constrain contour points; *x*-*y* and polar (circular) grids are available. Grid units can be inches, centimeters, or screen units.

Manual and numerical control: Positioning, attitude, and scaling can be controlled numerically or by hand.

Fast screen refresh: The 3D world is redrawn quickly.

Optional tool-lock: Normally, each tool gets one use. But with the CapsLock key down, any tool selected will remain active until another tool is selected.

Contour tools: Tools include the rectangle, polygon, and Ngon. The latter starts as an oval composed of a series of points. The number of Ngon tool points can be set, from 6 to 48, prior to using the tool to attain a desired smoothness.

Symmetrical and asymmetrical rendering and editing: It's possible to render a bilaterally symmetrical outline with one tool and then edit each side independently with another tool.

Tween animation: Tweening automatically generates intermediate versions of an object from one user-set state to another. This is useful for rapidly creating animated sequences. Playback options include **Write to Paint File** (which saves successive frames as individually numbered Paint files), **Write to Scrapbook** (which saves successive frames as Scrapbook pages), **Shadow** (see below), **Object Edge** (which displays edges defined by lines), **Project Image** (see below), **From Object's View** (which displays as if the object were a camera), and **Fast Tween** (which draws a simple box to represent the object). Redraws cannot be stopped, which is especially inconvenient during long tween sequences.

Shadows: Objects can cast shadows onto other objects, based on the position of the light source. Shadows are properly rendered as darker hues of the surface upon which they fall. However, old shadows of moved objects don't disappear from a shadowed surface unless the shadowed surface is moved, or somehow forced to redraw.

Project Image: This feature enables a 3D object to be "wallpapered" by a graphic contained in the clipboard. It's a method for adding textures and special shading effects to objects. Projected images are wrapped around objects. However, a projected image does not stay on the object onto which it was originally projected if the object is redrawn for any reason. The projection disappears and must be specifically reapplied with the Project Image command. The clipboard-resident projected pattern is not saved with a *Swivel* document. When the object is reopened at a later time, the effect cannot be automatically reproduced.

Variable degrees of freedom: Degrees in pitch, roll, and yaw can be established for each object. These limits can be relative to the object itself, to a linked object, or to the world. These are editable at any time. Motion can be locked on any or all axes.

Movable pivot point: Each object has its own pivot point. This helps to produce precise rotation effects. The pivot point can even be outside its object.

Color: Color can be assigned to the background or to any object using a color wheel to choose from the full 16.7 million possible colors.

Selecting: Objects can be selected with mouse or keyboard. By using the left and right cursor keys, you can select each object in the work space in turn. By using the up and down arrows, the parent or child object in a hierarchy can be selected. But there is no one-step way to select all objects.

Fully editable contours: Objects may be defined and edited at any time.

There is no transformation that freezes an object's lines, so every object's contours are always editable. This is true even if an object is linked to another.

Simultaneous multiaxis rotation: This feature is much like holding an object in the hand and rotating it. It's elegantly implemented and intuitive, and it saves lots of time.

Duplicate Link: This feature makes duplicates of a selected object, but modifies its size, position, and attitude based on size, position, and attitude relative to the original (parent) object. This capability, for example, can produce a series of objects, each growing in size, and slightly rotated from the preceding one.

Mirroring: Mirroring while duplicating allows, for example, a left hand to be produced from an existing right hand.

Inheritance: Characteristics, including position, attitude, scale, color, and form, can be passed on from one object to a duplicate (child). This feature helps produce regularly sized and spaced objects.

Sizing to fit: Size to Fit mode will show *all* objects in the 3D world in an automatically resized 3D space.

Color Gallery Figures 22 through 24 in the center of the book were produced with Sw*ivel 3D.*

Pro3D (2.0)

This veteran Macintosh shaded solid-modeling tool continues to evolve. It currently runs only on the Macintosh 512, Plus, and SE. As this book went to press, the full-featured Macintosh II version was still under development, but many of its new features were operational and were demonstrated. This overview will focus on its major features and strengths.

Pro3D has three basic modes: object creation, object positioning/editing, and world viewing. Its two primary tools for making new objects are the Lathe, which spins an outline about a horizontal axis, and the Profiler, which forms solids by connecting any number of cross sections that you create. With both tools, you define and reshape wireframes with *MacDraw*-like lines and handles. In the Lathe and Profiler modes there are tools for drawing accurate arcs, aligning a series of points, smoothing bumps, and moving, resizing, revolving or deleting any group of handles. The Profiler is one of *Pro3D*'s strengths, allowing the construction of completely irregular objects with very fine control over the surface texture.

Pro3D's objects are true solids. Several objects can be permanently merged into one, or one object can serve as an "Antimatter" carving tool to form a hole, or to partially scoop out material from a "Matter" object. Completely departing from real-world sculpting, when two antimatter objects are merged, only their intersecting parts remain. *Pro3D* employs a merge-like process to emboss, or stamp, the shape and color of one object onto another — continent-outlines onto a spherical surface, or numbers onto a billiard ball, for example.

Its world viewing mode has excellent controls for zooming in and out, orbiting, and spinning, all with numerical feedback in 1-degree increments. This feature can be used for creating smooth animation sequences by capturing successive changed views.

Pro3D Features

Editable, storable object outlines: From these any number of solids can be rendered. Outlines are not irreversibly converted to solids; they serve only as templates.
Multicolored objects: These can be rendered from a single outline.
Eight light sources: The intensity of each light source is variable and is independently positioned.
Four simultaneous views: These four views facilitate precise positioning of objects relative to each other.
Simultaneous scaling: There is simultaneous scaling of solids in all three dimensions.
Facet-blending on output to printers and other devices: This economically reduces the crystalline appearance of 3D objects without employing a lengthy true smooth-shading process.
Colored backgrounds: *Pro3D* also offers colored backgrounds.
Point-only rendering of objects: This feature, showing only vertices (dots), is nearly instantaneous and operates in addition to solid, shaded, and wire-frame rendering.
Repeat last move: This command speeds and simplifies animation recording.
High-resolution PICT: This feature offers high-resolution PICT at 4000 by 4000 pixels.
Export formats: *Pro3D* exports images in Paint, PICT, TIFF, and EPSF formats.

"Drawings" Gallery figures 11, 12, and 14 and Color Gallery figure 21 were created with *Pro 3D*.

Clip3D

This application comes from the developers of *Pro3D* and *Easy3D*, and reflects, in essence, the manipulation and viewing half of *Pro3D 2.0*. *Clip3D* is used to view, illuminate, combine, and arrange 3D color or monochrome clip art produced with *Pro3D 1.1* and *2.0*, and *Easy3D*. This tool offers a well-rounded but limited modification of object attributes. It can't, however, import objects as editable outlines.

3D art can be produced by the user, or purchased as categorized volumes from Enabling Technologies or as an entire library on CDROM published by NEC Home Electronics. Clip art objects include 3D fonts, architectural building blocks, maps, industry and currency symbols, posable human figures, and office furnishings and equipment.

Clip3D Features

Import formats: *Clip3D* reads *Pro3D* and *Easy3D* files.
Position: *Clip3D* positions objects anywhere in space.
Full 3D rotation: *Clip3D* has the capacity for full rotation of individual objects.
Color: Objects can be assigned color individually.
Four light sources: Each light source has independent on/off switch, position, and brightness.
Viewpoint: The viewpoint (camera) can be positioned anywhere around the 3D scene.
Variable perspective: The variable perspective effect has a range from zero to medium.
Reads *Pro3D* and *Easy3D* files.
Export formats: *Clip3D* exports in Paint, PICT, TIFF, and EPSF formats

Other Applications

Other powerful 3D applications include *Dimensions* from Visual Information and *Video3D* from Macromind (see the "Products" appendix).

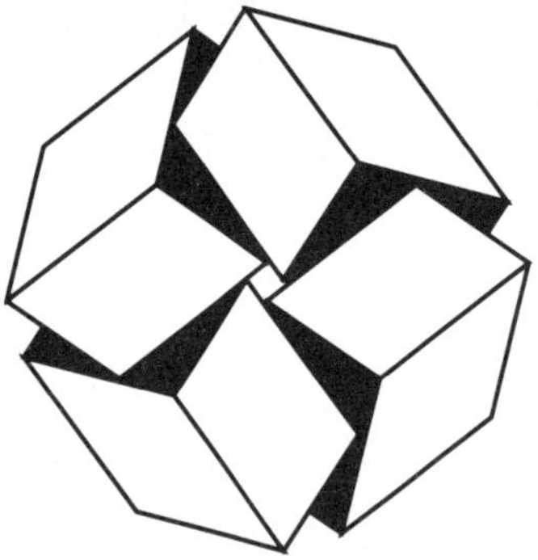
1

2

3

4

5

6

DRAWINGS

1 **Cutting Edge Logo** by Jack Davis. Executed with *MacDraw* using different line weights to form the simple logo design.

2 **Dancer** by Jim Pollock . Drawn in *MacDraw.*

3 **SDSU Standoff** by Jack Davis. Drawn with *MacDraw* using the freehand and polygon tools to achieve a "paper cut-out" effect.

4 **Sparrow** by Jack Davis. Drawn with *MacDraw* using a series of smoothed polygons. This is a good example of achieving a PostScript-like drawing effect, in this case Bezier curves, using a QuickDraw-based program. This file occupies only 4 K of disk space.

5 **Verbum Logo** by Jack Davis. Composed in *MacDraw* using basic geometrics and the freehand drawing tool. The Snap to Grid feature made possible the precise alignment of straight lines and curves.

6 **Gas Station** by Jack Davis. Created from scratch with *MacDraw.* The letters were drawn using the oval tool and smoothed polygons.

7

8

9

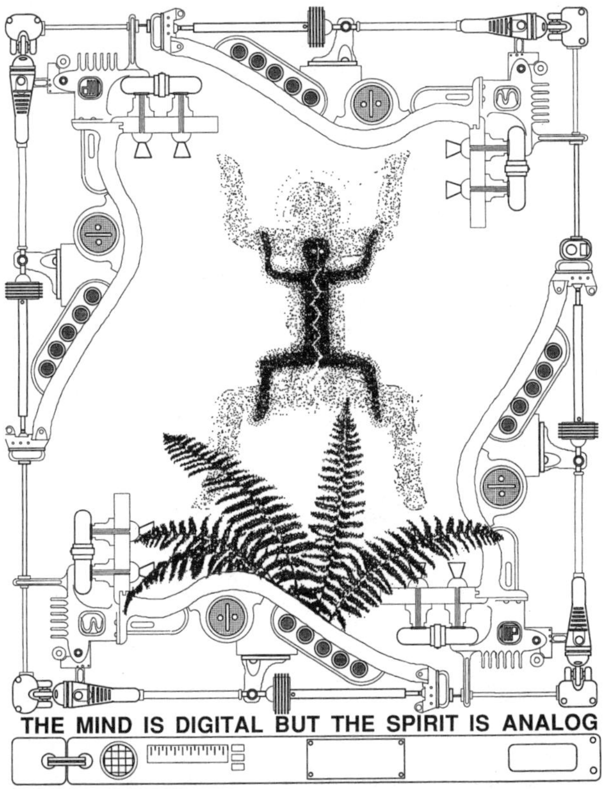

10

7 **Totem** by Christopher Kreidel. Rendered with *Canvas*. "Modular" heads were composed of grouped objects to create different totem designs.

8 **Masks** by Ida Candeleria. Drawn with *Canvas*, using the drawing features.

9 **The Last Supper** by Edgar Acadamia. Drawn with *Canvas* using silhouette forms with contrasting grays.

10 **The Mind Is Digital but the Spirit Is Analog** by Michael Green. Drawn with *Draw It Again, Sam*, using several layers to compose and assemble the different elements. The "engineering forms" were executed in the draw mode, and the aboriginal figure and the fern were rendered in the paint mode.

11

13

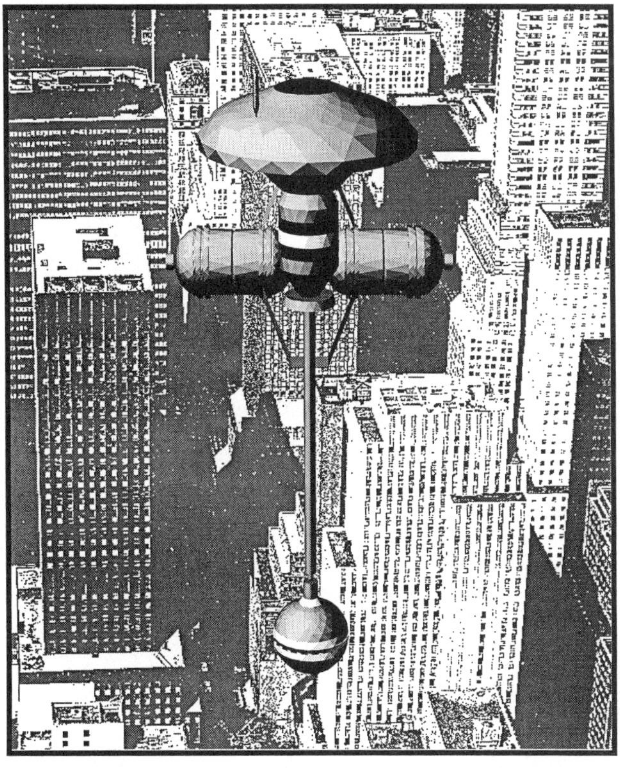

14

3D GRAPHICS

11 **Earth Crystal** by Jack Davis. Constructed in *Pro 3D*. The embossed Earth image and geometric framework were created separately and then assembled.

12 **Integrated Microwave Logo** by Jack Davis (from an original logo by Tim How). Rendered with *Pro 3D*. This logo was used in a brochure for the client as an illustrative element. Six different versions were reproduced, each shown from a different perspective and with a different lighting source.

13 **KHQ-TV Logo** by Brad Pettit. Rendered with *Super 3D*. Note the beveled edges, made easy with the 3D capability. (Design used with permission of KHQ-TV in Spokane, Washington.)

14 **Space Probe Over New York** by Pepe Moreno. Created in *Pro 3D*, the "probe" was then superimposed over a scan of a photo in *GraphicWorks*.

CHAPTER 6

PostScript Illustrations

PostScript is a a page-description language — a language for conveying the instructions for drawing the elements of a graphic. It's rich with features that can help generate spectacular effects with both text and graphics. With PostScript you can define screens, graduated gray-scale fills, freely rotated text, text aligned along any curved path, and much more. Ultimately, the PostScript code is interpreted by a printer or other device to form an image.

COMPACTNESS AND RESOLUTION INDEPENDENCE

Because a PostScript image is stored not as the image dots themselves but as a *program* for drawing the image, PostScript graphics and fonts take up less disk space than bitmapped graphics, for example. And they can easily be scaled up or down with no loss of resolution. When magnified, they don't become jagged as bitmapped (paint) images do. Regardless of the screen resolution of the input device, PostScript graphics are always rendered at the resolution of the output device. Any PostScript-compatible printer can render an image from any PostScript file.

Before the advent of PostScript-based applications, artists were forced to wrestle one-on-one with the actual PostScript language to produce their graphics. PostScript code is pure text, as removed from the finished graphic image as a recipe is from a cake. So, even more than with any other programming adventure, there were trials, errors, and surprises of every kind. Figure 6-1 is

Figure 6-1. A picahedron (by Tony Smith) surrounded by a twisted ribbon (by Toby Thain), both produced by programming in the PostScript language.

an illustration composed of elements by Australian Mac artists Tony Smith and Toby Thain, programming in PostScript.

Applications Such as *Cricket Draw, Adobe Illustrator,* and Aldus's *FreeHand* are written with PostScript effects in mind. They bridge the gap between high-quality concepts and high-quality graphics by giving the artist direct visual control of PostScript features through a user-friendly Mac interface. PostScript illustration applications translate the on-screen objects, and manipulations of those objects, into pure PostScript code. A PostScript-based program may also allow you to manually edit the code in the PostScript files it generates so you can modify or create effects that are not directly supported by the application's user interface.

Mel Ristau

TAPPING THE POWER OF POSTSCRIPT

Each PostScript application furnishes its own method of access to the powers of PostScript. Even those that are most similar have as many differences as they have similarities. So the commonality of the attributes discussed here should be very broadly interpreted. Identifying the strengths of each application involves making a subjective judgement based on the individual artist's needs, working style, and even patience. Some powerful features in one application may be awkward to access or painfully slow to achieve and print.

All the PostScript applications covered in this chapter perform in an **object-oriented mode**, in which each item can be moved or altered independently. They also allow the user to precisely specify most attributes of an object, such as **line width, pattern, color,** and **percent intensity**. Their tool palettes include **text, primitive shapes** such as rectangles and circles, and **freehand lines**. All of the programs supply transformation tools for **rotating** and **skewing**, although they operate differently in each application.

Every PostScript application discussed allows key attributes to be specified by both **mouse** and **numerical control**. **Grouping** and **ungrouping** of paths and objects are vital functions, and are fully supported in a similar fashion by all. Each application offers **enlarged** and **reduced views**, though the extremes vary from program to program. Edge-bound **rulers** with variable size units are universally available. The Shift key serves as the universal **constraint** button for drawing equilateral or equiradial objects, and for limiting movement to precise vertical, horizonal, or angled axes.

WYSI(Not Always)WYG

The **WYSIWYG** (what-you-see-is-what-you-get) mode is supported by all as either an editable or a noneditable view. The developer's decision about whether to provide a working WYSIWYG mode seems to have been at least partly based on whether the screen rendition of complex PostScript effects would be unacceptably slow or unfaithfully rendered. PostScript files will print differently on various output devices. Spectacular effects and subtle gradations can be acheived with a high-resolution printer, but the display of those effects on the Macintosh II screen, at 72 dpi, can hardly do justice to the finished, printed product. Current developments in display technology will render true-to-print working screen views soon.

File Format #3: PostScript and EPSF

Most PostScript-based applications save their images as encapsulated PostScript format (EPSF) files. In EPSF the image is saved in two forms — PICT (see "File Format #2: PICT" in Chapter 5) for screen display and PostScript (ASCII text) to be sent to PostScript output devices such as most laser printers. Pure PostScript files are of course more economical than EPSF when it comes to disk space, but without the PICT information they can't be displayed on the screen.

APPLICATIONS

Cricket Draw

Of all the PostScript applications, *Cricket Draw* has the user interface most similar to that of an object-oriented QuickDraw application like *MacDraw*. However, its special effects, many of which are WYSIWYG, place it well beyond the capabilities of QuickDraw applications. Its tool set consists of basic geometric primitives, plus several tools for quickly producing objects that require several steps with other programs. Its prowess with graduated shadows and object fills is outstanding (see Figure 6-2). Being PostScript-based, it also offers precise control over line width, pattern, and intensity.

Cricket Draw has some drawbacks. It produces only single-page documents, and reductions and enlargement of the screen image are limited to between 25 and 400 percent. Smoothed objects are redrawn very slowly, and *Cricket Draw*'s color support is limited: only black, red, blue, green, cyan, magenta, and yellow are available. And the program doesn't allow attributes of grouped objects (as a group) to be changed. *Cricket Draw* is also infamous for slow printing speeds.

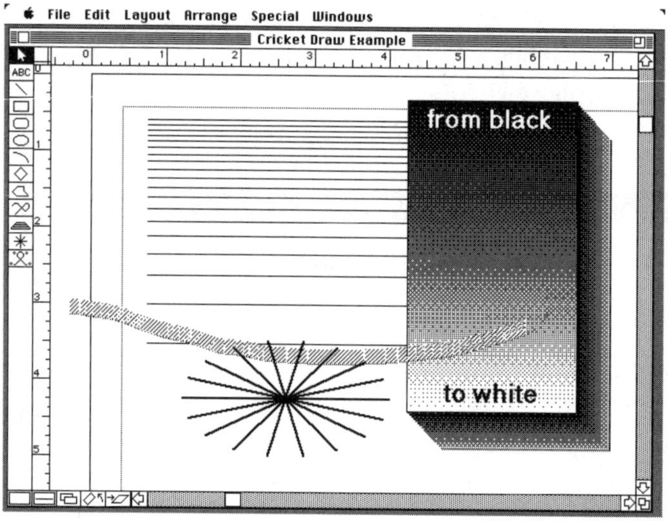

Figure 6-2. Among *Cricket Draw*'s features are gradient fills, starbursts, grates, and text bound along a path.

Cricket Draw Features

Graduated shadows: All filled objects and text can be provided with graduated shadows. Shadows can be of any length, extend in any direction, start at any intensity, and end at any intensity.

Gradient fills (fountains): Fountains make linear, evenly spaced transitions; they can be radial (extending from the center outward) or logarithmic (as in cylinder shading). They can be specified to start at any intensity and end at any intensity. The direction of the gradient is set by dragging at the appropriate angle.

Starburst tool: This tool can produce any number of lines at any angle.

Grate: Grates can be formed of any number of lines, evenly or logarithmically spaced. Linear (washboard) or radial (concentric circle) patterns can be made.

Diamond: The diamond is basically a rotated square, but its proportions can be changed as it's resized.

Bezier curves: Curves can be defined with four points.

Line management: Lines can be drawn in widths of 0.05 through 99 points, with an intensity of 0 to 100 percent black or the primary additive or subtractive colors (see Chapter 2 for a discussion of color mixing). Arrowheads can be installed on any line, including freehand lines.

Screen effects: For faster screen refresh, screen effects can be placed and then suppressed until the later stages of refinement.

Text handling: *Cricket Draw* allows the use of mixed text (varied fonts, styles, and sizes) in one block. It provides automatic word wrap, automatically beginning a new line when the text exceeds the line length. Text can be rotated to any angle or bound along an irregular path. (Text bound along a path appears as gray-filled rectangles on screen rather than as text characters.) Text can be filled with the basic colors at a uniform intensity, and full shadowing effects can be applied.

Rotation and skewing: Degrees of rotation and skewing can be set numerically or by mouse. Rotated objects can be resized proportionally only — that is, they can't be stretched or compressed in one direction only — unless they are rotated back to their original position.

Smoothing: Both polygons and freehand objects can be smoothed, but smoothed-object redraw is exceptionally slow.

Additional vertices: New vertices can be added to existing polygons.

Alignment of objects: *Cricket Draw* uses the standard object-oriented interface for aligning objects.

Grid and rulers: These devices offer predictable measurement and alignment. Rulers can be graduated in inches, centimeters, picas, or points.

Access to PostScript: PostScript procedures are available via a PostScript window and a Help function.

"PostScript Illustrations" Gallery Figures 1, 7, and 11 were produced with *Cricket Draw.*

TIP

Using *Illustrator* to Mask an Image

Draw the outline of the mask shape. With the shape selected, choose No Fill and No Stroke from the Style/Paint menu, and check the Mask box. Draw or import the image to be masked. Add color or other attributes to it. Then drag the mask shape into the correct position on the image. Select everything (the mask and the image to be masked), and group them to produce a finished, masked image.

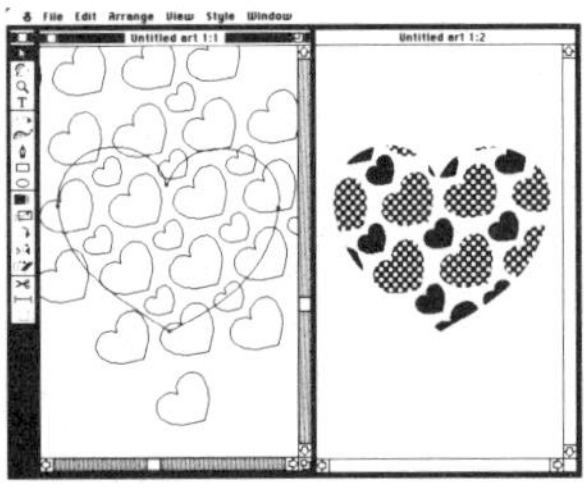

Adobe Illustrator '88

Unlike *Cricket Draw* but like *FreeHand, Illustrator* (Figure 6-3) is a path-oriented application — it lets you define objects as a series of curves and corners, and it permits very precise control over the image elements. (After you've drawn a square, for example, you can operate either on the square as a whole, or on one or more of the lines that make it up. For instance, you can cut out a piece of one side of the square and add a dimple, if you like, and then enlarge the whole square, dimple and all, and move it somewhere else.) One of *Illustrator*'s main functions is to help render smoothly defined line art by tracing over a bitmapped template, such as a *MacPaint* document.

Illustrator '88 operates through an elegant interface. Its menus are few and relatively short, and the icons in its tool palette are clear and well-ordered. Its relatively simple working window is less intimidating than that of most paint programs; it invites experimentation. The key (literally) to its higher powers is the Option key which, for every tool, allows precise customization of effects. *Illustrator*'s functions work with unique smoothness and rapid feedback.

In exploring *Illustrator '88,* we found only a single drawing layer and no familiar alignment grid. Also, there is no way to perform one-step fountain fills. Fountains had to be established using the shape/blending tool, and the process required several steps.

Adobe Illustrator '88 Features

Bitmapped template: Paint images can be imported and used as a template for tracing with Bezier curves. Tracing can be done by hand or automatically. Simply clicking on the perimeter of a bitmapped template instructs *Illustrator '88* to trace its edges and produce a Bezier curve outline that can then be freely edited. The tracing retains excellent fidelity to the template's curves, and saves a great deal of manual work.

Always accessible basic tools: Selection, hand, and magnification/reduction tools can be activated while using any other tool.

Shape blending: Shape blending is a kind of tweening capability (for filling in transformational stages between an original object and the object it's finally transformed into). Two objects, differing in size, shape, color, rotation, and position can be bridged with a number of automatically rendered intermediate objects. The attributes of the two original objects are transformed gradually. For example, a small green rectangle can be progressively transformed into a large magenta oval. An image made up of several objects can be transformed into another by shape blending the individual objects.

Freehand drawing tool: This tool defines a shape in a natural drawing motion, which the program converts to appropriate combinations of joined curves.

Curve segments: Segments can be cut from a curve and then copied and pasted.

Scissors tool: The scissors can clip a section from a path to permit another path to be spliced into the opened gap.

Path reshaping: Control points are provided for reshaping, or a path can be dragged between anchor points. Paths can also be split or joined to form closed shapes.

Transformation: Transformation can be applied to a single object or cumulatively to successive copies of an object. For example, an object can be copied five times, and then all copies can be reduced at once.

Constraining: Objects can be constrained along axes at any angle. This makes it easy to render complex objects that lie along a slanted plane.

Magnification and reduction: A wide range of working magnifications and reductions are easy to access with a menu selection or control keys.

Multiple views: Several views of the same document, including side-by-side WYSIWYG and working views, allow the user to see a preview of the final product as it's being edited.

Color attributes: Lines and fills are assigned colors numerically as percentages of cyan, magenta, yellow, and black, or as any one of the 747 PMS (Pantone Matching System) custom colors. The resultant color then appears in a window. (A color wheel would have been easier to use.)

Movable tool palette: The palette can be dragged anywhere on screen.

Resizing: Resizing can be proportional or not, and original line widths can be preserved or scaled with the resized object.

Text effects: Kerning and leading functions are provided, and text can be modified using most of the transformations that can be applied to other objects. (Text transformations are slow, however, and there's no simple way to place text along a path.)

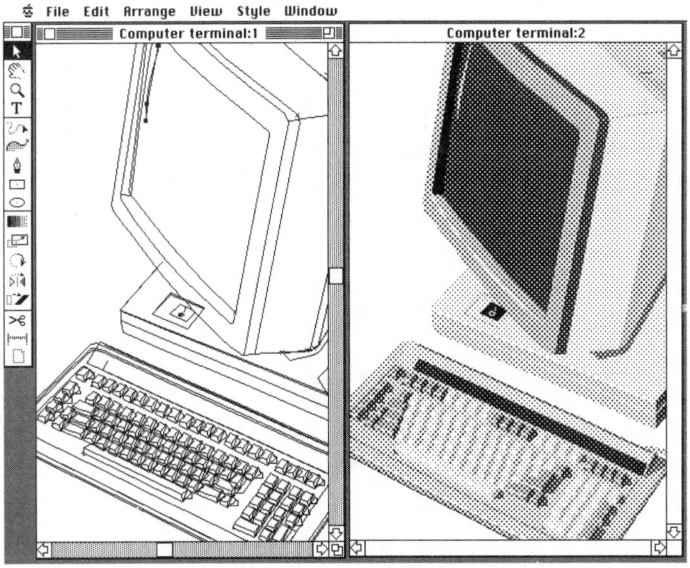

Figure 6-3. Two *Illustrator 88* windows showing artwork (left) and preview (right) views of the of an illustration.

Move, rotate, resize, reflect, and skew: These manipulations can be done by hand or by specifying exact numerical values relative to a click-point. Resizing can be proportional or disproportional. Numerical transformations allow extremely precise changes.

Import formats: *Illustrator 1.1* files can be imported for direct editing.

Export formats: Images can be saved as PostScript, Mac or IBM EPSF, or *Illustrator 1.1*–compatible files.

"PostScript Illustrations" Gallery Figures 2 through 5, 12 through 15, 17, and 19 through 21 were prepared with *Adobe Illustrator*, as were Color Gallery Figures 16, 27, 28, 30, and 34 through 36.

Aldus *FreeHand* (2.0)

FreeHand is an exceptional rendering tool. It lets you define objects by combining several types of joined lines (curve, angle, and combination). It also features a freehand tool that can define a shape in a natural drawing motion, which the program converts to appropriate combinations of joined lines (Figure 6-4). Another of its strong points is its ability to work in WYSIWYG mode, which includes full color. Complex work is made easier by its 200-layered environment. *FreeHand* combines some of the features of *Cricket Draw*, such as curved text paths and fountain fills, with those of *Adobe Illustrator '88*, such as curve control and multiple transformations.

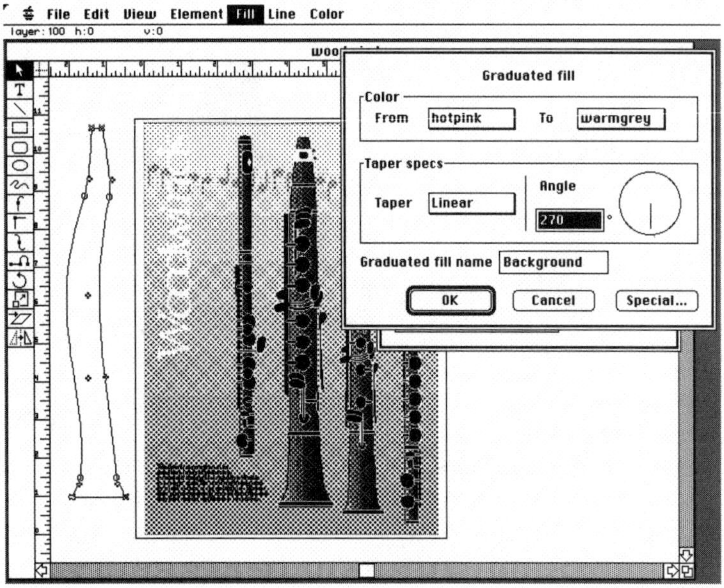

Figure 6-4. A *FreeHand* window showing the graduated fill dialog box.

FreeHand has powerful text-handling capabilities. You can bend text along a path, and edit it while it's joined to the path. Letters can be filled with custom patterns or colors, and you can choose from any number of fonts, styles, sizes, and alignments. Type fonts, sizes, and even colors can be mixed within a single text block, and multiple text blocks can be formatted simultaneously. Text can be kerned automatically.

FreeHand Features

Working WYSIWYG: Work can be done in the WYSIWYG (preview) mode or in basic line mode.

Magnification and reduction: A wide range of enlarged and reduced views are provided.

Import formats: *FreeHand* reads TIFF and PICT as well as *Illustrator 1.1* files. PICT files can be fully edited, and TIFF files can be enhanced and colored.

Bitmapped templates: Bit maps can be used as tracing guides or traced automatically in whole or in part. They can also be transformed.

Shape blending: Like *Illustrator, FreeHand* can blend one object or color into another in user-defined increments.

PostScript programming: Custom PostScript lines and fills can be defined by writing PostScript procedures.

Repeated multiple transformations: The duplicating function can duplicate not only an object, but also any transformation performed on it.

Color management: Pantone®, process color and spot color are provided. Models include RGB (red, green, blue), CMY (cyan, magenta, yellow), and HLS (hue, lightness, saturation). User-defined colors can be named and saved in color libraries. A defined color can be lightened with a 0 to 100 percent tint change.

Clipping paths: To produce a cut-out view effect, or custom fill, one object can serve as a cookie-cutter for another object that acts as the "dough." This is a powerful tool and a great time saver.

Print options: Options include color separations and combined images, with customizable halftone screens, and flipped and negative imaging.

Layers/UnDo Command: Up to 200 layers can be used, with full control of visible and active (editable) layers. Up to 100 levels of UnDo are allowed.

Page size: Page size can be selected from a set of standard dimensions, or it can be user specified (up to 3000 by 4000 points).

Custom lines, fills, and colors: The user can define lines, fills, and colors and add them to the menus. This essentially provides style sheets for colors and lines, which can be used to make global changes to styled objects without selecting them.

Line join: Separate tools are provided for each type of line join — corner, curve, and combination drawing tools. Line joins can be changed from one type to another (curve to corner, for example). Line segments and points can be added to or removed from a path.

Interactive text-attribute control: The user can adjust proportions, kerning, letter spacing, and word spacing.

Text-shaping effects: Text can be placed along (joined to) any path, with the effect visible on screen. Reshaping the path also reshapes the grouped text.

Freehand drawing tool: The freehand tool automatically fits curves and corners to a path you trace.

Fountains: Graduated area fills can be radial, linear, or logarithmic.

Rotate, resize, reflect, and skew: These changes can be made by hand or by exact numerical values relative to a click-point, the center of a selection, or a numerically specified coordinate. Resizing can be proportional or not. Line weights can be preserved or scaled with the resized object. Basic shapes can be resized without choosing special tools.

"PostScript Illustrations" Gallery Figures 6, 8 through 10, and 18 were produced with *FreeHand. FreeHand* was also used in creating Color Gallery Figures 21, 25, 26, and 32.

LaserPaint

LaserPaint (Figure 6-5) clearly endeavors to be the jack-of-all-trades graphics application, and achieves the result you might expect according to conventional wisdom. Its **paint mode** includes standard tools that work in rectangular paint zones called "bit-boxes." It has an **object-oriented mode** that includes objects composed from Bezier curves, straight lines, arcs, and even spirals. It also features a separate **text mode** for defining text blocks and their attributes, such as justification, kerning, leading, and columns. Its ability to auto-flow text around irregular objects is unique among graphics applications. Its **"Goodies" mode** provides special effects such as mirroring, resizing, and rotation that can be applied to some types of graphic elements. The four modes of *LaserPaint* can be accessed with control keys or menu selections, but not, as some paint-draw applications allow, by clicking on a specific type of object or by selecting a mode from some ever present palette.

LaserPaint's strongest feature is probably its ability to perform **color separations** on paint, draw, and PostScript images.

The program's combined capabilities are unmatched by any other graphics application. But it has its limitations, many in its user interface. Generally, intuition doesn't work, and most operations that ought to be performed with a single step require more. Using *LaserPaint*'s admirable mix of features requires considerable patience, both in wrestling with its unorthodox interface and in waiting for effects and redraws to occur. If you'll be using *LaserPaint*, it may help to know about some of its quirks in advance:

Figure 6-5. One stage of *LaserPaint*'s color selection process.

- There's no Undo capability. This is a most serious shortcoming, especially if you've invested a lot of time in detailed changes and then you make one mistake. Reverting to the last saved version can help, but it takes time to retrain yourself to Save every few seconds.
- The interface is excessively modal. Vital tools like rotation and resizing must be accessed through a separately invoked palette. The cursor changes to indicate the current mode, but this metaphor, along with some others in this interface, is overworked and confusing.
- Dialog boxes are unnecessarily large and do not respond to standard actions like tabbing through fields.
- The selection tool is buried at the bottom of the screen, and a prominent "info" button (where the selection tool could have been placed) opens a dialog box containing low-interest data like the already visible document title, size in bytes, free memory, number of objects, and so forth.
- Paint mode has no marquee, only a lasso tool. And with color TIFF images, a lassoed selection that's dragged

elsewhere becomes an unrecognizable hash of color pixels.

- In FatBits, the drawing color can't be changed and the pen is the only tool that can be used.
- Cropping of bit maps is permanent once the crop tool is deselected. Fine-tuned cropping is awkward and unpredictable, requiring excessive motion.
- Some of the typical PostScript transformation tools are lacking — for example, skewing and freely angled mirroring.
- Screen refresh ranks among the slowest, even for scrolling through a sparsely populated document.
- Response to free-form tools is generally slow. The eraser, pen, and airbrush tools lag signifiantly on the starting stroke. The action takes a moment to work, and brush strokes must be slow to avoid angular paths.
- Entering text is also extremely slow, especially in a fully justified text box.
- Resizing handles appear only on two corners of an object, limiting flexibility.

LaserPaint Features

Import formats: *LaserPaint* can import images from *MacPaint*, 300 dpi TIFF, PICT, and PICT2, as well as ASCII text.

Tool palette: The palette configures itself according to the screen size.

Editable palette icons: Icons can be customized at any time.

Registration, trim, and fold marks: These cues can be separately set and printed.

Navigation and zooming: Along with scroll bars and control keys, a floating palette is provided as a navigating tool.

Grouping: Grouping occurs automatically (and only) when some action is performed on a selected set. The set must then be ungrouped in order to make changes to individual objects.

Stacking: Stacking of objects is flexible. An object can be made frontmost or backmost, or stepped through a stack one level at a time.

Duplication combined with transformation: Transformation of copies as they are produced can be numerically specified with controls for offset, angle, number of steps, and degree of rotation. Specifications are set by holding down the Command key when selecting the menu item.

Stencils and masks: Stencils and masks can be made from objects and used like real-world paint shields or guides.

Spirals: Spirals can be automatically created from three points and can then be inserted into paths.

Arcs: Arcs drawn by center/radius can be inserted into paths.

Dashed lines: The intervals between dashes can be customized.

Text effects: Text effects include text on a path with upright or angled letters, colored and patterned text, variable leading, kerning (kerning can be varied within a text block), and full justification options (text flow around objects is also a selectable justification option). Text size can be as large as 7000 points. Eleven preset shadow effects are provided.

Columns: Columns of variable width and spacing can be set up. A number of predefined formats are available.

Graduated fills: These fills are created with a special airbrush in the object/PostScript mode. Both linear and radial fills are supported. The user can choose the color range and number of steps.

Resizable eraser: The eraser can be resized to allow better adjustment of a deleted area.

Airbrush: This feature can be used in "bit-boxes" and to retouch TIFF images. It has a variable pattern diameter and flow. (When the airbrush flow is increased above 5, the sprayed pixels become progressively larger squares.)

Process and spot color: Four-color separations, or up to 256 spot color plates can be produced. The program can use Pantone Matching System (PMS), 8-bit CYMK, or 24-bit colors.

Export formats: Files can be saved as PostScript, EPSF, compressed or noncompressed TIFF, or ASCII text.

"PostScript Illustrations" Gallery Figure 16 was produced with *LaserPaint*.

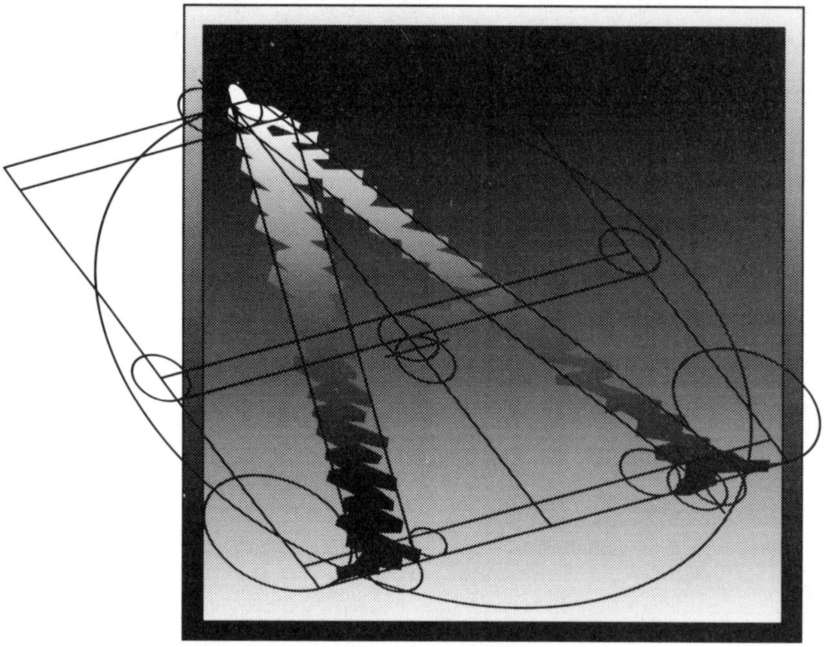

1

2

3

4

5

ILLUSTRATIONS

1 **Ramp A** by Jack Davis. Completed in *Cricket Draw*. The original "A" was drawn in *MacDraw* and brought into *Cricket Draw* as a PICT file, where the graduated screen ramps were added. The "squiggle" line was drawn as a closed polygon to allow for the graduated fill effect, since lines can't employ the fill effects.

2 **Verbum Logo** by Jack Davis. Prepared in *Adobe Illustrator*. This logo was achieved in three steps: (1) The original kerned type was output on the LaserWriter. The laserprint was then scanned and used as a bitmapped template to create the outline type stencil. (2) The masking type stencil was then filled with white. (3) The stencil was then superimposed on a scanned halftone in *PageMaker* to create the final image.

3 **The Art Collector Logo** by Calvin Woo Associates Inc. Executed with *Adobe Illustrator*. This custom logo type design was assembled from type.

4 **Hopkins Arabians Logo** by Deborah Hopkins. Designed and produced in *Adobe Illustrator '88*.

5 **California Pizza Logos** by John Odam. Drawn with *Adobe Illustrator*. The top version of this series of logo ideas includes a bitmapped treatment of "California" that was achieved by scanning a hand-drawn image.

6

7

8

9

10

11

6 **Aging and Mental Health Logo** by John Odam. Created with *Free-Hand*. The program's special-effect line screen was used to form this logo.

7 **Zap!** by Jack Davis. Finished in *Cricket Draw*. The initial drawing was traced from sketches with a digitizing tablet in *MacDraw*. A PICT file of the image was then imported into *Cricket Draw*, where the graduated screen effects were added.

8 **Sandy Hill Logo Comps** by John Odam. Produced with *FreeHand*. This series of three different logo concepts for a preschool shows a range of *FreeHand* capabilities.

9 **Spec Logo** by John Odam Created in *FreeHand*. This logo concept for a software company was created using repeated elements on a grid.

10 **Anthropology Headline** by John Odam. Generated with *FreeHand*. This textbook logo was designed using the shadow type feature and a truncated ellipse to form the swash.

11 **Windy** by Malcolm Thain Rendered in *Cricket Draw*.

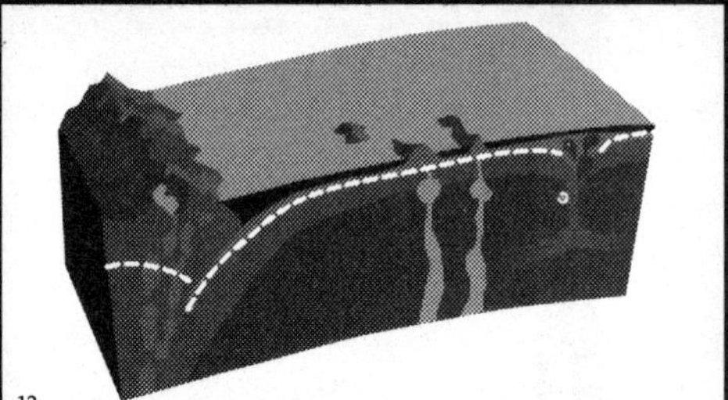

12

13

14

15

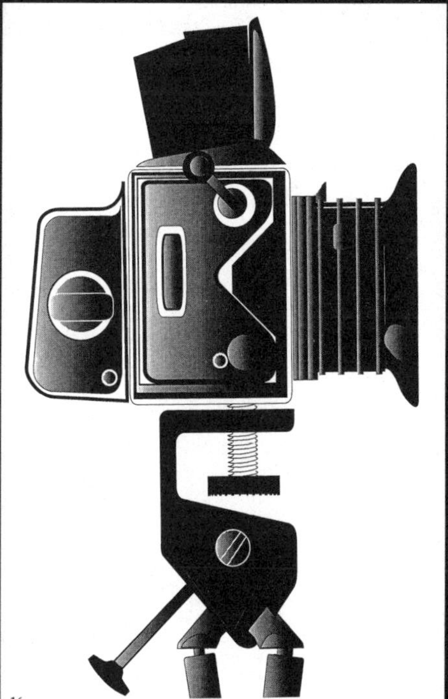

16

17

12 **Earth Section** by John Odam. Rendered in *Adobe Illustrator.* This illustration shows an excellent use of screens.

13 **Profile 3** by Jack Davis. Drawn with *Adobe Illustrator*. The dash pattern option was used to achieve the "string of pearls" line effect.

14 **Auditions Today** by Christopher Kreidel. Created in *Adobe Illustrator '88.* The template for this piece was a scan of the artist's original inked drawing, which was then traced and modified.

15 **Boy Series** by Jack Davis. Created in *Adobe Illustrator.* The template for this piece was a scan of a 1930s illustration, which was then traced and modified.

16 **Camera**. An illustration produced with *LaserPaint*, showing the program's powerful screen capabilities.

17 **Pasternec Logo** by Susan Merritt of Calvin Woo Associates Inc. Developed in *Adobe Illustrator.* This mark is a good example of the symmetrical precision that can be achieved by duplicating and rotating forms.

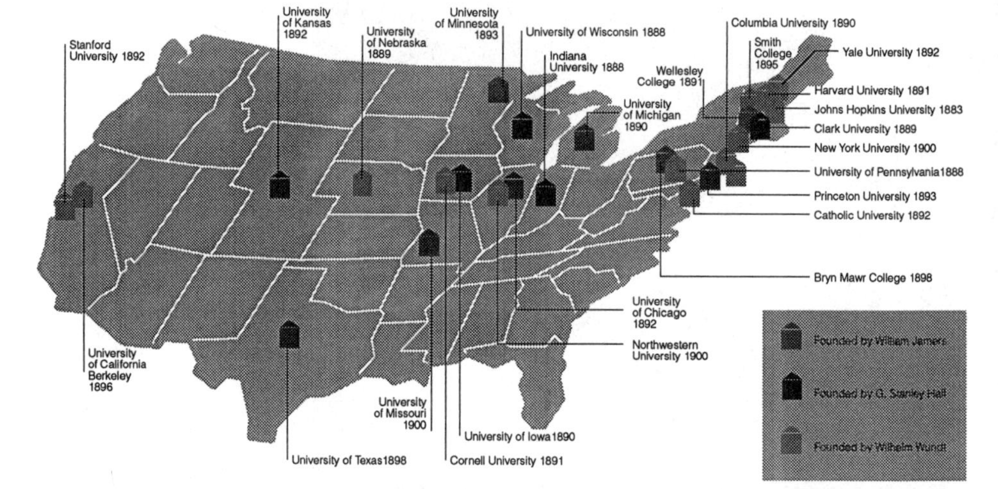

Stanford University 1892
University of Kansas 1892
University of Nebraska 1889
University of Minnesota 1893
University of Wisconsin 1888
Indiana University 1888
Wellesley College 1891
University of Michigan 1890
Columbia University 1890
Smith College 1895
Yale University 1892
Harvard University 1891
Johns Hopkins University 1883
Clark University 1889
New York University 1900
University of Pennsylvania 1888
Princeton University 1893
Catholic University 1892
Bryn Mawr College 1898
University of Chicago 1892
Northwestern University 1900
University of California Berkeley 1896
University of Missouri 1900
University of Iowa 1890
University of Texas 1898
Cornell University 1891
Founded by William James
Founded by G. Stanley Hall
Founded by Wilhelm Wundt

18

LINOTRONIC
Zip Marketing News

19

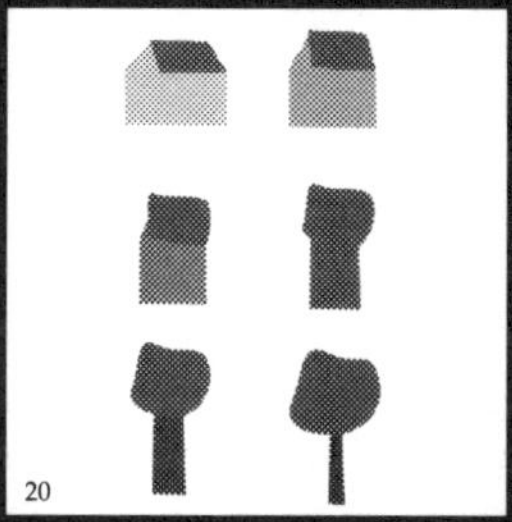

20

21

18 **U.S. Map** by John Odam. Drawn with *FreeHand*. All type was also added with *FreeHand*.

19 **MacOffice** by Laslo Vespremi. Executed with *Adobe Illustrator*. This detailed illustration was used for a story in *MacWeek*.

20 **Treehouse** by John Odam. Drawn in *Adobe Illustrator '88*. This simple illustration shows the Blend feature in action, whereby two figures composed of the same number of polygons can be used to generate intermediary stages, combining their respective forms and colors.

21 **Pearlcorder** by Bert Monroy. Drawn with *Adobe Illustrator*. This amazingly bold and detailed illustration occupies only 27K of disk space.

CHAPTER 7

Digitizing

Just as bitmapped artworks can be considered the electronic equivalent of painting and object-oriented creations can be thought of as representing technical drawing output, digitized images can be thought of as the equivalent of photographs — images produced by the action of light and captured on the electronic medium of the magnetic disk.

It almost seems as though we couldn't keep digitized images from finding their way into the Mac II, even if we wanted to. Uses for digitized images include illustration, page layout, product catalogs, employee files, advertising comps, and tracing templates. Each use has its own requirements for image quality, resolution, color, throughput, and method of digitizing. Fortunately, there are digitizing devices suitable for every end use, and every budget, with more and better ones emerging. Accompanying the flood of digitizers and digitized images, there are several very capable retouching and enhancement applications available.

TYPES OF DIGITIZING HARDWARE

A digitizing system is a combination of hardware and software designed for importing photographlike information into the computer. There are several fundamentally different kinds of digitizing systems: flatbed and sheet-fed scanners, and video-digitizing systems. Scanners read information from printed pages (photos, books, and so on) and create Mac files from that information. Video-digitizing systems make Mac files from input from video cameras. (A new type of scanning system — digitizing from 35 mm slides — is described in "The First of Its Kind — BarneyScan Color Slide Digitizer" on page 138.)

Some scanners and other digitizing systems can create and store on disk, images with up to 256 shades of gray. (See "File Format #4: TIFF and Related Formats" on p. 134.) With that many shades, and even with fewer than that, it's possible to

File Format #4: TIFF and Related Formats

Scanners produce TIFF (tagged-image file format) and related file formats. TIFF images are a type of bitmapped image in that the file describes each dot in the image. TIFF files store a **gray map**, specifying the level of gray (brightness) associated with each dot. Some digitizing programs have their own proprietary methods of storing gray-map information. However, TIFF has become a widely accepted standard file format used by most of these programs.

Page-layout programs read a TIFF file in two parts — a low-resolution version for the screen representation, and the complete file that contains the gray-scale information. You must have the separate TIFF file in the same folder as your page-layout file so the page-layout program can "link" the TIFF file when printing.

NOTE: Many programs save the TIFF format; but TIFF formats vary, and can lead to trouble.

render on-screen gray-scale images that are very close to the photographic images we're used to seeing. (For a description of how the Mac II displays gray-scale images and stores the information to produce them, see "Gray Scale" in Chapter 1.) Some digitizing systems even produce color images. It's also possible to output scanned images (in positive or negative form) on devices with resolutions from 300 dpi to 2540 dpi, with printed results that range from roughly rendered newspaper-quality to smoothly toned magazine-quality images.

Scanners and video digitizers come with software that translates the input to a form the Mac II can use. Some of these programs do little more than import the images (which is really pretty impressive in itself). Others do much more than that. This chapter describes several digitizing systems as well as two natural companions to gray-scale images, the gray-scale editing applications *ImageStudio* and *Digital Darkroom.* These image-processing programs allow various degrees of picture modification, from simple contrast and brightness control to sophisticated effects well beyond the capabilities of conventional photo retouching.

Flatbeds

Flatbed scanners accept printed originals, which are laid face down onto a glass surface. During scanning, one of two things happens: either a tightly-packed array of light sensors (on the other side of the glass) sweeps across the face of the original item, or the platform onto which the original has been placed sweeps across the top of the scanner, on precision tracks, over a stationary light-sensor array. Either way, the sensors record the attributes of thousands of points on the original image.

The spacing of the individual light-sensing points in a scanner's array determines its maximum resolution. If 300 sensors are packed in 1 inch of the sensing array, then that scanner's best resolution is 300 dpi.

Flatbed scanners can handle a wide variety of originals, including pages of bound books, product boxes, collages, mounted art, glossy photos, and even damaged items. Moreover, the original can be oriented at any angle. This kind of flexibility makes flatbeds generally preferable to sheet-fed scanners.

Sheet-fed

Sheet-fed scanners are faced with the same mechanical task as flatbed scanners: that is, to move an image past a set of light sensors. They feed the original *through* the scanner and advance it, using pinch rollers, past a fixed set of sensors. Again, the maximum resolution is determined by the density of sensors.

The sheet-fed models prevailed during the entry of scanners into the consumer market. But the current trend indicates a preference for flatbeds. Sheet-fed scanners can accept only flat originals of a limited thickness, and in fairly sound condition. Material from books and magazines is out of the question unless it's first cut out or photocopied. The orientation of originals is also somewhat limited, and it's difficult to position an original so that it will feed precisely vertically to prevent vertical and horizontal lines from turning out stair-stepped.

Sheet-fed scanners generally cost about 30 percent less than comparable flatbeds. Their price advantage, however, should be seriously weighed against their significant limitations.

Video

Video digitizers represent a somewhat broader class of image-capturing devices than scanners. As marketed, the devices may consist only of an interface box which accepts video inputs from cameras or VCRs; or a video digitizing system may be complete, including a camera, platform, and interface module.

Michael Gosney

The forté of camera-based units is their ability to "scan" ordinary 3D objects and scenes. Using cameras implies access to the tools of the photographic trade: lenses of various focal lengths, filters, lights, and special-effects devices. Best of all, the image-to-be is not frozen in time and space, so the contents, framing, and lighting of a shot can be precisely controlled. Some video digitizers read an image quickly enough to capture live action. Some are slower, and require a little old-time photographic rigor on the part of a live subject, but not much. Capture speed, predictably, affects the unit's price.

Videotaped images are suitable candidates for digitizing with such devices. Fast readers can capture a single frame of live action, while slow readers can be accommodated by freezing a given frame, a capability common to most VCRs.

Generally, the types of video digitizers that are suited for real-world imaging, are not at their best when scanning line art. Lighting and focusing become important limiting factors, and their sensor arrays simply are not optimized to provide the same kind of resolution that flatbed and sheet-fed scanners handle so well.

WHAT YOU GET FROM DIGITIZING SYSTEMS

Digitizing systems vary in the kinds of images they produce, both in the resolution (dpi) and in the nature of the information stored for reproduction of each dot.

Resolution

You can't render a cat's fine whiskers with a broad-tipped marker. Digitizer manufacturers know this, and build their machines with the capability to capture as much detail as possible within their cost constraints. We can think of the digitized image as a mosaic of thousands of point-sized photographs. The smaller and more tightly packed the pictures, the better and truer to life the mosaic image will look. This aspect of digitizing is called **resolution**. Digitizers can achieve resolutions from 30 dpi to 600 dpi and beyond.

Types of Digitized Images

Digitizers can save their images in the form of gray-scale information, halftones, high-contrast files, or color files.

Gray-Scale Images

Each pixel of a gray-scale image file has a specific gray value. When the image is displayed, those gray values are converted to corresponding *displayed* gray values. Since digitized images are most often gathered into other document forms such as page layouts and mixed art compositions, it's preferable to save black-and-white images in gray-scale mode, which gives the most flexibility for modifying or printing the digitized image later, with any of a variety of editing programs, or by using the adjustments for brightness, contrast, and halftone screens that are built into some desktop publishing applications.

Images saved as gray-scale files are relatively large in file size, but they retain information that can be used to modify them in very powerful ways.

Halftones

Some systems convert captured images to halftones before sending them to the Mac. The transmitted image has already been screened and now consists of halftone cells — neatly arranged clumps of variable numbers of black bits. Those clumps containing more bits than others are larger and appear darker. The grays of the original image are roughly reflected in these halftone cells.

The storage space required for a given picture in halftone rather than gray-scale form is significantly reduced. Instead of a **deep bit map** which relays true gray scale at several bits per pixel, the dithered form is a simple 1-bit-per-pixel rendition that creates the illusion of gray scale when you look at it.

Saving an image as a halftone can be a great help if the image is headed straight for the printer, or for an application that can't handle gray-scale images, or if you need to optimize image storage space, even at the expense of true gray scale. But generally, it's desirable to choose the gray-scale format over halftoning, to retain the greatest quality control and editing power over an image.

The First of Its Kind — BarneyScan Color Slide Digitizer

The BarneyScan Color Slide Digitizer is a self-contained unit that accepts only 35 mm slides (including glass–mounted ones), and scans them at a resolution of 1000 lines per image inch, in 16.7 million colors, or at 256 levels of gray. The actual image is captured at 1024 by 1530 pixels, and can be rendered in various software–converted pixel dimensions from 512 by 760, to 2048 by 3048. One scan pass, which takes about 50 seconds, is needed for gray-scale capture. For full color, scan time is about three minutes. Magazine-quality output is achievable if the final size of the scanned and printed image is 4 by 6 inches or less.

The BarneyScan interfaces with the Macintosh via a Nubus card. To fully evaluate the resultant color image, without the effects of color banding, it should be viewed with 24-bit video hardware, although this is not a necessity.

The unit has a very limited input format, but for uses where 35 mm slides are the main original imaging medium, as in publishing and color separation, it's an ideal vehicle for translating a photo into a file. Combined with editing and color-separation software, the BarneyScan drastically reduces the cost of color reproductions.

Software

Touch-up editing must be done with other programs. The included software has these global image manipulation capabilities: **cropping, centering,** and **rotation** by 90-degree steps. The software saves the image in TIFF, RIFF, PICT, and PICT2 formats, as well as its own native format. **Color, brightness,** and **contrast** can be corrected. An image can be modified from its stored resolution to a new resolution between 512 by 760, and 2048 by 3048.

High-Contrast Images

A high-contrast image, by design, is devoid of grays. This kind of image is very useful for scanned line art, where there aren't supposed to be any grays. High contrast is achieved by **thresholding** each image pixel. If the pixel is lighter than a specific shade of gray, then it's converted to pure white. If it's darker than that shade, it's converted to black. The shade of gray that's used as the deciding factor is called the **threshold**.

As with halftoning, the result is a flat, 1-bit-per-pixel bit map with no gray areas. The advantage of this image form is not just that it's more compact than gray scale. It's also essential where pure line art is to be represented, or where the next step involves an automatic tracing process provided by applications like *Adobe Illustrator '88* or *SuperPaint.*

Color

Digitized color images can be captured and saved in several modes, each with distinct advantages and costs. With the appropriate hardware, 24-bit-per-pixel color images can be produced. These are as storage-intensive as they are lifelike. Fortunately, you can choose to scan in 8-bit color mode, which is more economical, requiring far less storage and less expensive imaging hardware.

The 8-bit mode can render up to 256 colors. Unlike 256 grays, however, that many colors are usually not enough to produce a photographic rendition of real-world scenes. Often, there may not be enough hues to render subtle transitions. So, for example, 60 different adjoining greens will be rendered as six greens, producing an effect called **banding**, which, as the name implies, results in distinct color bands, abrupt jumps in hue, with definite borders instead of seamless blends.

But there are cases where banding may be a desirable effect, or where it may not show at all. It's also possible for the image-processing software to automatically create a 256-color palette that's customized for the scanned image and can better reproduce its specific color transitions, minimizing banding.

Although color scanners offer a full spectrum of imaging options, if you need "living" color output, your choices are not as broad as with gray-scale work. For example, you can't opt for high contrast or 64 colors to save storage space.

File Sizes

Files produced by digitizers are necessarily large. They must contain enough detail to faithfully render the original subject. If that subject is line art, then many image dots per inch will be required to reproduce smooth curves and fine lines. If the original item is a photograph, each image dot must contain enough information to reproduce its proper shade. If the digitized image is to be reproduced in full color, its image dots must contain even more information. In a nutshell, digitized graphics make large files. Anyone who uses digitized graphics very much will feel the need for at least one large-capacity storage device (see Chapter 23), and one with removable media is preferable, because, regardless of the capacity of a disk, it will almost certainly fill up — long before you expect it to. Optical storage devices promise immense space. These, by design, will have removable media.

Here's an example of how the different kinds of image storage affect file size. A 5-by-6–inch area of a seascape was scanned at 75 dpi on a Sharp JX450 color flatbed scanner. Various scanning options were used, producing several grades of image files:

- Black-and-white, 1 bit per pixel: 63K
- Gray-scale, at 8 bits per pixel: 166K
- Color, at 8 bits per pixel: 139K
- Color, at 24 bits pixel: 836K

(Note that the resolution was 75 dpi. At 300 dpi, the sizes of even modest color files can begin to make a 100 Mb disk seem cramped.)

To make a decision about how to optimally scan and store an image, you must weigh the requirements of a project, the limitations of the hardware and software, and the nature of the image itself.

ADJUSTMENTS TO DIGITIZED IMAGES

Once you have an image digitized, there are several ways you can modify it — either with the software that comes with a digitizing system or with specialized image-processing software.

Not every image captured by a digitizing system is picture perfect. Sometimes the original image is at fault. Sometimes the scanner's limitations are exceeded. For whatever reason, you may want to change the results. Unlike a printed photograph, which can't be gracefully altered, digitized images are much more editable.

Some of the classes of modifications that can be made using the scanner software or a gray-scale image editor are contrast, brightness, gray-scale transformation, and gamma correction.

Scanned photo of Lynette Berry by Tom Vollic.

Contrast

Increasing contrast will reduce the number of grays in the image. Light grays shift toward white, and dark grays shift toward black. Decreasing contrast does the opposite; deriving more grays from apparently white and black areas.

Brightness

Increasing brightness uniformly lightens all the tonal values. Decreasing it uniformly darkens all the tones.

Gray-Scale Transformation

This capability is present in gray-scale editors and in some scanner-driving software. Each pixel of a gray-scale image file has a specific gray value. When the image is displayed, stored gray values are converted to corresponding *displayed* gray values. It's normal, and usually desirable, to have black show as black, and 50 percent gray show up as just that. In other words, the grays in the image file are usually displayed as they are, untransformed.

But sometimes it may be advantageous to transform or edit specific stored gray values to other gray values — for example, displaying a 50 percent gray pixel as a 70 percent gray pixel, or a black pixel as a white pixel. The ability to substitute specific gray levels for other levels gives very fine control over the appearance of an image, and can be used for minor adjustments or special effects.

Gamma Correction

This adjustment can be used with difficult images with particularly dark or light areas that contain detail that lies within a narrow range of grays. With 256 grays available, normal distribution results in perhaps only 10 percent of the grays being assigned to the problem area. Gamma correction offers a way to assign a greater number of grays, say 128 from the 256 available, to that area. With that many grays, it will be possible to render the subtle shades of a region and bring out detail that can't be seen with simple contrast and brightness adjustments.

DIGITIZERS AND THEIR SOFTWARE

There are many suppliers of scanning hardware, particularly of flatbed-style scanners.

Following are representative products for each category of scanning system for the Mac II. All of these are proven products from reliable companies, but you should evaluate the range of products available to you based on price, performance, availability, and appropriateness to your needs. For some, the inexpensive ThunderScan system offers everything necessary for occassional sheet-fed scanning, while others may need the flexibility of video scanning offered by *MacVision*, or the color capability of the Sharp JX450.

Datacopy 830 Flatbed Gray-Scale Scanner with *MacImage* (2.0)

The Datacopy 830 is a 75 dpi to 300 dpi flatbed scanner capable of resolving 64 shades of gray. It interfaces with the Mac via the SCSI port, and it's driven by a versatile software package. The hardware has built-in contrast control, and is capable of converting the scanned image to a halftone, high-contrast bit map or a true gray-scale file before sending it to the Mac.

Figure 7-1. The Datacopy 830 flatbed scanner.

Datacopy also markets two powerful 400 dpi flatbed scanners capable of resolving 256 shades of gray. Model 840i has built-in image processing that relieves the host computer of these intensive activities. Model 840 offers the same image-capture performance, but lacks internal processors, operating more like conventional scanners in this respect.

The package that comes with the Datacopy scanner is called *MacImage*. It offers powerful editing and adjustment capabilities, but at a relatively high additional cost. It has a wealth of features, but it lacks the retouching tools of the two gray-scale editors covered later in the chapter.

MacImage Features

Halftone editor: The editor allows you to construct your own halftone cells.
Automatic default settings: Automatic defaults for resolution, contrast, and other attributes are provided for the various gray-scale modes.
QuickScan: This mode allows rapid scanning to obtain a guide for determining which part of the image is to be finally scanned.
Pixel-level editing: Pixel-level editing is provided for dithered images.
Adjustment: Attributes of pre-existing images can be adjusted. This removes the limitation of a single opportunity to modify an image before saving it.
Output formats: Images can be saved as RIFF, TIFF, EPSF, IMG, and other formats.

ProViz High Speed Video Digitizer

ProViz is a video-digitizing system that accepts color or black-and-white input from a video camera or VCR, and captures a 640 by 480 pixel frame in 1/30th of a second. It transmits a captured frame to the Mac in about 1 second via the SCSI port. The system can be optimized for line art, 16 or 256 grays, or color. The line art mode, however, still produces output that contains some grays.

Figure 7-2. The ProViz video digitizing system.

The ProViz hardware incorporates brightness and contrast adjustments, a video input port, and a video output port for a monitor or a VCR. The hardware-software combination also has the ability to convert an image stored in the Mac into standard video output that can be sent to a monitor or to a VCR.

The *ProViz* software provides the necessary control of the hardware via the Mac, as well as basic processing capabilities.

ProViz Features

Periodic capture: Frame scans can be captured at *n*-second intervals.
Basic editing: Cut, Copy, and Paste are provided.
Dithering: Dithering control affects the final appearance of the captured image.
Halftone controls: Controls provide for selection of screen type, frequency, and angle.
Printing: Captured images can be printed immediately, without saving.
Export formats: Images are saved as Paint, TIFF, EPS, ThunderScan, and ProViz formats.

(Figure 7-2- ProViz scanner, photo)

Sharp JX450 Flatbed Color Scanner

Hardware

The Sharp JX450 is capable of scanning originals at resolutions of 75 to 300 dpi, and capturing 256 gray or color levels or 16.7 million colors. The item to be scanned is placed on a sliding bed and passed over the sensing array. It's illuminated by three light sources, which, in color mode, flicker in turn to allow the separate collection of red, green, and blue information.

Scanning an 8-1/2-by-11-inch original at 300 dpi in 24-bit color takes about 100 seconds. The bed can accommodate reflective (printed matter) originals up to 11 by 17 inches. With an optional unit, the JX450 can also scan transparencies up to 8-1/2 by 11 inches. Under software control, the JX450 can scan any rectangular region of the imaging zone. To interface with a Mac II, a special "GPIB" board, available from Sharp Electronics, is required.

Naturally, the best way to view 24-bit color input is with 24-bit color output hardware, such as the RasterOps board and monitor. But it's possible, through image processing, to convert a 24-bit color image to a best-fit 8-bit color image that can be viewed with less expensive hardware and edited with a variety of available color bit-map painting applications.

Software

Sharp bundles *PixelScan* with the JX450. This program can be used after the image is captured and saved as a PICT2 file. It converts its 24-bit color image to one with 8-bit color or gray scale and saves it as a PICT2 or *PixelPaint* file. There are no editing or refinement tools in the program, but it can be instructed to optimize the converted colors for on-screen viewing or for printing.

Reducing 16.7 million colors to 256 while retaining the original image requires careful analysis and action by *PixelScan*'s sophisticated algorithm. The results may not always be ideal, but it's an excellent bridge between the two worlds of color.

A driver for the JX450 is incorporated in *LaserPaint Color II*, which can also perform basic pixel editing on the scanned image, produce color separations, and save the file in several formats.

Other independent drivers for this scanner, such as *Chromascan*, are also available. These will offer increasingly sophisticated capabilities, deriving maximum advantage from the the JX450's hardware functions.

The Sharp JX450 was used for "Digitized Art" Gallery Figure 12 and for Color Gallery Figures 16, 22 and 31.

ThunderScan Printer-Accessory Scanner

ThunderScan turns an ImageWriter printer into a gray-scale scanner that can sense 32 shades of gray at resolutions up to 288 dpi. This high resolution is obtained by specifying a 400 percent magnification during scanning, and then reducing the scanned image to 25 percent. The ThunderScan hardware consists of a small interface box and a reading head that temporarily replaces the printer's ribbon cartridge. As the original to be scanned gradually feeds through the normal paper path, like a single sheet of paper being printed, the reading head makes repeated horizontal passes, sensing and sending gray values to the Mac via the printer cable. The same basic mechanical motions are used for reading as are typically used for printing.

Figure 7-3. The ThunderScan window showing a scanned image being modified for improved contrast.

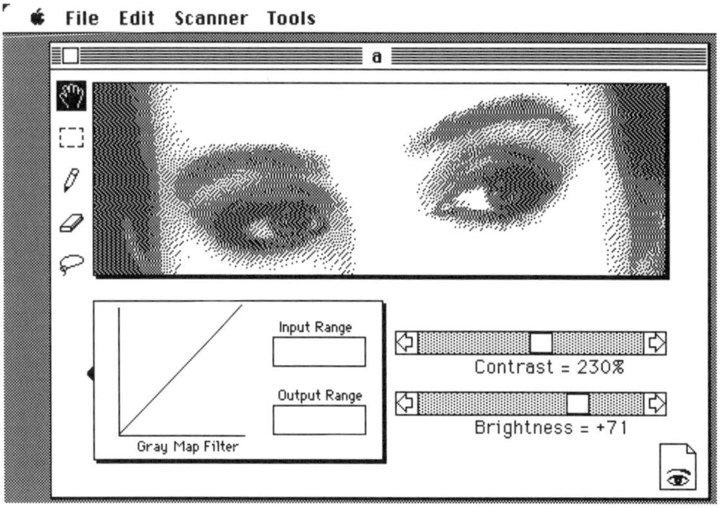

The mechanical condition of the ImageWriter and the physical nature of the scanned original strongly affect the quality of the final image. If feed-rollers slip, or if the head motion mechanism has excessive play, distortion will be introduced. The software has been designed with these factors in mind, and offers several options that can compensate for mechanical imperfections.

ThunderScan has the same limitations as sheet-fed scanners, in that it can accept only originals that can be passed through a curved-path roller mechanism. It's also considerably slower than ordinary sheet-fed ones, but if the original feeds smoothly, the final quality of its scanned images is generally excellent.

This veteran Mac imaging tool has earned its popularity with its simplicity, reliability, excellent software, and a price that's roughly one-tenth that of other scanners. If the scanned images are to be output to a 300 dpi printer (such as a LaserWriter), ThunderScan's 32 grays are not a limiting factor, because that's the best such printers can render.

The *ThunderScan* software was designed to complete a self-contained package. It's capable of pixel-level retouching, as well as manipulating brightness and contrast. Because ThunderScan reads and stores unfiltered gray values from the original, the full range of available modifications can be made to an image even after it's been scanned and saved.

ThunderScan Features

Selection tools: Marquee and lasso are provided.
Pencil: This tool is provided for turning dither pixels on and off.
Eraser: The eraser is used for clearing large swaths of image.
Navigation: A hand tool is provided for navigating around the image area.
FatBits: This mode is for detailed work.
Magnification and reduction: Images can be enlarged up to 800 percent and reduced to 25 percent.
Gray-scale interpretation: Any image gray shade can be converted to any output gray shade by means of a curve drawn with the mouse.
Contrast and brightness: Controls are provided for these two attributes.
PostScript: *ThunderScan* provides several PostScript effects and features: **halftone screens** — line or dot screens adjustable in frequency and angle; **frames** — rectangular, triangular, or circular; **rotation** — of an entire image in 1-degree increments; **captions** — added to the bottom of the image; **statistics** — printed to indicate the final settings of the printed image, such as dpi, brightness, and contrast; **custom effects** — written in PostScript and applied to the image.
Output formats: Images can be saved in Paint, TIFF, EPSF, and ThunderScan formats.

MacVision (2.0) Video Digitizer

MacVision is a video-digitizing system that accepts black-and-white input from a video camera or VCR, and captures a 640-by-480-pixel frame. The user can vary the gray-scale resolution: 4 bits (16 grays), 6 bits (64 grays), or 8 bits (256 grays) per pixel. The captured image is sent to the Mac II via one of the modem or printer ports. This process can take from 4 to 20 seconds, a long time compared to SCSI-based digitizers.

This unit is low in price and offers capabilities that make it adequate for many users. Its capture speed is well within the reasonable range for most digitizing devices.

The *MacVision* software controls the hardware and can perform several key functions in adjusting and modifying the captured image.

MacVision Features

Import formats: *MacVision* imports TIFF (from PC or Mac).
Cut and paste: Image sections can be cut and pasted within the application.
Gray-scale interpretation: Any image gray shade can be converted to any output gray shade by means of a curve drawn with the mouse.
QuickScan: This mode allows rapid scanning for faster feedback during focus, lighting, and composition.
Dithering: Special dithering effects provide a number of stylized patterns.
Image resizing: Images can be sized to from 25 percent to 1600 percent of the original scanned measure prior to saving.
Output formats: Images are saved as Paint, TIFF, EPS, and RIFF (Raster Image File Format) formats.

MacVision was used in the creation of "Digitized Art" Gallery Figures 1 through 3.

GRAY-SCALE EDITORS

In many respects, gray-scale editors round out one's collection of artist's tools. There's simply no substitute for their photo-retouching powers. Simply put, gray-scale **editors** import a file, alter the image by applying special effects to selected areas and by using artists' tools, and then save and output the image. Their ability to modify the reality reflected in a photograph, to produce seamless transitions, and to create other-worldly worlds constitutes reason enough for the Macintosh II artist to own and master these magical software implements.

To make the best possible use of gray-scale image processors, you need a monitor that's capable of displaying true grays, as opposed to dithered black-and-white pixel images (see "Gray Scale on a Black-and-White Monitor" below.) With gray-scale monitors the effects of contrast and brightness changes are instantly displayed throughout the entire image, and very subtle tonal differences are visible. The on-screen image reflects a very close approximation of what will be printed.

Gray Scale on a Black-and-White Monitor

On black-and-white displays (or on any monitor in two-color mode), the Mac II must dither changes in contrast and brightness, and so renewal of the display is slower. The necessary pixel dithering is coarse, which means gradations of gray are not rendered smoothly, especially through the lighter shades. With the limitations of black-and-white displays, it's difficult to predict what the printed image will look like. Feedback from several test prints will be required before you achieve the intended effects.

Importing Files

Gray-scale editors can usually accept images in a variety of formats including Paint, PICT, TIFF, and ThunderScan. They can read black-and-white images and synthesize shades of gray by diffusing (changing the light levels) of adjacent pixels.

Manipulating the Grays

Gray-scale editors provide **selection tools** with which to surround an area of the image so it can be edited — moved, copied, cut, or modified by **darkening, lightening, blurring**, or **sharpening**. Editing can be performed through a wide range of **magnified and reduced views** with **instantaneous on-screen feedback. Navigation tools** that allow you to move around inside an image include a zoom-in/zoom-out function, scroll bars, and a hand cursor.

Gray-scale image editors all allow full manipulation of the gray scale, using **contrast and brightness** sliders and fully editable gray-map interpretation. Any image shade can be substituted for any other shade (white can be shown as black, medium gray as light gray, and so on). This capability alone raises these editors above ordinary photo retouching. Several different gray scales can be permanently applied to selected areas of a single image to help optimize local contrast and brightness or to add spot special effects.

Artists' Tools

The conventional **paintbrush** in various sizes is supported for applying a selected gray shade to cover any part of an image. **Smart brushes** can be instructed to apply gray paint only to specific image shades or ranges of shades. Other intelligent tools are used like brushes, but unlike brushes, they can darken or lighten, by specified degrees, any area they pass over.

Brushlike **blurring tools** are supplied for smoothly blending or blurring adjacent grays, an effect that's vital to retaining an unretouched look. Several sizes of **texture pick-up tools** can copy the pattern of an area and then duplicate the pattern elsewhere. These "rubber-stamp" tools can extend uniquely textured surfaces to fill gaps or simply to add more area, and they can create special effects well beyond realism.

Built-in special effects include **posterization** and **equalization.** Posterization dramatically increases contrast so that only black and white remain. Equalization distributes the full gray scale used in an image over a selected area; this technique helps bring out detail from a relatively flat region.

Saving the Retouched Images

Gray-scale editors can save images in a variety of file formats: Paint, EPSF, and TIFF. They can also scale a saved image and export a selected area only. They offer a selection of **halftone printing options**, including dot screens, patterns, and angled screens. And they can print a selected portion of an image, which saves time in previewing a printed effect.

ImageStudio (1.0)

This first-class gray-scale editor carries conventional photo-retouching to new heights. Its tools — the water drop, charcoal, and blending finger, for example — are intuitive and responsive and produce predictable, lifelike effects. (Unfortunately, the selection tools [lasso and marquee] are limited in their usefulness — they don't automatically scroll past the window edges, and any conventional scrolling action deselects the selection.)

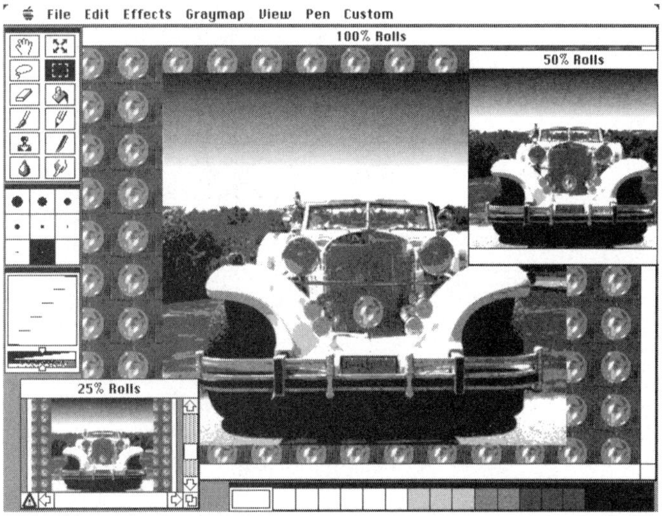

Figure 7-4. Multiple magnifications of an image in the *ImageStudio* window.

ImageStudio successfully achieves its prime objectives of smoothness and seamless blending of image elements so that conscientiously applied photo retouching is virtually undetectable. Its wide range of menu-driven magnification and reduction (there's no key-driven size option) help to retain photo realism by providing working views from panoramic down to a single pixel (Figure 7-4).

ImageStudio is also an excellent stand-alone graphics program. At its simplest level, it could be dubbed the *MacPaint* of the gray-scale world. But exploring its depth through its elegant user interface reveals that it offers much more. The user can get help by Option-clicking on a tool, or through well-ordered choices from the "About..." selection from the apple menu. And *ImageStudio*'s user's manual is exceptionally clear.

ImageStudio Features

Grays: A total of 256 gray shades are supported. (The LaserWriter is capable of producing 32.)

Import formats: *ImageStudio* can import Paint, TIFF, ThunderScan, and FOTO (from *PageMaker 1.2*) files.

Page-level rotation: The whole page can be rotated left or right 90 degrees to reorient scanned images.

Multiple views: Different image sections can be displayed at various magnifications simultaneously. When a change is applied, all views are updated.

Undo/redo: This comprehensive function works even after the mouse is idly clicked or a new tool is selected (but not yet used).

Resizing: A selected rectangular area can be resized by cutting it and pasting it into a block of predetermined size.

Cropping: This function deletes all parts of the image that extend outside a selected area.

Flip and rotate: Vertical and horizontal flip functions are provided, as well as left and right rotation of rectangular areas.

Invert: The Invert command retains gray-scale control while making a negative of a selected area.

Filters: These can be used to blur, sharpen, diffuse, soften, trace edges, and produce a star-lens effect.

Area fills: The paint bucket can apply solid fills, graduated fills, or borders only. The fill can be a gray shade or a user-defined fill pattern.

Fine control of tool attributes: Tool attributes like diameter, pressure, timed flow, transition from light to dark, and modifying only those image shades darker than the selected gray, or lighter than the selected gray, can be precisely controlled.

Background shade: The user can define the background shade. This allows more control over what gets painted, because tool attributes can be set to paint or not paint onto the background shade. For example, to use the old-fashioned coloring book as a metaphor, you can paint over part of an object without "coloring outside the lines."

Soft-edged brush: This tool applies a soft-edged stroke of a selected shade according to set preferences.

Pencil: The pencil is sharp-edged, but otherwise follows the same rules as the brush.

Charcoal Darken/Lighten: This mode allows darkening or lightening of an area with progressive strokes.

Rubber-stamp tool: This tool can apply custom imprints such as leaf patterns. It can also copy a section of the existing image for use in extending a subject's hair, for example, or creating or extending a streaked surface.
Water drop: This tool dilutes, softens, and blends everything it touches.
Finger: The finger tool blends by directionally pushing one image shade into another adjoining gray.
Polygon tools: Created by using the Shift key in conjunction with the pencil, brush, rubber stamp, or eraser, polygon tools draw connected straight lines in their currently set modes and shades.
Custom tools: Existing tools and attributes can be combined to form custom tools, which can then be saved as named items in a menu. Custom tools make extensive special effects possible.
Halftone screens: Line and dot types may be one of several program default formats, the printer default format, or a custom-specified type.
Special dither patterns: These patterns can be applied to files saved in Paint format. A preview function can display the final printed effect.
Compressed files: Images can be saved in compressed form so that they occupy one-third the space of noncompressed files.

"Digitized Art" Gallery Figures 3 through 13 were prepared using *ImageStudio*.

Digital Darkroom

Digital Darkroom is a technical gray-scale editor that combines a few familiar metaphors with some power features that have no obvious real-world counterparts. Its emphasis is *editing what's already there* rather than creating a new image. It provides a wide variety of selection tools, and it can select multiple *unconnected* areas of an image. *Digital Darkroom*'s image-modification tools are extremely powerful. Great care has been taken to provide tools that permit changes to blend well with the unaltered regions of the image. *Digital Darkroom* redefines "pasting" by offering extensive control of the overlap effect; for example, it lets you specify to what degree the stationary element and the element pasted over it will dominate the final image (Figure 7-5). The same kind of selective control can be used in painting with its gray-scale brushes.

There are also limitations in navigating in *Digital Darkroom*. Magnification and reduction are exclusively key driven, and scrolling with the hand cursor is slow.

But *Digital Darkroom*'s weaknesses are far outweighed by its talents for selection, controlled distortion, overpainting, and gray-scale alteration. These can save hours of hand-powered trial and error, and can quickly produce effects that can't be achieved with any other Macintosh application to date.

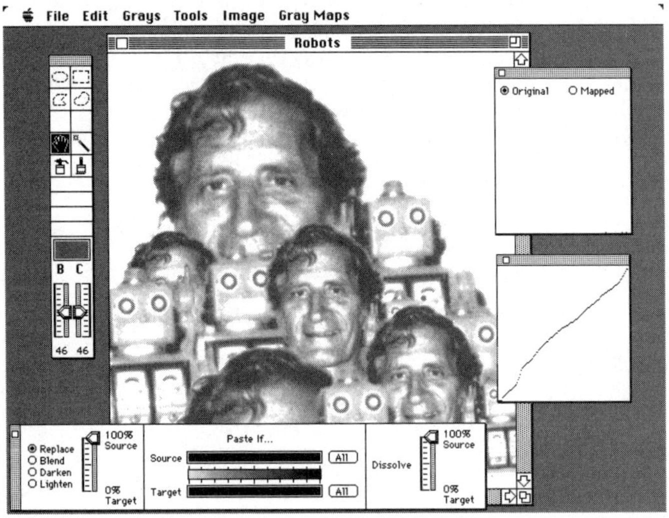

Figure 7-5. A "ghost" created by blending a pasted selection with the underlying image in *Digital Darkroom.*

Digital Darkroom Features

Grays: 256 gray shades are supported. Although the on-screen limit is 128 shades, the printed image can contain 256. (Remember that the LaserWriter is capable of producing 32.)

Import formats: *Digital Darkroom* imports Paint, TIFF, ThunderScan, PICT, and PICT2 formats.

Selection tools: Manual selection tools include a rectangle, an oval, a freehand region (lasso), and a polygon.

Magic wand: When this tool clicks on a spot, it seeks the edges of an area containing approximately the same shade of gray, and then selects it. The selection can be altered with the other selection tools, or the magic wand can be instructed to continue its search, extending the already selected region.

Inside or outside editing: The user can choose whether the selected or the nonselected area(s) will be modified by an edit operation. This makes it easy to make sweeping alterations in an image while keeping small areas unchanged.

Selection refinement options: With this outstanding set of options, any number of selections of any shape can be simultaneously active, including a selected region with a deselected hole in it. Choices include:

- **New,** which deselects any currently selected areas and activates a new one.
- **Add,** which retains all current selections and adds a new one, contiguous or not.
- **Refine**, which keeps selected the overlapping region of two selected areas and deselects the rest.
- **Subtract**, which deselects the overlapping region of two selected areas, leaving the rest of the two areas selected.

Deselecting tool: This is a necessary part of the tool kit; it helps remove regions from the selected set.

Scissors tool: This tool can cut a selected area into two parts. It's handy for partially deselecting, or for performing two different operations on portions of a selection.

Filters: *Digital Darkroom* provides filters to blur, sharpen, find edges, darken edges, and despeckle (despeckling removes from a selected area any scattered pixels that don't match the general shade of the region).

Darken/Lighten settings: The user can specify the number of gray shades by which to increase or decrease the intensity of an image area. This setting works with the additive and subtractive brushes and with the Darken/Lighten Region commands. There are separate Darken/Lighten controls for the brush and for overall image effects.

Transformations: Transformations of a selection include:

- **Rotate,** which rotates the selection left or right in 90-degree steps.
- **Flip,** which creates a vertical or horizontal mirror image.
- **Free rotation**, which provides very powerful and clean rotation.
- **Stretch, Distort, Slant, Perspective,** which allow a selected image to be stretched or shrunk, squeezed, and sheared. These options can create the illusions of depth and shifted viewpoint. Combined with free rotation, these features permit a kind of surrealism — allowing major alterations of photo images while retaining the look and feel of reality.

Paste controls: These controls are a shining example of customized effects. Sliding scales (0–100 percent) and instant visual feedback help to fine-tune the product of two overlapping images. For example, a 50/50 blend of the underlying image and the pasted image produces a ghostlike result. Paste controls allow:

- **Replacement,** which replaces the underlying image with pasted image.
- **Blending,** which merges the two images.
- **Darkening,** which darkens the underlying image with the darker patterns imposed by the pasted image.
- **Lightening**, which lightens the underlying image with the lighter patterns of the pasted image.
- **Dissolve,** which provides pixel dithering of the two images. Two "spectrum" bars are used to further specify which gray shades of the pasted image will be applied, and which gray shades in the underlying image will be modified by the paste operation. These bars allow extremely fine or broad control over the final effect.

Brush modes: There are many powerful and varied ways to use the paintbrush. The brush can:

- **Apply** a selected (opaque) gray shade over the surface.
- **Darken or lighten** an area gradually in user-specified steps.
- **Blur,** softening and averaging gray values.
- **Smudge**, pushing one gray tone into another.

Texture: An area can be textured with a pattern first picked up (using the Option key) from another area of the picture. (This feature helps to create or patch large areas of randomly textured grays, or to obliterate unwanted details by painting them over with a background pattern.)

Stamp: An area can be stamped with a brush-shaped "cookie-cut" of another area of the picture (first picked up by using the Option key). (This feature helps create or patch areas with distinct patterns such as flowing hair, feathers, and pebbles.)

Nudge: This editing function moves the selected area one pixel width to the left or right, up or down. It eliminates "overshooting," making precise adjustments easier.

Paint/Fill: These controls work essentially like the Paste controls. Basically, two parallel gray-scale bars let the user select the range of grays that will be allowed to serve as paint, and the range of image grays that will be allowed to receive the painted shades.

Masking: Masking a region with a pattern produces an effect like screening, but on only a selected portion of the image. (The mask patterns are not real screens but standard-looking Macintosh fills.)

Autotrace: This specialized tool converts all selected regions of approximately equal grays into outlined objects. The outlines can be Bezier curves, or QuickDraw polygons. The resulting collection of objects can be imported into programs such as *MacDraw, SuperPaint, Adobe Illustrator*, and *FreeHand*.

Enhance edges: This command darkens all prominent dividing lines between different gray regions.

Halftone screens: Screens include round dots, lines, and square dots, with variable angles and variable numbers of cells per inch (the resolution of the output device is the limiting factor). Images can also be printed as dithered bit maps.

Advanced halftone and standard halftone printing: Advanced mode creates a printed image that is significantly sharper looking than the normal halftone screen, and reveals more descernible detail. Printing, however, takes several times longer than with a normal halftone screen.

Compressed files: Images are saved in archived (compressed) form, which requires less disk space.

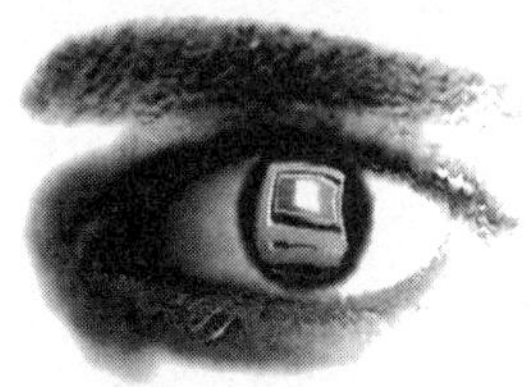

1

2

3

4

5

6

DIGITIZED ART

1 **Self Portrait** by Jack Davis. Recorded from live subjects using *MacVision*, the two high-resolution video scans were then combined, distorted, and retouched in *ImageStudio.*

2 **Get 1** by Paul Rutkovsky. Originated in *MacPaint*, printed on a LaserWriter, and redigitized with the *MacVision* video scanning system for the exaggerated pixelation effect.

3 **Quad Portrait** by Mike Uriss. Scanned with *MacVision*, this photo was then modified in *ImageStudio.*

4 **Victorians** modified by Jack Davis. Scanned with 16 shades of gray and brought into *ImageStudio.* Hundreds of modifications were made to the original image. In many cases, adjacent areas were selected with the lasso tool, copied, and moved into position. These areas were selected, and the Soften or Diffuse filter was used to blend edges. Further retouching was done with finger tools.

5 **Hokusai vs. Godzilla** by Jack Davis. Created by scanning the Hokusai wave and Godzilla head, combining the images in *SuperPaint*, and adding the gray shades with the paint bucket in *ImageStudio.*

6 **Through a Rain-Streaked Pain** by Jack Davis. Created by scanning a photo and modifying it in *Image-Studio.* The finger tool was used to smear the grays, the selection rectangle (marquee) was used to delete sections, and the water drop tool was used to soften the resulting edges.

7

8

9

10

11

12

13

7 **Rebel II** by Pepe Moreno. Rendered in *GraphicWorks* and brought into *ImageStudio,* where the gray-scale highlights were painted in.

8 **Eye Surf** by Mike Uriss. Scanned as two images that were then combined in *ImageStudio* for soft blending and special effects.

9 ***Verbum 1.3* Logo** by Ed Roxburgh. Created by inking the letters by hand (using brown ink to retain a textured appearance), and then scanning the original image and modifying it in *ImageStudio.*

10 **Australia's Challenge to the Americas Cup** by Daryl Isaacs. Created in *ImageStudio* by combining two scanned photos: the catamaran sailboat and the duplicated cruise ship in the water.

11 **Earth Apple** by Jack Davis. Scanned from two photographs at 150 dpi with 8 bits of gray-scale information. The two images were then combined and retouched in *ImageStudio.*

12 **Platt College Ad** by Jack Davis. Scanned from a photo with a Sharp JX450 flatbed scanner at 150 dpi, the image was brought into *ImageStudio,* where other images were pasted in on the computer screens in the foreground. The edges of the photo were blurred with the water drop tool. The file was then placed in a *PageMaker* layout, which was printed on the Linotronic as a negative at 2540 dpi.

13 **King Arjuna** by Serban Epure. Scanned from a hand-drawn image, the bitmapped file was then opened in *ImageStudio* and painted over with gray screens using the brush and charcoal tools.

Chapter 8

Desktop Publishing

The goal of desktop publishing (DTP) applications is to furnish the space and tools to design, assemble, edit, and precisely fine-tune a layout. They're typically used for the complete cycle of design, comping, and production of finished, camera-ready art. Most often, the process involves elements created with a number of different applications. With their talent for importing and managing diverse graphics and text formats in one document, they simplify the development of ad layouts, brochures, posters, manuals, books, and mixed (electronic) media art.

Throughout the electronic layout process, they strive to present an accurate view of each page as it will appear in print. Like many other types of Macintosh applications, they support a variety of page sizes; their range extends to tabloid, and beyond.

Their powerful text-formatting capability sets DTP applications in a different league from word processors. In addition to supporting standard character and paragraph styles, they offer a wide variety of column options. They allow you to distribute a body of flowing text among disjointed blocks anywhere in a multipage document, and the blocks act as freely movable objects. Edited text automatically reflows through whatever patchwork of blocks it resides in.

While it's by no means indispensable, a large screen display is very useful for working efficiently with DTP programs. All applications support a sufficient range of page reduction (and even magnification) so that two facing pages can be viewed on any size screen, but using a smaller screen costs the extra time it takes to zoom out to see a full page and then zoom in again to continue detailed work. All reduced views are fully functional, though, allowing you to freely arrange elements and even edit text, as long as you can read the reduced text well enough to work with it.

Although DTP applications support the ImageWriter printer (see Chapter 11), many of the effects of kerning (tightening the space between two adjacent letters), screening, and using fine lines and halftones can't be rendered very well with its relatively low resolution.

The environment of DTP applications is peppered with terms from (what else?) the publishing industry, most of which relate to text and its formatting: kerning, leading (space between lines of type), letter spacing (general spacing between letters), pica (a measure of line width and height), gutter (the space between columns) — terms like these help extend the metaphor. These words soon become familiar to the novice, and they help acclimate the seasoned conventional publisher to this new desktop world.

ART COLLECTORS

Desktop publishing applications, by nature, specialize in importing documents produced with a wide range of graphics programs, from the earliest *MacPaint*, to the high-end PostScript-based tools like *Adobe Illustrator* and *FreeHand*. They also cheerfully accept 300-dpi images from scanners and gray-scale documents from applications like *ImageStudio* and *Digital Darkroom* as long as the graphics are saved in generic file formats like Paint, PICT, TIFF, and EPSF.

The graphics creation tools of most DTP applications are limited to **lines** (rules), **frames**, and **ovals**. Those basic shapes, however, can be rendered in a variety of line **types** (dotted, dashed, multiple), thicknesses, and patterns. Imported graphics can be cropped and scaled, and some applications provide means to modify the contrast and brightness of imported graphics.

DTP programs with minimal graphics-editing talents can easily be supplemented with powerful graphics-crunching desk accessories (DAs) with much of the power of graphics applications (see Chapter 19). And with *MultiFinder* and sufficient memory, you can work on your layout and access *all* the power of the application(s) that produced its artwork without having to close your DTP file to do it.

A WAY WITH WORDS

DTP applications can directly import a variety of native text formats also — from word processors like *Word* and *MacWrite* as well as the international currency of computers, ASCII text. Most DTP programs support a workable set of **word processing functions**, including spell checking and automatic end-of-line hyphenation, so that text can be entered directly from the keyboard.

All justification options (left, right, center, and full) are supported, as well as control of the finer attributes of text formatting like leading, kerning, letter spacing, and tabs.

A combination of **paragraph and character formats** (indentation, tabs, font [see Chapter 18], and leading, for example) can be defined, named, and saved as a **style sheet**, and any number of style sheets can be defined for a document. The typical styles for a layout might include one each for body text, headline, subhead, and caption.

A style sheet can be applied to any number of paragraphs, which instantly take on the assigned format. The power of style sheets becomes even more apparent when you decide to modify some aspect(s) of a style. When you do, all paragraphs with that style automatically reflect the change, without a click of extra effort.

Although DTP software offers the opportunity to enter and edit text directly from the keyboard, it's generally better to prepare any text that's longer than a short paragraph in a word processor, and then import it. Entry and editing functions work faster in word processors.

TIP

Moving Through the Layers

In *PageMaker* you can select any object within a set of layers by Command-clicking. The program goes through the object levels one at a time while you click.

PAGE MAKEUP

To help with the placement of graphics and text, DTP applications provide both **passive and active guidelines** that overlay the on-screen page. (Passive guidelines are present merely as a visual clue for lining up elements, while active guides "grab" the elements you place on the page and line them up for you.) The **column metaphor** is used, and you initially specify how many columns your document or page will have. With some DTP applications you can also specify how many **horizontal** divisions a page will have.

Column guides provide the initial reference for the start of text insertion and for where word wrap occurs. When a text block is first defined, it will size itself to the column guides. You can later shift the text block anywhere in the layout and freely resize it.

For layouts that contain a number of identical attributes, you can create **master pages** — templates whose characteristics are passed on to other pages. Left and right (even/odd) master pages can be set up with different or identical format. Pages can be automatically numbered.

Each application lets you toggle on and off the activity (magnetism) of its vertical and horizontal guides. When the guides are active, layout objects will snap to the nearest guide. When guides are inactive, objects are allowed to settle anywhere on the page.

Measurement and positioning tools include **vertical and horizontal rulers** divided into inches, picas and points, metric units, or other measurements. As you move the cursor, sliders on each ruler indicate the cursor's position, or the position of an active object. Vertical and horizontal guidelines can be installed to serve as steady baselines for text or graphics. Typically, vertical and horizontal rulers have an adjustable zero point for accurate sizing or positioning of different elements on a page.

Vertical and horizontal **grids**, which can act as magnetically as column guides do, can be established and toggled on and off. Their horizontal and vertical steps can be defined in a variety of units.

Many DTP applications provide **layering**, which allows you to move overlapping elements upward or downward in the "pile," so that you can more easily grab and manipulate them.

TIP

Avoiding Distortion in *PageMaker*

When using paint graphics in *PageMaker*, you have to be careful about resizing the graphics, or some patterns will distort. *PageMaker* has a special option to constrain the resizing of paint images to sizes that don't distort. This is accomplished by holding down the Command and Shift keys while resizing the image.

DTP APPLICATIONS

PageMaker (3.0)

PageMaker furnishes a comfortable and flexible environment in which to operate (Figure 8-1). Compared to most other page-layout programs, it's the least rigorous for the user, requiring little preparation before most actions, such as importing text or graphics. Column width, for example, can be altered at any time simply by dragging the guides.

Overall, it's a smoothly operating seasoned professional. It doesn't wield the same raw power as *Quark Xpress*, but its balance of features and ease of use have helped *PageMaker* emerge as a favorite DTP application among a wide variety of users.

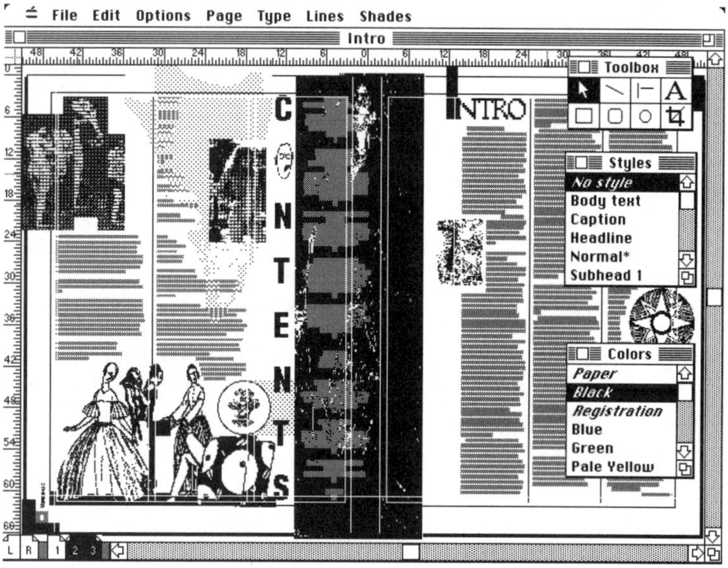

Figure 8-1. The *PageMaker 3.0* page-layout window, including the tool, style, and color palettes.

PageMaker has a versatility that goes beyond the Mac II. It accepts IBM PC *PageMaker* files (formatted text, bit maps, TIFF files, and PostScript images within the layout are directly compatible). It also accepts PC word processor files from *WordPerfect*, *Wordstar 3.3*, and *XyWrite*, as well as DCA format files.

> **TIP**
>
> **Saving Space**
>
> When saving files in *PageMaker* and most other page-layout (and also word processing) programs, use the Save As option every so often instead of Save. This procedure saves a considerable amount of disk space. To see how much, Save the file and check its size by choosing Get Info from the desktop File menu; then use Save As and check again.

PageMaker 3.0's drawbacks are few, and most of them can be compensated for. It has no spell checking, but this function can be accomplished in a word processing program before text is imported. There is no option for numerically specifying sizes, but elements can be shaped using the pointer, the rulers, and the crosshairs that automatically follow the pointer and indicate its position on the rulers.

Maximum page size is tabloid (17" x 22"). Maximum file size is 128 pages.

PageMaker Features

Pasteboard space: The program provides "table space" around the page layout, where you can set graphic and text elements temporarily, so that they're in view as you decide where to place them. Although visible to the user, elements in the pasteboard space don't print as part of the page layout.

Alignment guides: An unlimited number of vertical and horizontal guidelines can be established.

Rulers: Units for vertical and horizontal rulers can be set independently of each other. The user can choose units from a standard set, or establish custom multiples of a half-point.

Color guides: Rulers and column guides display in color.

Graphics formats: *PageMaker* can import a full range of Mac graphics formats: Paint, PICT, PICT2, TIFF , and EPSF. Elements from *Jazz, Easy 3D, MGM Station CAD,* and *Excel* can be brought in through the clipboard.

Drawing tools: Lines, rectangles, rounded rectangles, and ovals are provided.

Frame and line character: Lines and frames can be produced in compound, dashed, and dotted patterns or in 10 percent gray-scale increments.

Intelligent scaling: Bitmapped graphics can be scaled in mathematically appropriate percentages to prevent interference patterns when printed at the resolution of the output device.

Gray-scale image control: *PageMaker* allows you to adjust brightness and contrast. Built-in special effects include dot or line screens variable in angle and frequency, negative (inverted), posterized (stepped gray-levels), and solarized (like the effect you get by briefly turning on the light during developing a negative in the darkroom).

Spot color: The user can produce overlays (one per color) using RGB (red-green-blue), CMYK (cyan, magenta, yellow, and black), or HLS (hue-lightness-saturation) color models.

Style sheets: *PageMaker*'s style sheets are compatible with those of *Word*. Any styling done in *Word* can be automatically imported with the text, and text exported from *PageMaker* to *Word* retains *PageMaker* style sheets also.

Automatic text-flow options: Text can be made to stop at obstructions or to skip over or flow around, behind, or in front of them.

Editable wrap-around (outset) border: By adding vertices to a basic rectangular border, a user can direct text around graphics.

Color text: The color text option is available and is also supported as a style sheet attribute.

Optional "greeking": To reduce the time it takes to refresh the screen when you switch to a reduced view of the page layout, greeking (simulated text) is used in the reductions, where real text would be too small to be useful anyway.

Specialized printer driver: The printer driver can be optionally employed to make optimal use of a printer's resolution, yield shorter print times, use an unlimited number of downloadable fonts, and interface better with nonstandard print spoolers.

Customizable printer interface: This interface uses printer description files that provide printer-specific information (page sizes, resolution, etc.) to the *PageMaker* print driver. Maximum use of a specific printer's features can thus be derived. As new printers emerge, their features and specifications can be relayed to *PageMaker* using description files.

> TIP
>
> **Printer Driver Pros and Cons**
>
> Smoothed polygons from draw programs don't print out correctly in PageMaker unless you use the Apple printer driver. But then you won't have the advanced kerning and justifying capabilities of the Aldus driver. You can't have it both ways.

"Publications" Gallery Figures 1, 2, 3, 5, 7, 8, and 10 were generated with *PageMaker*.

Ready,Set,Go! (4.0)

Ready,Set,Go!'s working style makes it easy to define a layout quickly. *RSG!* subdivides the page with blocks rather than columns. Blocks provide both vertical and horizontal snap-to guides, and any text or graphic frame will instantly be adjusted to fill any guide blocks it touches (Figure 8-2).

Prior to placing any text or graphics, the user must place appropriate frame types on the page. The block-based scheme imparts a certain rigidity to the layout process, but for many purposes it's a positive feature.

RSG! has comprehensive word processing features and can be used to generate all the text required. Its response to text modifications is among the fastest of the DTP applications.

Figure 8-2. The *Ready,Set,Go!* page-layout window, showing a finished page spread incorporating bitmapped graphics.

However, in some respects *RSG!* is less versatile than *PageMaker*. For example, it does not import *Word* paragraph formatting, and it exports text only as ASCII files. Style sheets can't be imported or exported. *RSG!* provides no paint tools, and although it supports color for imported graphics, it provides no color-generation tools of its own.

Among *RSG! 4.0*'s little inconveniences are these: removing a style from text is tricky, requiring careful selection of all affected text; and changes in page view (reductions and enlargements) always shift to the upper left corner of the page, regardless of the current position of the cursor.

Maximum page size is tabloid (17" x 22").

RSG! Features

Grid-based layout: *RSG!*'s reliance on a grid system allows quick, accurate placement of text and graphics blocks. Grid specifications include several preset choices, but can be fully customized.

Resizing: Scaling is specified numerically; rescaling by mouse is not an option.

Object alignment: Like *MacDraw*, *RSG!* can align objects by sides or centers.

Hand cursor: This tool provides an efficient way to navigate through currently open layout pages.

Graphics formats: Paint, PICT, PICT2, TIFF, and EPSF can be imported.

Graphics handling: Picture blocks (frames) receive imported graphics. The blocks can be resized to crop the contents, and the image can be shifted inside the block.

Fill/Pen patterns: 52 preset patterns are provided, including 10 percent gray-scale increments.

Frames and lines: Compound, dashed, and patterned lines may be used; patterns include gray scales in 10 percent increments.

Style sheets: Extensive choices of character and paragraph formatting are allowed. Defined styles can be applied with menu or with Command key combinations.

Importing text: Text can be brought in from *MacWrite*, *Word*, *Works*, and *WriteNow*; ASCII text can also be imported.

Automatic text-flow options: Text can be made to flow around rectangular or irregular graphic elements. Text reflows automatically if a graphic element is moved.

Type styles: Font sizes up to 255 points can be used. Styles that can be originated within the program include standard options plus Strikethrough, All Caps, Small Caps, and white type on black.

Word processing: Features are comprehensive and speedy.

Search and replace: The search functions can find character formats (bold, italic, and so on), tabs, and Returns. This function works within a single block, several blocks, an entire set of linked blocks, or an entire document.

Spell checking: A suspect word is highlighted and suggestion(s) for correction are made. This function works with single blocks, several blocks, or an entire set of linked blocks.

Glossaries: Frequently used phrases can be invoked with a dialog box or code key sequence, providing a quick alternative to retyping.

"Continued" notes: When blocks of text must be split between pages, "continued" notes are automatically added; they're updated as linked text blocks change location.

PostScript file: *RSG!* transmits its layouts as pure PostScript files. This allows faster printing (because the file is sent in the printer's native language [see Chapter 10]). It also allows the layout to be transmitted and received by modem as an ASCII file and sent to any PostScript device without that device having *RSG!* installed as an application.

"Publications" Gallery Figure 4 was created with *Ready,Set,Go!*

Quark Xpress (2.0)

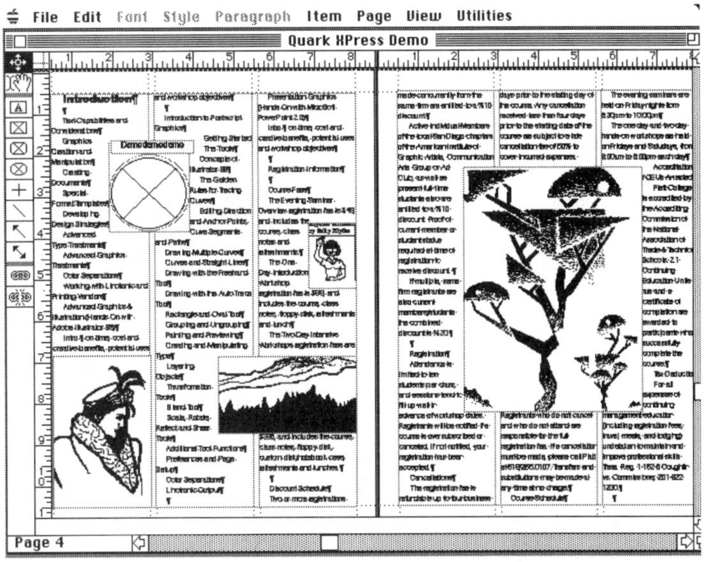

Figure 8-3. The *Quark Xpress 2.0* page-layout window, showing predefined blocks for text and graphics.

Xpress is a powerful layout package. Unique among the DTP applications is its hierarchical management of layout elements. Blocks contained within other blocks are handled as "daughter" items. Wherever the outer blocks go, the inner ones go along. This feature permits the use of complex layout blocks that can be shifted as units, remaining otherwise undisturbed.

In addition to its hierarchical layout management, *Xpress* uses hierarchical menus. A selected menu-bar item reveals a submenu off to one side, offering options relating to the initial menu-bar item.

Xpress is a column-based application, but it requires blocks (or frames) to be predefined within the layout before text or graphics can be entered or imported (Figure 8-3). Its word processing capabilities and typesetting options are excellent, and they support extreme precision.

Xpress offers extensive options for controlling the final rendition of imported graphics. Color management is its graphics strong suit. In addition to importing and displaying color images, it allows any object, including text, to be tinted or gray-scaled. It's capable of producing true color separations from its layouts. Unfortunately, *Xpress* provides no paint tools.

Xpress provides a much larger maximum page size than *PageMaker* or *RSG!* — 48" x 48".

Xpress Features

Object-measurement display bar: This tool shows the dimensions of a selected object.

Graphics formats: *Xpress* can import Paint, PICT, PICT2, TIFF, and EPSF formats.

Elaborate frame styles: A variety of frames are supplied, and more can be created with the Frame Editor (and creator) application. Graphics frames can be rectangles, round-corner rectangles, or ovals.

Lines: Several line patterns are provided, including lines with arrowheads at the ends.

Built-in smoothing: This feature for smoothing bitmapped graphics is especially useful if the output device you're using doesn't have smoothing capabilities.

Cropping and scaling: All graphics formats can be cropped and scaled.

Gray-scale image control: Contrast and brightness of imported graphics can be manipulated, and line and dot screens and posterizing and solarizing effects can be added.

Color management: *Xpress* provides both spot color and process color using RGB, CYMK, or HSB (hue-saturation-brightness), as well as the printing industry's ink standard Pantone Matching System (PMS). It can also display digitized graphics in color.

Importing text: Text can be brought in from *MacWrite, Word, Works,* and *WriteNow;* ASCII text can also be imported.

Automatic text reflow: When an embedded graphic is shifted, text automatically reflows around it.

Type styles: Text sizes can range up to 500 points. The standard styles are provided, as well as All Caps, Small Caps, Strikethrough, and white type on black. Tabs can have optional leader characters.

Color text: Text can be gray-scaled or tinted.

Optional "greeking": To reduce the time it takes to refresh the screen when you switch to a reduced view of the page layout, greeking (simulated text) is used in reductions where real text would be too small to be useful anyway.

Search and replace: Search can be based on character formats (font name, style, size, etc.). The function works through an entire set of linked blocks, or an entire document. Wildcard characters can be used.

Horizontal scaling of text: Text may be stretched or compressed horizontally from 25 to 400 percent by letter, word, line, or block, to solve tight-fit or loose-line problems.

Paragraph-to-paragraph spacing: Paragraph spacing may be specified independently of line leading.

"Continued" notes: When blocks of text must be split between pages, "continued" notes are automatically added; they're updated as linked text blocks change location.

Spell checking: A suspect word is highlighted and suggestion(s) for correction are made. This function works with single blocks, several blocks, or an entire set of linked blocks.

Color separations: Registration marks are included in the color separations.

"Publications" Gallery Figure 6 was created with *Quark Xpress.*

Other Applications

Simple page layout can be accomplished in software other than page-layout programs — for example, Microsoft *Word, FullWrite, MacDraw,* or *SuperPaint.* Gallery Figure 9 is a good example of a layout accomplished completely with *FreeHand,* a PostScript graphics program.

For the production of long documents (books, manuals, catalogs) that require substantial text and formatting control but not as much design flexibility, there are powerful publishing programs such as *Interleaf Publisher.*

For more sophisticated color layout capabilities, the Mac II–based Lightspeed system offers a complete turnkey solution (see the Product appendix).

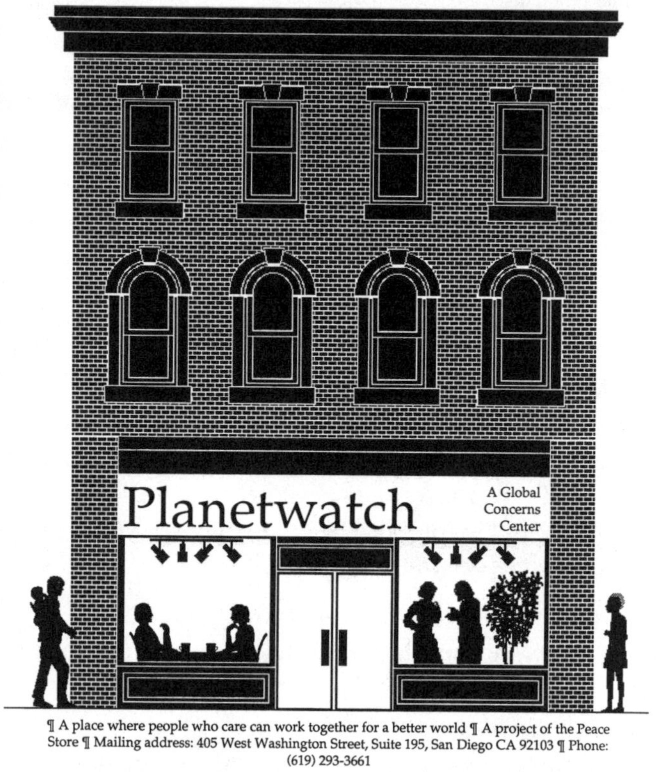

Planetwatch
A Global Concerns Center
¶ A place where people who care can work together for a better world ¶ A project of the Peace Store ¶ Mailing address: 405 West Washington Street, Suite 195, San Diego CA 92103 ¶ Phone: (619) 293-3661

1

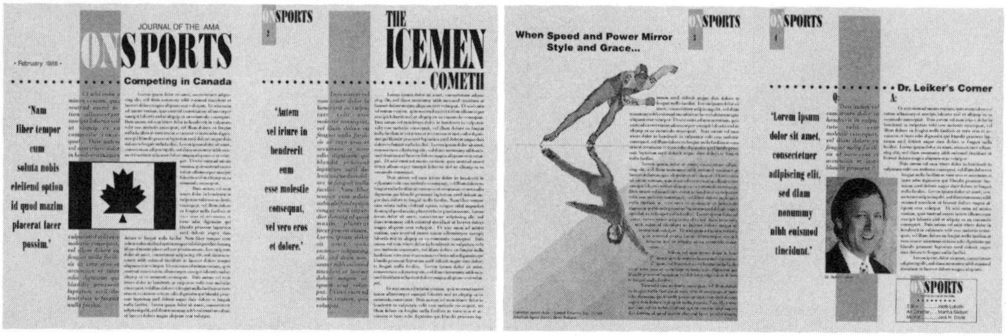

JOURNAL OF THE AMA
ONSPORTS
Competing in Canada
'Nam liber tempor cum soluta nobis eleifend option id quod mazim placerat facer possim.'
ONSPORTS
THE ICEMEN COMETH
'Autem vel iriure in hendrerit eum esse molestie consequat, vel vero eros et dolore.'
When Speed and Power Mirror Style and Grace...
ONSPORTS
ONSPORTS
Dr. Leiker's Corner
'Lorem ipsum dolor sit amet, consectetuer adipiscing elit, sed diam nonummy nibh euismod tincidunt.'
ONSPORTS

2

PUBLICATIONS

3

4

1 ***Planetwatch* Newsletter** by John Odam. Created with *PageMaker.* This is the cover of a one-color newsletter illustrated throughout with bitmapped graphics produced in *SuperPaint.*

2 ***On Sports* Newsletter** by Martha Siebert. Designed and assembled in *PageMaker.* This design for a four-page newsletter uses type and graphic elements created in *PageMaker,* as well as several types of imported graphics: the flag is an *Adobe Illustrator* piece, the skater is a gray-scale composition executed with *ImageStudio,* and the halftone was touched up with *Digital Darkroom.*

3 **Invitation** by Michael Gosney. Prepared in *PageMaker,* using a clip art image and type.

4 **Restaurant Ad** by Jack Davis. Designed and produced with *Ready,Set,Go!* The tree image in the logo was scanned with *Thunderscan* and assembled in *Ready,Set,Go!*

Let's Celebrate Science!
February–March 1988
Reuben H. Fleet Space Theater and Science Center
Balboa Park
15th Anniversary

5

4 4 MacWEEK May 24, 1988 WINDOW ON
FINANCIAL MANAGEMENT
TAKING CONTROL OF YOUR MONEY
BY LAWRENCE STEVENS
MacWEEK May 24, 1988 4 5
WINDOW ON
FINANCIAL MANAGEMENT
Determining where the dollars go, Page 44.
Whether it's for business or personal use, tracking household expenses or a stock portfolio, there's a Mac package to help you keep track of your budget. The money you save may be your own.
LAPTOPS
A Mac for the road, Page 50.
The problems of developing a true laptop Mac have yet to be completely resolved.
How to get data from a non-Mac portable, Page 51.
NEXT WEEK
Property management
Micro-mainframe links
MACS IN DEPARTMENT THAT CAN COMMUNICATE WITH MAINFRAME OR MINICOMPUTER

6

5 **"Let's Celebrate Science" Poster** by Michael Gosney. Designed in *PageMaker*, using scanned images. This 11" x 17" poster was printed in black ink and reversed white areas with a background of silver ink. The radar dish is a TIFF file that was purposely printed as the low-resolution version to achieve the desired pixelated effect. It was printed on the L-300 as base art with overlays.

6 ***MacWeek* Magazine Spread** by Laslo Vespremi. Designed and produced with *Quark Xpress*, which accommodates the publication's 11–3/4" x 13–1/2" page size, and allows for precise type handling.

7 ***Verbum 1.2* Cover** by John Odam. Designed and produced with *Page-Maker*. The screen gradations on the bars were executed in *CricketDraw*. The large VERBUM at the top of the page was created by typing each character on its own *PageMaker* text field and positioning the fields with slight overlaps. Letters of the small VERBUM were also created and placed individually and, where necessary, were reversed out using *PageMaker*'s Reverse Type command.

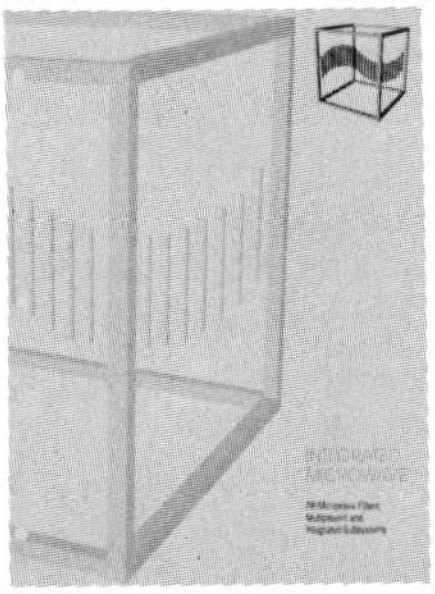

8

9

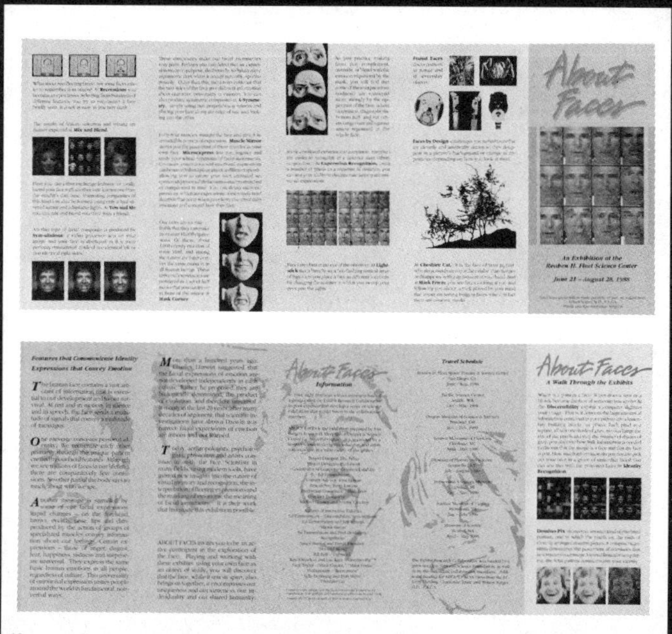

10

8 **Integrated Microwave Brochure** by Michael Gosney. Designed and produced with *PageMaker*. This cover for a four-color brochure uses a 3D version of the company's logo rendered with *Pro 3D*. The logo was used as a design element throughout the brochure in a variety of rotations.

9 **"The Other California" Brochure** by John Odam. Developed entirely with *FreeHand*. This four-color brochure cover shows how in some cases production of single panels can be accomplished completely in a PostScript illustration program because these programs have sophisticated type-handling capabilities. The cover was separated directly out of *FreeHand* on the Linotronic L-300.

10 **"About Faces" Brochure** by Michael Gosney and Daryl Isaacs. Created with *PageMaker*. The background face illustrations for this four-color brochure were converted from hand drawings into *Adobe Illustrator '88* documents using the Auto Trace tool on bitmapped scans of the drawings. The various photos and illustrations were scanned in for ease in designing on screen and were used as position prints within clean black masks that served as windows at the stripping stage. The full sheet size was 9" x 20", which required a custom APD file to run on the Linotronic at full size (normally limited in *PageMaker* to 11" x 17").

Color Gallery

For what seemed like many years, people spoke with reverence of the future "color Mac" – a mystical machine that someday would do all the things the original Mac did, but in spectacular high-resolution color. That someday arrived in 1987 when the first Mac IIs were shipped. The early Mac II owners were frustrated by the lack of software that could take advantage of the machine's color potential. But gradually, software developers brought out new and upgraded products that made color on the Mac the new standard of quality for the personal computer industry.

For artists, this powerful color technology means that illustrations, layouts and even scanned photos can be developed and output in accurate color. With 3D graphics, presentations, color separations, and animation, the color Mac is realizing dreams faster than we imagined possible.

The Color Gallery showcases sample works, following the same order as the preceding chapters, from paintings to desktop publishing layouts. The images are reproduced in various ways (see notes on page 196): transparencies shot from the screen, film recorder output, prints from color thermal printers, and offset printing from digital color seps.

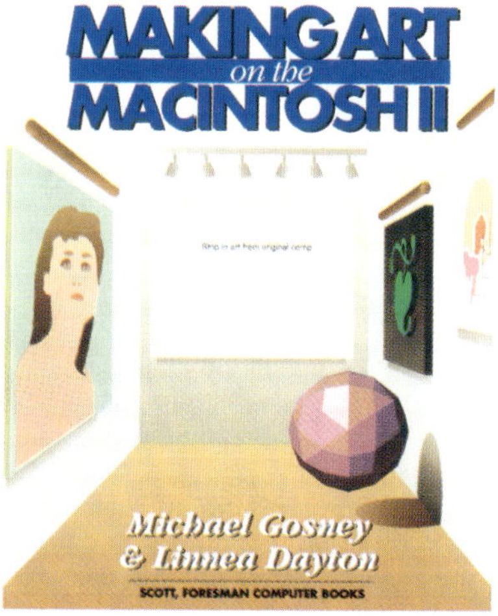

Proof of *Making Art on the Macintosh II* cover from a QMS ColorScript 100 color PostScript printer. The negatives were produced on the Linotronic L-300 at 2540 dpi and used for printing the final cover.

1

2

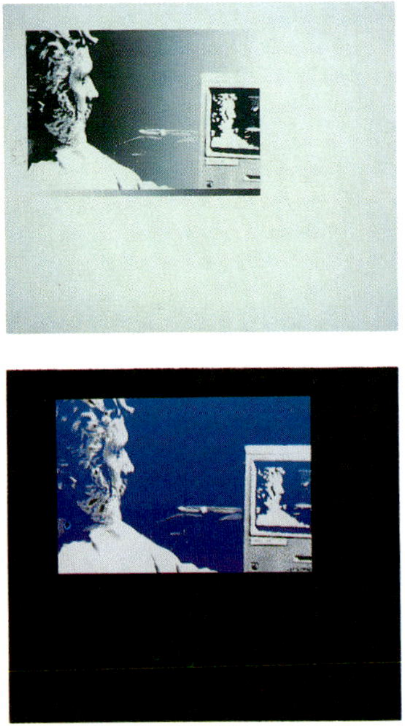

3

4

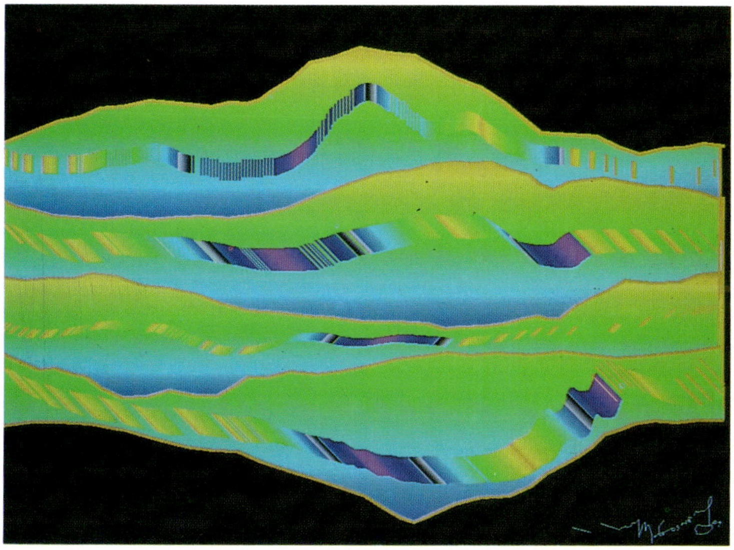

5

6

1 *Verbum* Logo 1 by Michael Gosney. This logo for *Verbum* magazine was created in *MacDraw*. It was colorized in *PixelPaint* using the paint bucket with color blend special effects.

2 *Verbum* Logo 2 by Jack Davis and Michael Gosney. This *Verbum* magazine logo was drawn by Jack Davis in *MacDraw*. Michael Gosney then stretched and colorized it in *PixelPaint*.

3 Mind Mirror by Michael Gosney. A bitmapped image of the profile and the scanned image on the Macintosh Plus screen were captured using *MacVision*. The file was brought into *PixelPaint* and modified using graduated fills. The gray version was filled with a gray palette, and the color version with a blue-to-purple blend.

4 Rings by Michael Gosney. This *PixelPaint* illustration was created by using the radial fill feature with a custom palette to generate the color rings. A section was selected with the lasso and moved.

5 Fractal Wave by Michael Gosney. This *PixelPaint* illustration was created using the fractal line feature and color ramp fills.

6 Un Cachet by Dominique de Bardonneche-Berglund. This subtle *PixelPaint* illustration was created by a talented Swiss artist who uses only the mouse to execute her lifelike digital paintings.

7

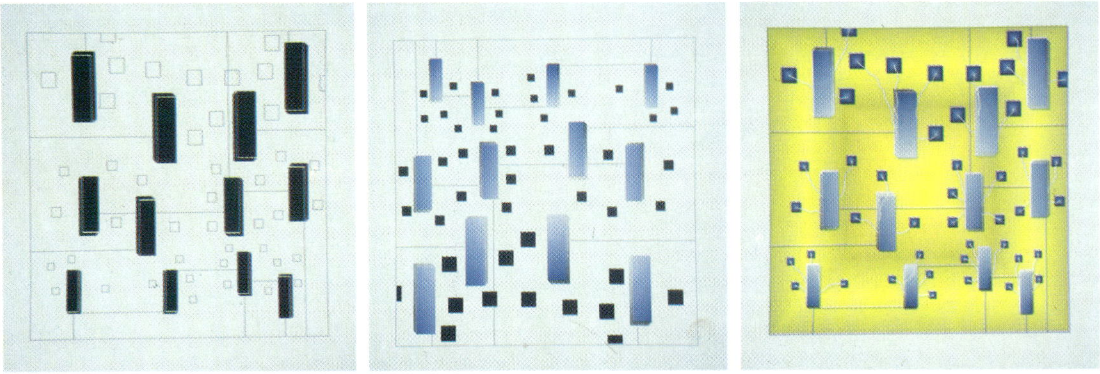

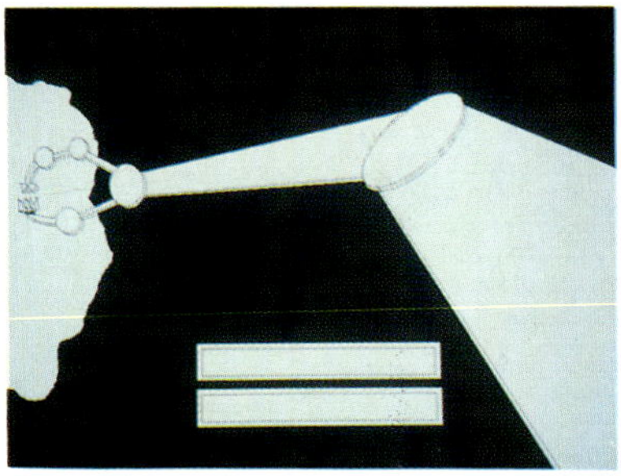

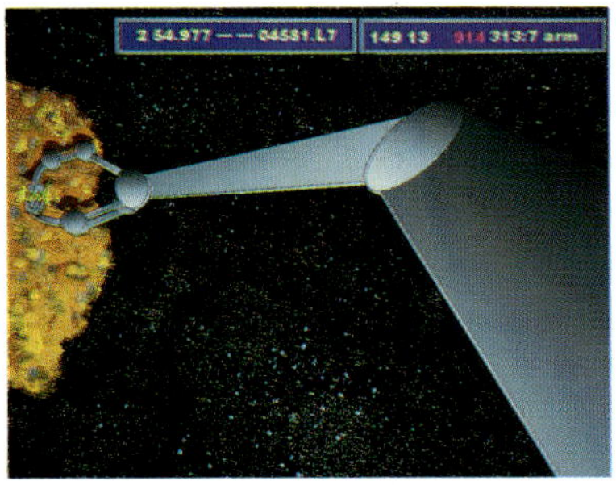

9

10

11

7 Networking by Michael Gosney. The first step in creating this illustration for a magazine cover was to generate the lines and rectangular shapes in *SuperPaint*'s draw layer. The image, saved as a PICT file, was brought into *PixelPaint,* where the color ramps were added with the paint bucket. Finally, a color background was added using the paint bucket with the Shapeburst effect.

8 Space Arm by Michael Gosney. This illustration for a magazine cover was created in *PixelPaint.* The main elements were drawn in outline and filled with the directional fill feature. The starry sky was painted using the airbrush and speckle airbrush with whites and grays, and the "alloy" was painted with the brush and airbrush.

9 Connection by Michael Gosney. This illustration for an article on "Mac-to-Mainframe Connectivity" was generated in the draw layer of *SuperPaint*. It was then brought into *PixelPaint* as a PICT file and colorized. The background color was created with a directional fill.

10 Window by William Lombardo. This *PixelPaint* illustration began with a scanned image of a face.

11 Ocean Planet by Ron Cobb. This illustration was created with *PixelPaint*.

12

Barb's Luncheonette
CARDS · STATIONERY · CANDY · BOOKS
PEPSI
384
CANDY

13

12 Le Silence by Dominique de Bardonneche-Berglund. Three reproductions of this *PixelPaint* illustration are shown here. The image on the left was generated with a Mirus film recorder. The image in the middle was shot from the screen of our SuperMac 19" Sony monitor as a 2-1/4-inch transparency (see "Shooting Transparencies from a Color Monitor" in Chapter 17). The image on the right was reproduced from a print off the Tektronics Color Image thermal printer. The film recorder creates a technically more precise image, with each "pixel" glowing vibrantly. The screen shot, however, actually reproduces the color and texture of the original more faithfully because it more accurately reflects the screen image the artist was using as she created her work. The Color Image printer works well with *PixelPaint* files, but sometimes has a hard time with blends and exact color matching.

13 Street Scene by Bert Monroy. This *PixelPaint* illustration was developed for exhibition at *Verbum* magazine's art show produced for Apple Computer's Imaging Sciences Offsite in March 1988. It later won first place in *Macworld* magazine's art contest. See Chapter 4 for the artist's detailed explanation of how the work was created.

14 Tarzan by Dominique de Bardonneche-Berglund. The artist used *PixelPaint* to create this vibrant piece. The Diffuse effect was used to give the flames a realistic appearance. The brown-to-green coloring of the leaves was achieved with the Shapeburst fill effect.

14

16

Computerized
Airbrush
ART

15

cinemax
Taking TV
To The Limit With...
Supercharged exclusive movies!
Breakthrough comedy specials!
Soaring music spectaculars!
Out-of-this-world original series!
Far-out film festivals!

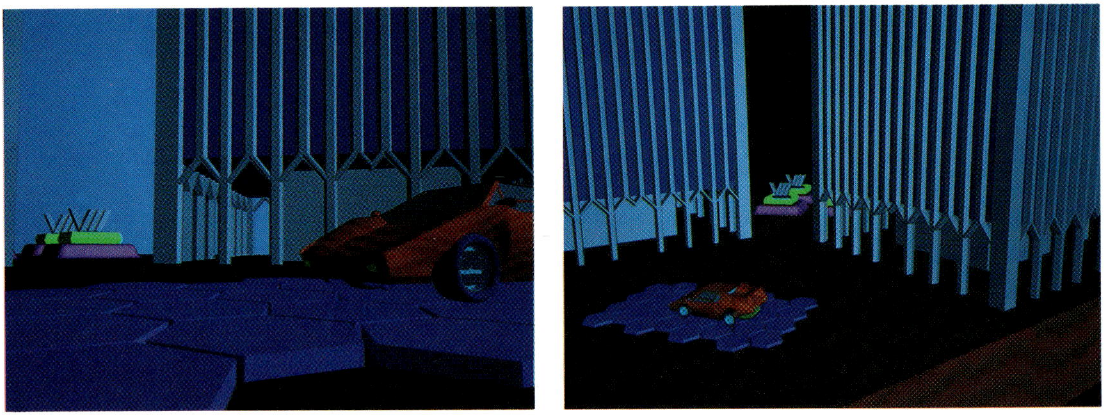

17

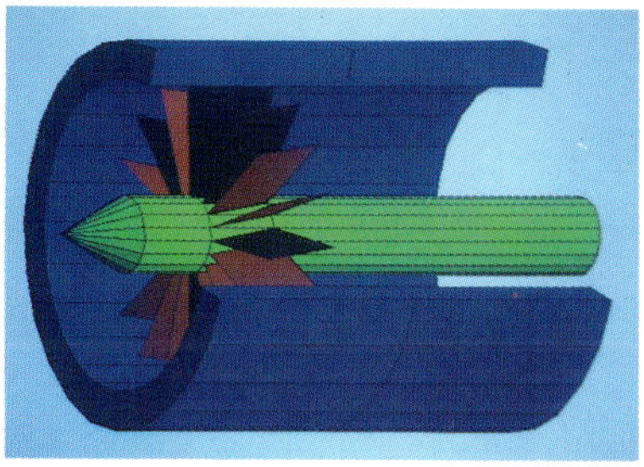

18

19

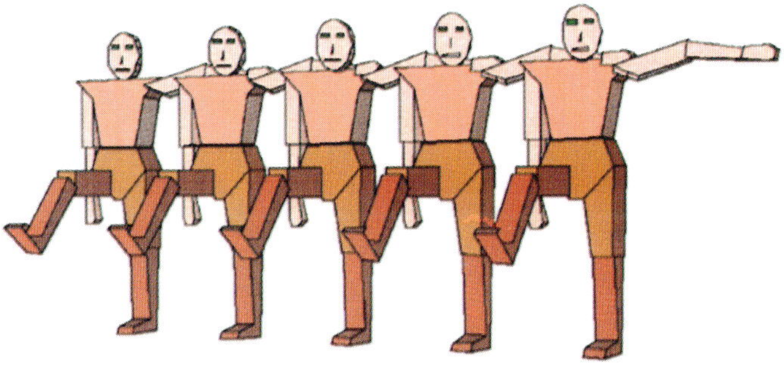

20

15 Cinemax Poster by Joseph Prieboy and Rich Godfrey. Using *MacPaint* and *GraphicWorks*, the artists created this piece at HBO, Inc. Creative Services as a comp. The client liked it so much that it was used as is, with the rough pixelation. The colors on the finished 24" x 48" poster were added with process color screens on press. It went on to win the 1987 Broadcast Design Award.

16 Computerized Airbrush Art by Daryl Isaacs. This *PixelPaint* illustration began in *Adobe Illustrator*. *PosterMaker Plus* was used for the special type effects. The line art and type files were imported, colorized, and embellished with the addition of the cloud backgrounds, which had been scanned from photos using a Sharp JX450 color scanner.

17 Lambo by Eric Popejoy. Two views of this 3D image are shown. It was created with *Dimensions*.

18 Turbine by Michael Martin. This *Super 3D* piece was rendered by the programmer of *Super 3D*. The component pieces were created separately as hierarchical objects and then combined. This image is part of an animated sequence illustrating the spinning turbine.

19 Can-Can Robots by Russell Schnapp. This illustration was rendered with *Super 3D*. The extruded forms can also be used in an animated sequence. The file was created using the program's hierarchical objects feature so that the five robots occupy the disk space of only one.

20 Furniture & Layout Plan by Robert White. This illustration started in *MacDraft*. The original piece was then brought into *Dreams*, (Innovative Data Design's mid-priced CAD package for the Mac II) where it was modified and enhanced with colors and color patterns.

21

22

23

24

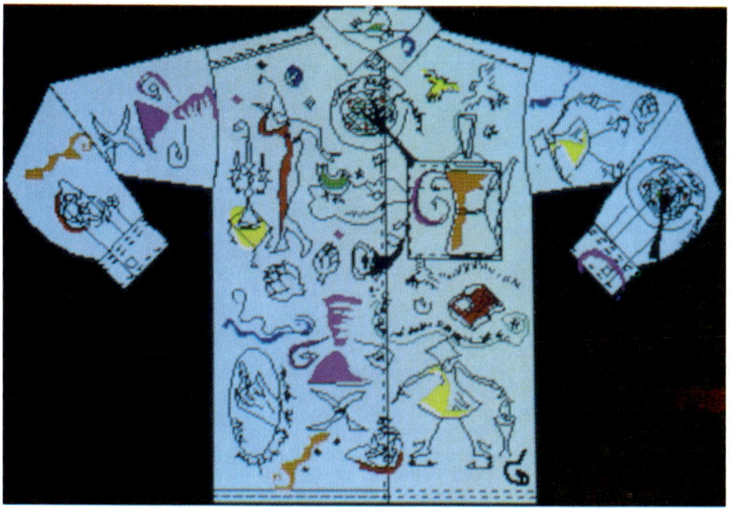

25

21 Spiralling PostScript by Jack Davis. The image was originally created in *Pro3D*, using its ability to rotate the "ribs" of an extrusion, thus forming the double helix. The file was then saved in EPSF form and brought into *FreeHand*, where the graduated ramps were added.

22 Ocean Couch by Jack Davis. The three objects, the reclining figure, the "geo furniture," and the moon, were constructed in *Swivel 3D*. The human figure consists of "linked" 3D objects, allowing for realistic movement of the arms, legs, head, and so on. Each of the three figures was given in its own image "wrapper" — water, turkey sandwich, and sunset, respectively — which had been scanned on a Sharp JX450 color scanner from photos. After being saved as PICT files, the three objects were brought into *PixelPaint* for the final composition, and the cloud background was added.

23 Stacked Tables by Young Harvill. This illustration was created in *Swivel 3D* by the software's programmer (an artist by trade, who began programming as a hobby). The pieces were created with the program's extrusion capability, and the shadows were cast using one of the built-in rendering effects.

24 Double Fresia by Young Harvill. This *Swivel 3D* illustration shows wireframe and shaded versions of the flower. The component units are linked so that the flower's movements can be animated to look natural.

25 Textile Print by Jackie Shapiro. This is one of a series of fashion designs created with *FreeHand* for the Minna clothing line.

27

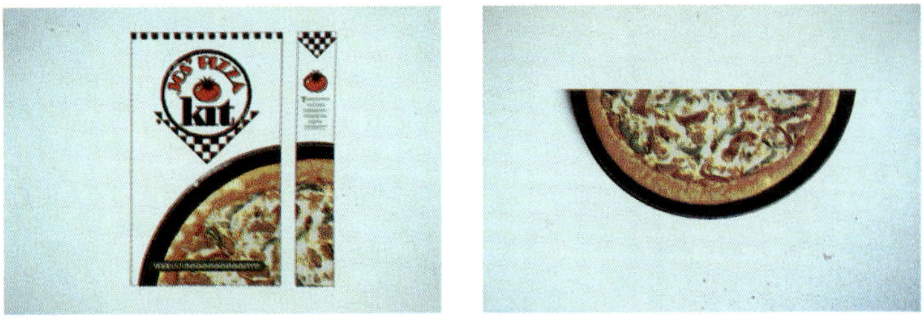
kit

H.P.BLAVATSKY
THE MYSTERY
Gottfried de Purucker
in collaboration with Katherine Tingley

26

HOTDANCE 88

28

29

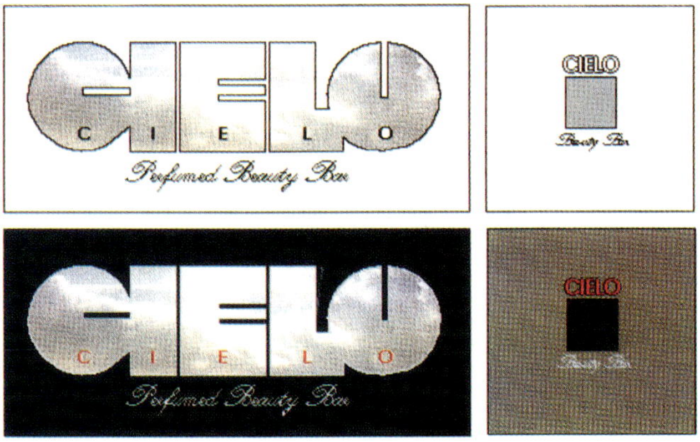

30

26 H. P. Blavatsky Book Cover by John Odam. The illustration and type for this book cover were executed in *FreeHand* and color separated for two-color printing on the Linotronic. To achieve this special effect of blending shades without the computer would have been very difficult and expensive.

27 Joe's Pizza Box by Mike Uriss. The label of this package was first designed and produced in *Adobe Illustrator '88.* The resulting EPSF file was then combined with the color photograph of the pizza in *PixelPaint.* The completed 2D package front and side were then slanted, and a top was added to finish the 3D mockup.

28 Hotdance by John Odam. Created with *Adobe Illustrator '88*, this piece shows an effective use of the merge tool. The tonal gradation on the legs was created by merging between the outer (dark) trapping line and a highlight line drawn down the center of the leg. The transform effect was created by flopping the original image and using the Blend feature to generate the intermediate images.

29 Easter Island by David Brunn. The original image was composed in *MacPaint 2.0* from digitized 35 mm slides (using MacVision) and then brought into *Modern Artist* and colorized.

30 Cielo Beauty Bar by Ida Candelaria. The line art for this design comp, including a custom typeface, was created in *Adobe Illustrator '88.* The EPSF file was then opened in *PixelPaint*, and a scanned photo was used to fill the letter forms. The artist used Command–Shift–Click with the lasso to select the interior of the letters, and then used the clipboard picture method to fill the letters.

31 

32

First Contact

■ *by John Odam*

Freehand

1. A one-minute lettering test drawn directly with the mouse. The highlights were added using the graduated fill effect to simulate wet paint. 2. A relic of World War II — and Verbum 1.2 — The venerable DC3 serves as a test bed for the clipping path feature of FreeHand. The outline, which was originally drawn in Adobe Illustrator, serves as a mask for various color schemes. Stripes and other markings can be drawn fairly broadly beyond the outline. This feature is obviously a time-saver when presenting alternatives in vehicle fleet color schemes for corporate identity programs.

3. Logo for a psychology manual, demonstrating the special effect line screen. 4. Dust jacket art for a philosophy book, showing off the graduated fills in color. A bitmapped scanned portrait was used on the base layer. The original was printed two-color offset in brown and blue inks. 5. Logo for a software company, using repeated elements on a grid. 6. Title for a brochure for a textbook series. The arch shape is a truncated ellipse. 7. Record album design with vivid color fills and colored type. The face was drawn directly with the mouse.

I drew Madame Blavatsky (4) the day I got the *FreeHand* beta version and sent her to the L-300 for separations. Apart from an irrelevant error message off-image and a missing ear lobe, the file whistled right through the printer and produced two sets of film positives the next morning. It wasn't until several weeks later when the press proofs of the dust jacket came back from the printer that the implications of what we had done hit me. I had produced a $500 airbrush illustration in 20 minutes and paid $25 for a color separation. Not only that, but the blending of two ink colors in graduated steps could not have been accomplished with airbrush without using all four printers ink colors, or by using camber some overlays in which the exact color scheme could not be previsualized. I felt the same rush of adrenaline that I had experienced when I first saw a Linotronic proof.

FreeHand is the first of a whole new generation of softwares that operate in PostScript and in color. Apart from its obvious color capabilities, *FreeHand* is a powerful program for the less glamorous but necessary monochrome and laser output work. It has largely supplanted the pioneering but bug-ridden *CricketDraw* for graduated tint areas and special screen effects due to the enormous increase in efficiency and printing speed over *CricketDraw*. I especially like the built-in invisible grid — a tremendous timesaver in logo design where repeated elements must align perfectly. Using fairly coarse grid intervals imposes an architectural structure on one's drawing that produces pleasingly strong, simple shapes. But the software is flexible enough to support complete spontaneity — a spontaneity that has some of the rough edges taken off through the magic of PostScript.

FreeHand users had better like menus a lot; there are menus within menus within menus. The type specifications box, especially, routes one through many cumbersome submenus. Giving colors names was another ritual that was hard to get used to. I soon realized I was going to run out of names long before I ran out of colors, and started calling colors Sid, Daphne, and Albert instead of Greyish, pinkish yellow, which doesn't fit the box. The color menus were thorough and logical, however, enabling monochrome screen users, like me, to specify color by typing in the mix of process colors.

I think I understand the reason behind including the Crayola crayon colors in the color library that comes with the software, giving the product an easy and friendly frame of reference. However, I very much doubt that [illegible] many children will need to operate color PostScript programs, and the professional artists and designers keep sets of Crayolas in their desk drawers.

When I had the opportunity to check some of my files on color monitors, I found that the color display was nice, if a little coarser than the resolution that one is used to expecting with the bitmapped programs such as *PixelPaint*. This was particularly noticeable in the graduated fills, which suffered from pronounced banding. But color PostScript users are not in the business of selling screen displays. It is the hard copy output that counts, and with *FreeHand* it is astoundingly good.

The toolbox, interface, and manual are all of the high quality we have grown to expect from Aldus. The tangent, curve, and straight line tools take more time to learn than the freehand tool, and I have not yet mastered them. They have the same quirky feel of the *Fontographer* tools (see *Verbum 1.1*). The freehand tool works beautifully, but I had difficulty stopping, starting, and backing up. When I tried to splice several line segments, the area would not fill properly. I soon discovered that the way to do it is not to stop drawing until the path is closed — to "ski" with the mouse. Not only did this speed up the drawing, but it gave a more confident, spontaneous quality to the line. But watch out, skiers, when you get to the edge: *FreeHand* doesn't scroll automatically!

With *FreeHand* it is possible to draw and edit in the preview mode. This is not an essential feature, but it's nice. Sometimes I can see what I am doing with a line better in its wire-frame mode without the clutter and showing effect of the total drawing on the screen.

There was a time once when you could tell which Macintosh application had been used to produce a graphic, but many programs on the market now are capable of producing the same end result with varying degrees of ease. Most of the graphics on this page could have been produced in *PixelPaint* or *Adobe Illustrator 88*, for instance. In the end, it is what best suits the individual user that counts. If you are already an *Adobe Illustrator* user, I would not necessarily recommend switching to a whole new software with some confusing similarities and overlapping functions. But if you are new to PostScript graphics, then *FreeHand* is the most accessible and capable program I have yet tried out, and I recommend it to you.

This illustration, and all others on pages 42 and 43 have been separated on a Linotronic L 300 and output in film negatives at 1270 LPI.

33

34

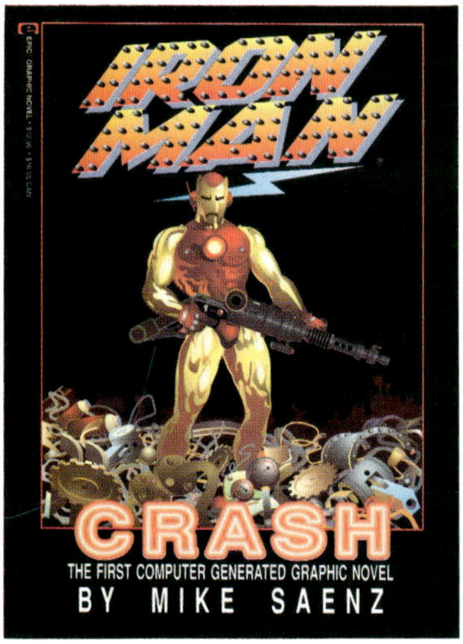

35

31 Museum Brochure by Darinda Collinsworth. This mock-up of a two-fold, five-color brochure for an exhibition on Impressionism began with photos scanned with the Sharp JX450 color scanner and combined in Aldus's *PageMaker 3.0*. The textures on the edges are enlarged portions of the Cathedral painting. The comp was then printed on a Tektronix color thermal printer.

32 *Verbum* 2.1 Page Spread by John Odam. This spread, executed with *PageMaker 3.0*, features several illustrations and logos drawn and colored with *FreeHand*. The final document in *PageMaker* was output as four-color process negatives at 2540 dpi.

33 MTV Logo by Stuart Sharpe. These frames from a *VideoWorks II* animation, which included music, were created using the program's built-in color paint utility.

34 Bugs Article by Jack Davis. To produce this design for a two-page magazine spread, the public domain clip art bugs were scanned and then colorized in *PixelPaint* using the Blend fill effect. The shadow was added using the Shadowing visual effect and a black screen pattern. The Push feature under the Special Effect brush menu was used to distort the color slightly. The headline was created in *Adobe Illustrator*, printed on a LaserWriter, and scanned in as a bit map to create the final 140-point type, which was then filled with a drop shadow. The greek type was added with the *PixelPaint* text tool.

35 Iron Man Graphic Novel by Mike Saenz. This work was illustrated and composed using various programs, including *Adobe Illustrator*, *Pro 3D*, and *GraphicWorks*. Color separations were made using the *Lithographer* program.

36 *Verbum 2.1* Cover by John Odam. This cover for the Spring 1988 *Verbum* magazine, including the custom type, was created entirely with *Adobe Illustrator '88*. The satellite/rose blend was accomplished by drawing the satellite and rose with the same number of objects and using the program's Blend feature to create six intermediate images. The cover was color separated on a Linotronic at 2540 dpi.

Color Gallery Reproduction Notes

Figures 1–10 Reproduced from transparencies shot from a 19" SuperMac monitor.
11 Reproduced from a color print from a Tektronix Color Image Printer, model 4693D.
13 Reproduced from a transparency shot from a 19" SuperMac monitor.
14 Reproduced from a color print from a Tektronix Color Image Printer, model 4693D.
15 Reproduced from the printed poster.
16 Reproduced from a color print from a Tektronix Color Image Printer, model 4693D.
17–21 Reproduced from transparencies shot from a 19" SuperMac monitor.
22–24 Reproduced from color prints from a Tektronix Color Image Printer, model 4693D.
25 Reproduced from a transparency shot from a 19" SuperMac monitor.
26 Reproduced from the printed book jacket.
27 Reproduced from a transparency shot from a 19" SuperMac monitor.
28 Reproduced from a print from a QMS Color Script 100 PostScript thermal transfer printer.
29–31 Reproduced from color prints from a Tektronix Color Image Printer, model 4693D.
32 Reproduced from the printed page spread.
33, 34 Reproduced from a transparencies shot from a 19" SuperMac monitor.
35 Reproduced from the printed book.
36 Reproduced from the printed magazine cover.

36

CHAPTER 9

Presentation Graphics

First there were graphics programs. Then page layout. And now there's **desktop presentation**. Many artistic efforts eventually become part of a presentation. After all, art is meant for showing. One aspect of desktop presentation is **frame layout**. Another is **animation**.

FRAME LAYOUT

Assembling a presentation from a variety of inputs and helping it flow in a somewhat logical order can be accomplished with a good object-oriented application, or even a desktop publishing package. But for the greatest ease and dedicated power, it's best to use frame layout, or **presentation**, software.

For "business" use, you may not need any more graphics power than the little that presentation software typically provides. If, on the other hand, a project requires bit maps or EPSF images, art must be imported from other applications. Presentation programs are capable of importing several of the common file formats.

The "leanness" of frame layout packages is precisely what makes them so valuable in terms of ease and speedy production of all the elements of a formal show. They provide enough tools and editing features to get the job done well — without too many frills to distract you from the task at hand.

Background graphics can be automatically applied to each slide. And you need change the background in only one view to affect all slides. Any color and set of objects can serve as a background. A frame can receive treatment as a slide view, a handout, and a speaker's note. Each of these is a printable product, and the content of these views is changed dynamically if the arrangement of presentation frames is changed.

The sequence of frames can be by altered by dragging thumbnail sketches or frame titles, just as you might shift 35 mm slides around on a tabletop to change presentation order.

This can be done minutes before show time, with the knowledge that related handouts will be properly sequenced, dated, and numbered.

Text blocks with tab stops and indentation controls make it easy to format bullet charts and hierarchical lists — another welcome strength of dedicated presentation software. Unfortunately, a text block can't be moved while you're working in the text mode.

You can use the Mac II as the show device by outputting the show to the screen, to a projection device, or to an electronic slide on an overhead projector. Slides can be shown at specifically timed intervals, or they can be manually sequenced using the mouse as the "change" button.

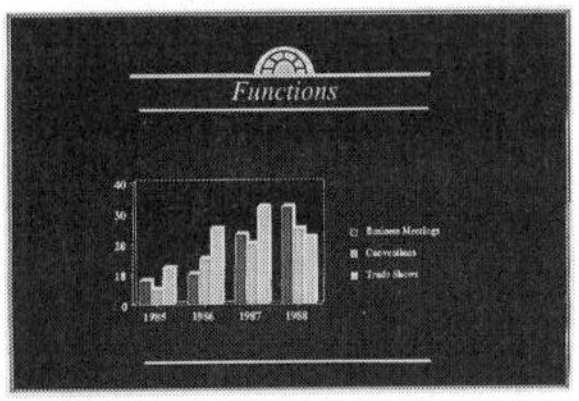

Each of the presentation packages reviewed here provides automatic links to download a presentation to slide-production service organizations, where high-quality slides can be produced, in 35 mm or overhead transparency formats, on film recorders (see Chapter 16 for a discussion of this technology) and quickly mailed back to the sender.

Cricket Presents (1.0)

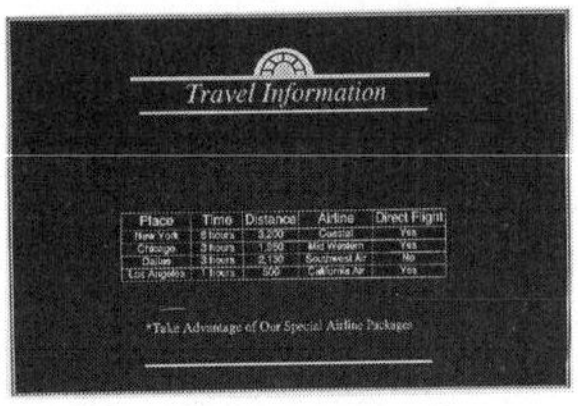

Courtesy Cricket Software

Cricket Presents is a high-end application that can be considered self-contained for most presentation work. It offers an object-oriented drawing environment, built-in graphing and data-table capabilities, and excellent text formatting. Its color capabilities should satisfy all reasonable requirements, and then some.

Its interface is a descendant of *CricketDraw*'s — polished and intuitive, brimming with easily accessible options.

Cricket Presents Features

Import formats: Graphics can be imported in Paint, PICT, and EPSF formats. Imported Paint format files retain their full document dimensions, even if most of the space is empty; fortunately, the empty space is transparent.

Multiple presentations: The ability to open several presentations at once simplifies comparison, cutting, and pasting. A Windows menu helps select the active set.

Ruler, grids, and guides: These guides can be optionally displayed and snapped-to. Rulers can have floating zero points. The grid and rulers can be customized with up to 99 divisions per inch. Inches, centimeters, or picas can be used as measurement units.

Full alignment options: Besides the standard options, this program allows centering of a selection within the frame. However, no rotation is available, not even by 90 degrees.

Zooming: You can zoom in and out by key, or with a lens cursor.

Cursor key navigation: Left and right arrows advance through the presentation or go back one frame; up and down arrows go to the first or last slide, respectively.

In-frame navigation: Navigation within a frame is limited to the hand tool.

Insert/Delete: A frame can be added to or deleted from a presentation.

Built-in graph generation: Data entered into a 5 x 25 cell matrix can be graphed in scatter, line, area, pie, column and bar, and stacked column and bar formats. (If a graph is changed from a column [vertical] to a bar [horizontal] type, the axis markers won't follow their respective axes and must be specified.) Titles, labels for axes, and legends can have their own fonts and styles (but all must be of the same color). In a line graph, point markers for each series of data can be chosen from 15 types. Attributes for graph lines can be selected from 64 colors and five widths. Display options include 3D, legend, and with or without vertical and horizontal grid lines. Completed graphs are resizable and can be exported.

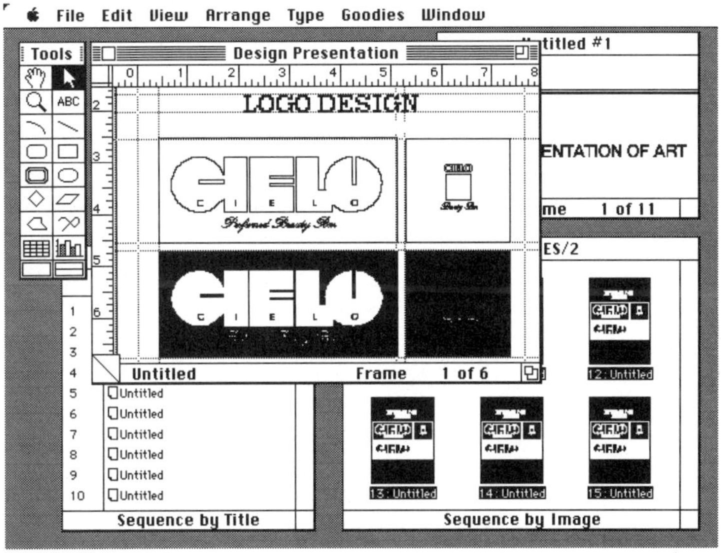

Figure 9-1. *Cricket Presents* allows you to sequence elements of a presentation by title or by image.

Built-in data table generation: You can create tables up to 8 rows by 8 columns in size, with separate control over the text attributes and color of column titles and data entries. Columns are resizable, and justification can be specified independently for each. Vertical and horizontal lines can be hidden or displayed and can be assigned a color. A background color for an entire table can also be specified. Unfortunately, table blocks offer no choice of line spacing — that's based entirely on the font selected for the table entries.

Object-oriented drawing tools: Tools include the rectangle, oval, polygon, arc, line, freehand tool, diamond, variable-tilt parallelogram, and multiline frame. Objects can't be smoothed.

Movable tool palette: The palette can be repositioned for convenience.

Multiline framing rectangles: Frames can be composed of up to three lines, each of a different color.

Arrows: Straight lines can be converted to arrows, both uni- and bidirectional, with a choice of three types of arrowheads.

Background: Background objects can be applied to all the frames of the presentation. In addition to objects, the background can be assigned an overall color as an absolute background for all other items.

High-powered text formatting: A text block can contain independently set paragraph formats, mixed fonts, styles, and justifications. Tab types include left, right, centered, and decimal. Normal and hanging indent are supported. Leading between paragraphs can be different from line-to-line leading.

Text sizes: Text up to 256 points is supported.

Extensive color choices: Color palettes contain 8 fixed hues and 56 customizable hues. Colors can be used for all graphic and text elements. A palette can be named and saved for later use.

Colorizing: Imported Paint and PICT images can be colorized. For object-oriented images, colors can be independently assigned to various fill patterns. Pattern fills can be converted to solid fills of the assigned color. (Once the fill patterns of a pasted PICT image are converted to a solid fill, they can't be converted back to patterns.) Lines and text can each be of a different color. The color choices for imported images are limited to the basic eight: white, black, red, green, blue, cyan, magenta, and yellow.

Frame color: Normally, frames are transparent to allow the background color to show through. Individual frames can be assigned (nontransparent) colors that completely mask the background color, but allow the background objects to remain visible.

Colored text: The full range of standard type styles is available in color, with the option of a clear or colored background.

Grouping and ungrouping: This feature allows more efficient management of completed or related objects in a frame. The attributes of grouped objects can't be altered.

Templates: Every element that can be manually rendered (charts, backgrounds, frames, and so on) can also be saved as a template and retrieved from a named file. All frames of a presentation (or a specified range of frames) can have a copy of a template applied to them. (This is basically a shortcut to importing the same template several times.)

Independent output of presentation elements: Frames (slides), handouts, and speaker notes can each be output on different devices. Output devices include the Mac II's screen.

Video Show mode: Time intervals between frames can be automated or manually triggered, with a choice of 13 special transition effects. Frames can be shown actual size or scaled to the size of the screen.

Speaker notes: Notes can vary in format from frame to frame.

PowerPoint (2.0)

PowerPoint provides the tools for assembling a first-rate presentation. Its strength is in tending to the inevitable chores of text formatting and embellishment, and positioning imported graphics. Its interface is nicely intuitive, with the frequently used functions and views accessible through ever-present icons.

Its graphics-generation capabilities are limited to a few geometric basics, but it will import a variety of file formats output by popular applications.

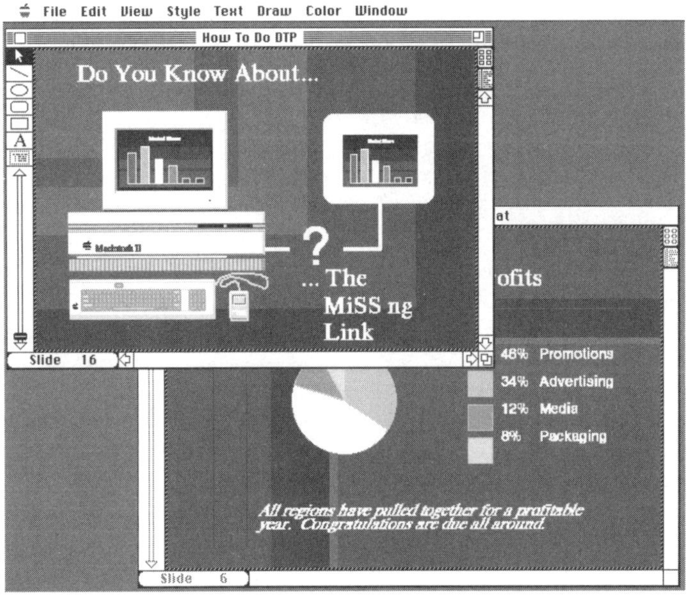

Figure 9-2. *PowerPoint* allows you to open more than one presentation at a time.

PowerPoint Features

Import formats: Paint, PICT, PICT 2, and EPSF formats can be imported.

Multiple open presentations: The capacity for opening several presentations at once simplifies comparison, cutting, and pasting. A Windows menu helps select the active set.

Grids and guides: Guides can be optionally displayed. An always-invisible grid can be optionally snapped-to to help with object alignment. The grid and guides are the only alignment aids.

Zoom in and out: Menu-selectable percentages are 33, 50, and 66 percent and full size. No key-driven zooming is provided.

Object-oriented drawing tools: Tools include the rectangle, rounded rectangle, oval, and line. No polygon, freehand, or arc tools are provided, and no rotation is available, not even by 90 degrees.

Tool availability: The palette is well organized, and the functions most frequently performed are accessible by clicking icons at the edges of the window.

Line width: Width can be chosen from six preset selections.

Multiline objects: All objects drawn with *PowerPoint* can be composed of up to three lines.

Arrows: Straight lines can be converted to arrows, both uni- and bidirectional.

Drop shadows: Drop shadows can be specified for all closed objects.

Patterns: There are 22 patterns (including black and white) for lines and fills.

Shaded backgrounds: Backgrounds filled with a graduated hue can have horizontal, vertical, or diagonal direction, or the background color can focus on the slide's title.

Text formatting: One block can contain mixed fonts and styles. Tab types include left and decimal. Normal and hanging indents are supported. Leading between paragraphs can be different from line-to-line leading.

Indentation: Five levels of indentation per text block are supported. Left

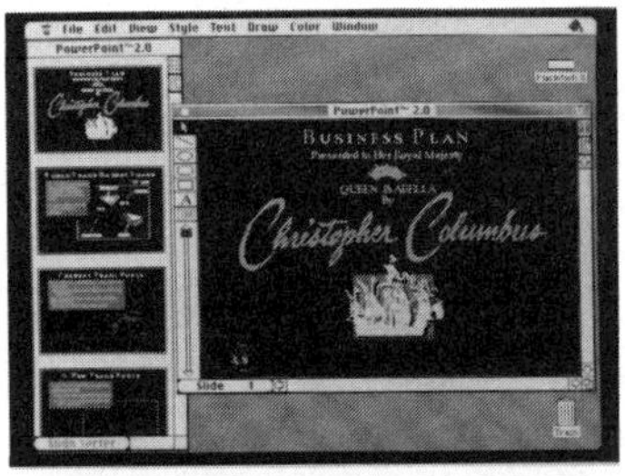

Courtesy Microsoft Corporation

margins of paragraphs at the same level are automatically aligned. Each level can have independently set spacing between its paragraphs.

Text sizes: Up to 127 points are supported. The font menu can be customized by adding selected fonts from the System's set. A default style can be specified for each font added to the menu.

Color management: *PowerPoint* provides full access to the Mac II's 16.7 million colors. Color can be assigned to objects at any time and later modified. Color effects are visible on screen.

Color scheme templates: Templates automatically assign colors to various elements of the presentation — for example, background, foreground, titles, and text. The color assignments can be modified later. A collection of 5000 color schemes is supplied.

Master objects: Designated objects can be applied to all the frames of the presentation.

Omit Master: This command can be used for individual frames to exclude the presentation's background.

Grouping objects and text: Text can be entered into an oval or rectangle, and it will be automatically grouped with the object. The **Size-to-text** option makes an oval or rectangle resize to completely contain its block of text. This can be a great time-saver.

Insert/Delete: You can insert a frame into a presentation, or delete it.

Slide show mode: The time interval between frames can be automatically or manually triggered.

Slide show controls: You can make the show proceed forward, backward, or to a specified slide number. Other controls can show or hide the on-screen pointer, invert the image, blank or restore the screen, or return to the slide show dialog box.

ANIMATION

Animation applications will be used increasingly in presentation work, for on-screen presentations, and for production of videotape programs. Currently, *VideoWorks II* has established itself as the Mac II standard.

VideoWorks II

VideoWorks II offers a unique package of high-powered animation tools. It single-handedly fills a significant gap in the Macintosh II's graphics software. Armed with *VideoWorks II*, you can add life to presentations by producing anything from a simple slide show with basic dissolves, to a multicharacter fully animated extravaganza, complete with full-color fireworks, scrolling backgrounds, little walking people, sweeping lights, and symphonic music.

VideoWorks II has a self-contained painting environment with basic capabilities. By design, this can be supplemented with imported art work produced with most of the full-featured Macintosh applications like *PixelPaint* and *MacDraw II*. Color scanned images can be also be imported. Such art can be used for backgrounds or as animated objects. Excellent 3D animation can be achieved by importing sequentially created frames from *Pro3D*, *Super 3D*, and *Swivel 3D*. Best of all, the best products of the best applications can all take part in the show.

It's possible to integrate real-world sights and sounds with animation in several ways: Video boards produced by both Mass Micro and Computer Friends enable the Macintosh II to display live video and to superimpose animated sequences. However, synchronization of the on-screen events must be done manually. High-quality sampled sounds can be integrated into movies with fine control by using *VideoWorks II*'s built-in sound channel.

For smoother animation of complex scenes you can use the *VideoWorks II* Accelerator, a MacroMind program that preprocesses a *VideoWorks II* movie and essentially stores entire screens as single frames. These can be played back very quickly, up to 30 frames per second. The accelerated version of the movie uses considerably more disk space; for example, a 200 K color movie can grow to 5 or 10 Mb and also require more RAM to achieve smooth playback.

A *HyperCard* interface program, *VideoWorks II HyperCard Driver*, also from

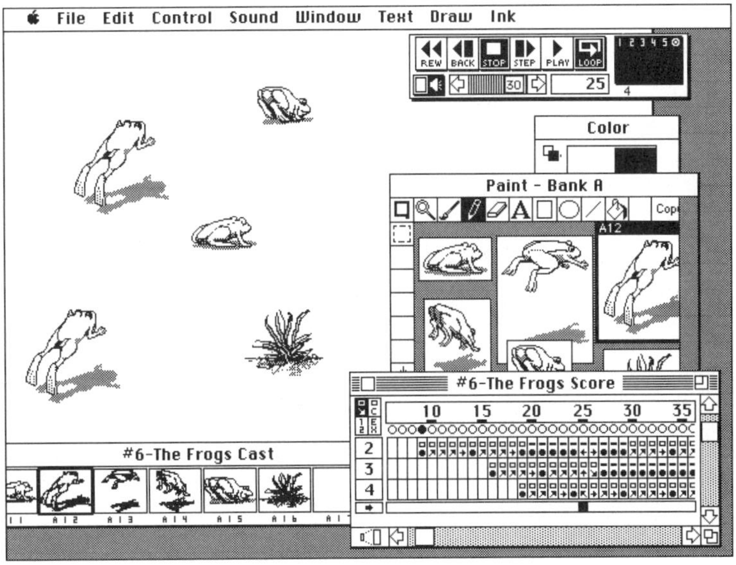

Figure 9-3. A *VideoWorks* sequence in development.

MacroMind, adds to a *HyperCard* stack the ability to invoke the playback of any *VideoWorks II* movie. During playback, the current card can serve as the movie's background, or can totally disappear; or the animated characters can move in front of or behind *HyperCard* objects.

VideoWorks II is unique among Macintosh software, but it doesn't take advantage of its virtual monopoly on animation. Its interface is carefully designed, refined, and flexible, although it can be somewhat intimidating at first. It's the kind of program that requires cracking the user manual to make full sense of the on-screen symbology, and to understand the sequence of steps needed to access its power.

VideoWorks II Features

Frame-by-frame animation: Each frame is positioned by hand and added to the movie.

Real-time animation: As an object is dragged with the mouse, its motions are automatically recorded.

Tween animation and motion: This process fills in intermediate frames between a starting and an ending position (and size) of an object.

Sound: Sounds can be imported from a variety of sources and synchronized with the action. Sound effects can even include speech from *MacIntalk* (a speech-simulation program).

24 channels of animation: Each channel allows control of an object on stage.

Specialized animation tools: Tools include: **registration points** for objects that require precise placement of substitute objects, which stabilizes pivot points and stationary zones from frame to frame; **cutting and pasting of sequences**, enabling object actions to be easily multiplied, shifted, or deleted; a **reverse sequence** feature, which reverses the motion and size-change of a selected set of frames, so that events like bouncing and shuttling from side to side need only one direction to be manually created (the opposite event can be synthesized by duplicating the first event and then reversing it); **animated film loops** that can be created separately and used as individual objects, vastly simplifying effects like walking people, flying birds, helicopters with spinning blades, or anything else that has built-in motion as it traverses the screen; **prioritized stacking order** of objects, based on their channel number, which allows objects to pass in front or in back of other objects (the stacking order can be modified by moving selected frames from one channel to another); **tweak tool**, which allows precise displacement of a selected object (the mouse is used to indicate the vertical and horizontal shift) and displays the precise numerical pixel offsets in x and y boxes.

Painting environment: Both black-and-white and color are available. The black-and-white mode has a typical set of tools, including an excellent variable-diameter airbrush, and special effects like free rotation, perspective, and distortion. The color mode uses the System's 256-color palette, but lacks the lasso, airbrush, and special effects tools.

Basic QuickDraw shapes: These primitives can be used as memory-efficient background objects.

Extensive overlapped-object control: Via selection of special ink modes, you can control how overlapped objects interact: for example, *Matte* renders unbounded white space transparent, *Or* essentially adds the pixel colors of overlapped objects to produce a third, and *Xor* reverses or complements overlapping parts of objects. There are many more.

Overview mode: This is a powerful tool for composing an animated production from existing elements. Among other features of this mode is the ability to use the same animation several times on the same screen, offset by some distance and delayed by some amount of time. The overview tools provide these capabilities: importing a variety of document types including Paint, PICT, PICT2, Glue, and *VideoWorks* movies, which are left in their original locations and only *accessed* during the use of the Overview mode; setting the location, delay, and duration of an image or animation, and, for animations, the number of repetitions; selecting the transition effect from one scene to another; choosing whether or not to include sounds related to a movie; adding new sounds to the current overview production.

Text management: Text management features include painted (bitmapped, noneditable) text on animated objects and editable, speakable text entered in a dedicated Text window. This latter type of text can be globally searched for and replaced, and normal justification and style options apply.

Variable playback speed: Speed can vary from 3 to 60 frames per second, although for complex scenes it may not be possible to achieve the highest speeds.

Full-screen movies: Movies can be played with no menu bar or other visible controls. The menu bar remains active, even when hidden.

Printing of animation frames: Frames can be printed at 100, 50 or 25 percent for use as storyboards.

OTHER PRESENTATION PROGRAMS

Other presentation programs include *Standout!* by Letraset, *Persuasion* by Aldus, and *More II* by Symantec (see the "Products" appendix).

Between one and two thousand years ago, block printing was invented in China. Raised characters were carved to make wooden blocks of text, and the characters were inked and pressed against paper to transfer the image. Then in 1045 something happened that could have caused a publishing revolution in China — but didn't quite. Pi Sheng, a printer, invented the first movable type. He made and assembled separate reusable pieces of clay type representing characters of the Chinese language. His idea was that the characters could be assembled and reassembled to make up new "pages." Good idea, on the face of it. But the Chinese language has thousands of characters, and it must have seemed like more work to sort, assemble, and maintain the clay pieces than to go on carving blocks, because Pi Sheng's revolution never really caught on, and block printing continued.

Nearly half a millennium later Johannes Gutenberg converted a wine press into a printing press in Germany. The Renaissance was in full flower, and hand copying and block printing couldn't keep up with the demand for books. Gutenberg's press with its movable metal type was recognized for the major advance in publishing efficiency that it was. And after a brief flirtation with the idea that the printing press was the work of the devil — after all, if God had wanted us to produce up to 300 copies of a page a day, He would have given us more hands to hold quills, wouldn't He? — the printing revolution took hold and the European printing industry began to grow.

Part Three

Printed Output

Today we have the Mac II, AppleTalk, phototypesetting, offset presses, and laser and ink jet printers, to name a few of the advances in print production, all of which make the printing process a lot easier than it was for the early Chinese or for Gutenberg and his colleagues. But our goals in printing are very similar to theirs: to get the copy set and printed along with line art. In addition to line art, our printed materials today are illustrated with halftones and color illustrations.

With the Mac II and today's printing technology, there's a whole spectrum of ways to accomplish our printing goals. Desktop publishers typically either follow the lead of traditional publishers, passing the printing process to professional printers, or use laser technology to do the printing themselves. At the traditional end of the spectrum is hand preparation and paste-up of camera-ready art (some of which may have been generated on the Mac II and stored on disk) for reproduction on an offset press. At the desktop end of the spectrum is electronic generation of fully camera-ready pages by means of graphics and word processing software, system fonts, and page-layout programs, followed by the printing of multiple copies on a laser printer or a higher-resolution imagesetter. Between these traditional and desktop "extremes" is a rainbow of combinations of traditional and electronic methods. (The rainbow even extends beyond the extremes, with technologies that allow output in the form of 35 mm slides and digital color separations.) The methods you choose for any particular publishing project will depend on the complexity of the printing job, the level of quality you are trying to achieve, and your equipment and production budgets.

Chapter 10

Laser Printing

A laser printer is an essential part of a Mac II system. It really makes more sense to have a laser printer without a Mac II than vice versa. In some instances, laser-printed pages can serve as camera-ready copy. More often, laser pages are used as comps or as proofs for copy to be printed on high-resolution imagesetters (see Chapter 14).

HOW LASER PRINTERS WORK

Most laser printers use the same technology that most photocopy machines use. The printing engines of both kinds of machines consist of a light source, an electrostatically chargeable metal drum, and mechanisms to make them work together. Photocopy machines use a photographic process to make an image of information from a master page; the image is then sent to the engine for processing. But in laser printing, the printer's software interprets the digitally coded information sent to it by the Mac II.

Laser printing has its parallels in the traditional printing process used by Gutenberg and his successors. In the laser printer (Figure 10-1) the laser replaces the human hand setting movable metal type. The drum replaces the type bed that holds the metal characters. And a combination of charged toner and heat replaces the traditional ink. Aimed at the metal drum, the laser electrostatically charges the drum surface to define the characters and other images to be printed. The charged drum rotates through the toner supply, and the oppositely charged toner particles stick to the charged character impressions. Toner-defined characters are transferred to a charged sheet of paper fed against the drum's surface, and heated fuser rollers bond the toner to the paper as the sheet passes out of the printer. This sheet can be used as the final printed page, or as the master for making a negative or positive plate for printing on an offset press.

LASER PRINTER CHARACTERISTICS

Apple's LaserWriter was the first laser printer made for the Macintosh. Its print quality, PostScript page-description language, resident fonts, communication connections, memory, speed, paper handling abilities, toner supply system, and service rating became the standards for measuring laser printer performance. More recently Apple has introduced the LaserWriter II printers, maintaining some of the old standards and setting new ones as well.

Figure 10-1. The LaserWriter II printer.

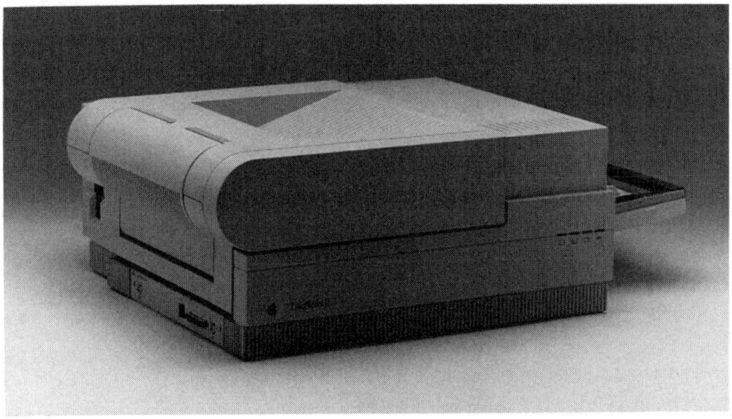

Print Quality

Regardless of how much time, effort, and hardware and software technology you and your Mac II put into preparing a document, the look of the final output depends on how well the printer puts it onto the paper. Laser print quality depends on three things: (1) how many discrete dots per linear inch (dpi) the printer produces, (2) how solid the black areas are, and (3) how cleanly the image is reproduced on the paper.

DPI

The LaserWriter set the laser printer standard at 300 dpi, and many other laser printers, including the LaserWriter II, followed it. A few printers print at higher resolution, for example 406 and 600 dpi. A 300-dpi laser printer prints 90,000 (300 x 300) dots to make a 1-inch black square, while a 600-dpi model prints 360,000. Comparing these two figures, we see that the 600-dpi printer provides four times the resolution. The higher-resolution printer can define lines and characters more precisely and can produce a higher-quality scanned photographic image. Alas, we don't get the extra quality free of charge. Higher-resolution laser printers cost more, often between two and three times as much as 300-dpi models. This is in part because they have a separate raster image processor (RIP), which translates the information to be printed, and a hard disk, which provides more memory for fonts and for faster printing. Besides transmitting more precise information to the printing drum, the higher-resolution printers use toner made up of smaller particles — for example, 8-micron particles rather than the 14-micron particles of the 300- dpi printers. This smaller particle size contributes to the crispness of printed type and the increased amount of gray-scale information that reaches the paper.

Black

How black is laser-printed black? And how black would you like it to be? The answer to the first question depends at least in part on which kind of print engine the laser printer uses (see "'Write-Black' Versus 'Write-White'"below), and the second depends on what kind of copy you typically want to produce. Comparing the output from printers of equal resolution (300 dpi, for example), black looks blackest when it's printed by a "write-white" engine. "Write-black" engines sometimes produce better gray-scale ranges. Halftones digitized by scanner from a continuous-tone black-and-white photo also vary in quality from printer to printer.

Besides the nature of the printer, temperature and humidity can affect blackness, as can paper characteristics (see "Paper Handling" later in this chapter).

"Write-Black" Versus "Write-White"

The Canon engine that serves as the basis for the LaserWriter, LaserWriter Plus, and several other laser printers is a "write-black" engine. That means that the laser beam charges those areas of the drum where the toner particles will adhere.

The Ricoh, Kyocera, and Canon LBP-SX (LaserWriter II) engines employ a technology that charges the white space areas of the drum to repel the toner. This "write-white" technology results in denser toner coverage and therefore blacker blacks.

TIP

Making Black Blacker

If large areas of solid black show streaks or uneven toner coverage, you can blacken the area by spraying the laser print with matte finish coating (fixative) for artwork. Follow the directions on the spray can. Work outdoors or in a well-ventilated space. Spray from about 18 inches away.

Clean

Even with excellent resolution and blackness, the printed image can become muddied by toner scatter, extraneous toner particles adhering to the paper in places where they aren't supposed to be.

PostScript

The PostScript language is a very versatile and useful one for desktop publishers, especially those who use a profusion of graphics or require sophisticated type treatments. In the printing process, the data to be printed is translated by routines in the Mac II's RAM into PostScript code and sent to the printer. The printer interprets the PostScript and prints the document.

At present, PostScript is a must for a laser printer used with a Mac II for desktop publishing. The original Apple LaserWriter used the PostScript language, and PostScript has become the standard for laser printers used with the Mac. Some printer manufacturers (including Apple, with the LaserWriter II SC) are marketing QuickDraw-based printers, which are faster and less expensive than PostScript-based ones, but not appropriate for intense graphics production. (See "PostScript Versus QuickDraw" on p. 214).

The version of PostScript varies from printer to printer, with later versions providing faster handling of bit maps as well as other improvements over earlier versions. Some manufacturers provide updates to their printers' PostScript at a relatively small cost. Apple has provided this "updatability" in its LaserWriter IIs' upgradable control boards, which can be modified or exchanged for more powerful ones.

Resident Fonts

Laser printers store a certain number of resident (built-in) fonts (characters of a given type family, style, and point size; see Chapter 18, "Fonts") in ROM. Four resident fonts were the standard set by the original LaserWriter. LaserWriter Plus and LaserWriter II provide 11 built-in fonts. These resident fonts print more quickly than other fonts, which must be downloaded to the printer by the Mac II. The page layout versatility and speed a printer provides are markedly affected by the number of resident fonts it has.

TIP

Fat Fonts

Write-white printers seem to add an extra pixel to the stroke width of printed characters, so regular-weight fonts appear demibold, for example.

Memory

The amount of RAM a printer has and the way memory is allocated are important for three reasons: (1) These characteristics determine how many fonts can be downloaded to print at one time, (2) they determine how much page description information can be stored and thus the maximum area of a page the printer can print, and (3) they determine how many characters (character/font/style/size/rotation combinations) the font cache can hold, and this affects printing speed.

Fonts that are not stored in the printer's ROM must be downloaded to RAM from the Mac II. So the amount of RAM that's set aside for fonts, or that can be "borrowed" from other functions and used to store fonts, determines how much you can vary the type styles in a printed document. A hard disk dedicated solely to printer support like that of the LaserWriter II NTX provides many more resident fonts.

The amount of RAM allotted for creating an image on the page is important in determining how large a page the printer can produce and how close to the edges the print can go. Typically laser printers leave an unprinted margin around all four edges of the paper. Some printers, such as the LaserWriter Plus, can borrow from the memory normally reserved for downloadable fonts. By choosing to restrict the number of fonts you use, you can make the printer image more of the page area.

PostScript Versus QuickDraw

Color QuickDraw is the graphics package built into the Mac II and resident in ROM (the other Macintosh computers use the original QuickDraw, without color). It controls the screen display of most drawing programs and also controls printing by QuickDraw-based laser printers. QuickDraw printers are less expensive than PostScript printers, but, at least at present, they're also less versatile. They cost less because the producers don't have to license PostScript from Aldus and they don't have to license typefaces because they've developed their own QuickDraw fonts. QuickDraw printers are limited in terms of graphics programs to bitmapped images such as those of *MacPaint* and object-oriented ones such as those of *MacDraw*, *MacDraft*, and *SuperPaint*. They can't be used with PostScript-based graphics software such as *Cricket Draw*, *Adobe Illustrator*, and *Fontographer*. Instead QuickDraw laser printers are the business professional's super letter-quality printer, and they serve well for high-volume output of *MacDraw* documents, for example. But they're not presently suitable for graphics-intensive production. If technology is developed for generating QuickDraw files from PostScript-based graphics software or if QuickDraw is rewritten to provide more functions, this proscription may be lifted. Another limitation of QuickDraw printers is that they're tied specifically to the Macintosh family of personal computers and thus don't allow easy networking with other pc's.

The font cache is a part of RAM set aside to "remember" characters as they are used in printing a document. The first time a character (with its font, size, style, and rotation characteristics) appears, its laser dot image is stored in the font cache so it can be retrieved quickly, rather than recreated, the next time it's needed. This speeds up the printing process. When the cache fills up, which it will when a large number of different characters are used in one document, the "oldest" characters in the cache are deleted to make space for the most recent. So for typographically complex documents, the bigger the font cache, the speedier the printing.

Speed

Printing speed depends not only on the microprocessor "brain" of the machine, the number of resident fonts, the version of PostScript used in the printer, and font cache size, but also on the graphic complexity of the material to be printed. Bitmapped graphics such as paint program output and scanned images, take longer to process than object-oriented or PostScript-generated images. (The differences between paint, object-oriented, and PostScript graphics programs are discussed in Part II.)

Communication Connections

A laser printer to be used with the Mac II should be able to connect easily with AppleTalk, and the more easily this connection can be made, the better. Ideally, the printer should have an RS-422 port to accommodate the standard AppleTalk connector. If you plan to include computers other than the Mac II in your network, you'll need other connectors (such as RS-232, parallel, serial, or Centronics parallel connectors).

Paper Handling

The versatility of a laser printer in handling paper depends on how many kinds and sizes of paper it will take and how the paper is fed into and travels through the machine. Some laser printers are designed to handle only plain xerographic paper in one standard size (8-1/2 by 11). Most can also accommodate bond paper and clear acetate sheets in at least two more sizes, 8-1/2 by 14 and A4 (210 mm by 297 mm). Still others can handle paper of more varied weights and thicknesses, such as card stock, colored construction paper, and even rice paper. While these kinds of paper may not typically be used in the desktop publishing efforts of a standard business office, they can be important to graphic artists from time to time. To successfully use paper of unusual thickness or texture, or of a size smaller than 8-1/2 by 11, you need a printer that allows manual feed of single sheets.

TIP

Printing Transparencies

Because laser printing uses heat to fuse toner to paper, you must be sure that any acetate sheets (transparencies) that you use won't melt in the machine. Acetate sheets for use with photocopy machines will work. You can use clear or colored sheets and print in more than one color of ink. To obtain the effect of depth, print on both sides of the sheet, using the Flip Horizontal function to reverse the type when you print the second (back) side. That way both colors of type will be readable from the front, and the second color will appear to be "dropped" behind the first.

TIP

Printing Paint Style Documents

Be careful of printing paint style (bitmapped) documents in the landscape mode on the LaserWriter printer. A document that would normally take a few minutes can take drastically longer to print. The technical reason relates to the mathematics of shifting each dot of the bit map. If you must print a document sideways, rotate the image 90 degrees in your painting program before you print.

> **TIP**
>
> **Toner Cartridge Replacements and Refills**
>
> If the service rating of your laser printer is 4000 copies per month, the cartridge life is approximately 2000 copies, and the cartridge replacement cost is $90, you may find yourself spending over $2000 a year on cartridges. Reputable cartridge-refilling services clean and refill toner cartridges for considerably less than the cost of new ones. And these services typically refill cartridges with more toner than most manufacturers put in initially. (If you see holes covered by tape in a refilled cartridge, it has probably been filled without cleaning and servicing. Don't use the cartridge, and avoid the service that filled it.)

The paper path of a laser printer is the route that the paper — automatically or manually fed — follows through the innards of the machine. A printer can have a straight or curved paper path. The LaserWriter and LaserWriter II printers use both kinds of paths — a curved path for paper fed from the paper tray and a straight path for manually fed sheets. Printers with curved paper paths only are limited in their paper handling abilities. They can't print envelopes, for example. Printers that use a straight paper path for automatic feeding take up more space in the work area, because the paper supply and the finished page hopper extend from opposite ends of the machine.

Toner Supply

The LaserWriter Plus and many other laser printers use replaceable toner cartridges that make toner replenishment relatively clean and easy. Printers with Ricoh and Kyocera engines, on the other hand, have toner bins that must be refilled with loose toner. This is a somewhat messier process and doesn't allow for using more than a single toner color (see "Color Printing," later in this chapter), because the bin can't easily be completely emptied of toner.

Service Rating

The **service rating** of a printer is the manufacturer's estimate of how many pages a laser printer can produce per month and continue to perform well. For example, the service rating of the LaserWriter Plus is 4000 copies per month. To exceed a printer's service rating may lead to mechanical trouble and may affect the manufacturer's warranty of performance.

A printer's **duty cycle** is the number of pages it can print before it needs replacement or at least a major overhaul. The LaserWriter II printers have a duty cycle of 100,000 to 300,000 pages.

PRINTER DRIVERS AND SPOOLERS

Printer **drivers** are programs that run in the Mac II and control the printing operation. LaserPrep, for example, is the printer driver Apple developed for the LaserWriter series. It contains common PostScript commands that the Mac II sends to the LaserWriter to be installed in RAM and used in converting information in a file into the instructions the printer needs to process the document. Other printer drivers are offered by developers outside Apple. The printer driver you use can affect the number of downloadable fonts your printer can handle, the quality of letter spacing, and the quality of printing for some graphics and special effects, for example. It can also affect how well a particular spooler works in your system.

TIP

Reducing Performance Degradation

Using a QuickDraw print spooler can cause performance degradation, slowing of Mac II foreground functions while printing goes on in the background. With *SuperLaserSpool* used in a network, this can be avoided if you specify that spooled files be stored on a hard disk attached to another Mac.

To someone familiar with what print spoolers do for a Mac network, the word "spooler" may conjure up visions of files being spun onto spools for storage like so much thread, and then fed through some metaphoric "needle's eye" to the printer, where they're applied to the tapestry of the page. But the word "spool" actually originated as an acronym for "simultaneous peripheral operations on line," back in the early days of computing when centralized computers ran jobs in batches for many different users. A **spooler** is software that uses part of the Mac II's RAM to intercept the file to be printed, to store it on disk, and then to pass it on when the laser printer is free to print it. The spooler can manage several files "waiting in line" to be printed, from a single Mac II or from several machines sharing a printer (see Chapter 3, "Making Connections"). Once the spooler has intercepted a file, it carries out its operations "in the background," and the Mac II user interface is freed up so you can go on to other tasks. A spooler thus reduces the amount of time a Mac user has to sit idle during the printing process.

While a spooler is reducing the waiting time associated with printing, it should be as unobtrusive as possible to the user. It should work automatically and should work smoothly with the applications and printer driver(s) used in the system.

It should spool files quickly (see "Spooler Speed" below). The spooler should conserve the Mac's RAM by storing its files in as compact a form as possible and by removing each temporary print storage file from RAM as soon as it finishes transmitting it to the printer. The user should be able to exercise control over the spooler: to change the order in which spooled files print; to spool files to be printed and then suspend the printing process until later; to specify printing priority among users of a network; to determine how many spooled files are waiting to be printed, when one starts printing, and when it has finished; to choose between printer drivers; to specify a backup printer in case the primary printer in a network is not available. The spooler should notify the user promptly and conveniently about problems such as paper jamming or running out.

Spooler Speed

Spooler speed is a measure of how fast the Mac II is returned to you, not how fast a page is produced by the printer. QuickDraw spoolers are speedier than PostScript spoolers. They capture and store the files to be printed in their QuickDraw (screen display) format, before the files are translated into PostScript for the laser printer. PostScript spoolers translate the files before storing them. What difference does this make? For a simple page made up of text only, probably not much difference at all. But for graphically complex pages, PostScript files can be much larger than QuickDraw files, so it takes longer (and more disk space) to store them (write them to disk). While the Mac II is writing to disk, you can't use it for other functions. *PrintMaster*, the print spooler application provided by Apple's *MultiFinder*, and *SuperLaserSpool* by SuperMac Technologies are both QuickDraw spoolers.

COLOR PRINTING

Color thermal transfer printers such as the QMS ColorScript print the four process colors (cyan, magenta, yellow, and black) in one pass of the paper through the printer (see Chapter 13). High-resolution color output is best done via professional color separation, either by traditional photographic methods or digitally (see Chapter 15). However, it's also possible to print in color by using cartridge-loaded laser printers for type or artwork that doesn't require precise registration. Color cartridges are available from printer manufacturers or from services that refill toner cartridges.

For printing in color, the graphics software makes a separate **master** for each of the colors. Masters can be separate documents or pages of a single document. After the first color is printed, the toner cartridge is replaced with one of the second color, and the printed sheet is fed through the printer again. Manual feeding provides the best registration the machine can produce. The process is repeated for each additional color.

CHOOSING A LASER PRINTING SYSTEM

At present, laser printing technology is developing quite rapidly, with new machines becoming available all the time. When you consider which printer to buy, you'll want to analyze your own printing needs, present and future, as well as your budget. Read current comparative reviews of laser printer systems, insist on demonstrations, and check with other users of the system you plan to buy to see how it performs for them.

Analyzing Your Needs

Whatever you're producing with your Mac II now, you'll probably be producing more of it in the future, and you can expect your work to grow in sophistication and complexity as you become more familiar with both hardware and software. As you analyze your printer system requirements, knowing the answers to the following questions will help you narrow the field somewhat:

- Do you need higher than standard (300 dpi) resolution? If you do, expect to pay more for it.
- Will you be printing relatively large solid black areas? halftones? This may affect whether you want a write-black or write-white printer.
- Will you be using the printer with computers other than Macs? Look for models with connectors appropriate for your system.

- What image size do you need? Will being able to print 1/4 inch closer to the edge of the page make a difference to you? Do you need to print on larger than standard 8-1/2-by-11 sheets? Make sure the printers you consider can provide the size and coverage you need.
- Will you be using a variety of type styles for most of the documents you print? If so, the number of resident fonts and the amount of memory for storage of downloadable fonts will be important.
- Do you expect your needs to change significantly within the lifetime (duty cycle) of your printer? If so, expandability and upgradability are important.
- Is it important to you to be able to print in more than one color? Look at printers with toner cartridges rather than bins.
- Print speed will certainly become important as you wait for the printer to produce the pages you design. If high-volume production will be critically important, then print speed is an important factor in making your choice.

Getting Current Information

The magazines (printed and electronic) that specialize in Macintosh-related interests, computer graphic arts, and desktop publishing periodically run comparative reviews of laser printers, drivers, and spoolers. Check recent issues for the most current information. (You'll find a listing of these publications in the "Publications" appendix of this book.)

Taking a Test Drive

Prepare your own disk or disks to use for printer demonstrations. A demo of your own materials will be more meaningful than test sheets provided by the manufacturer or dealer. Use examples typical of the work you do in terms of complexity (number of type styles and bit maps), typical halftones, and line art, as well as examples that push the upper limits of what you want to produce. Bring along all the kinds of paper you want to use with your printer, to find out whether the printer can handle it and how it will look laser printed. Also bring along software you use often, so you can try applications, printer, driver, and spooler together.

At the demos, compare print speed for a first page alone as well as for a several-page document. In a document of uniform complexity, the first page takes the longest, so manufacturers' claims for number of pages per minute are not necessarily meaningful for the documents you plan to print. The best way to compare is to time the printing of the same documents by several printers.

During its demonstration, notice how much noise a printer makes. Will it fit conveniently in the work space you have available? Is it easy to operate? Does the documentation that comes with it tell you clearly what you'll need to know — how to set up the printer, dislodge paper jams, and maintain and troubleshoot the system? Check to see how often the toner cartridge has to be replaced and what it costs. Find out what the warranty promises, whether the machine comes with a service contract, and if so, how much it costs. What kind of support do the dealer and manufacturer provide?

Asking Around

Before you make the final decision to buy, check with others you know who are already using the printer. Or ask dealers for names of contacts with printing requirements like yours and experience in using the printer. Finally, choose a dealer with a reputation for customer support — one with a staff who will be able to help you operate your system now and expand it in the future.

CHAPTER 11

Dot Matrix Printing

The original Apple ImageWriter was the dot matrix impact printer sold with the original 128 K Mac. Perhaps almost as much as *MacPaint,* the ImageWriter was responsible for the computer graphics revolution the Mac started, because it reproduced exactly the 72-dpi images created on the Mac screen. Artists could paint an image and immediately print it out on paper. Today second- and third-generation ImageWriters — the ImageWriter II and ImageWriter LQ (for letter quality) are available. The ImageWriter II (Figure 11-1) still prints at 72 dpi, or 144 dpi at high resolution. The LQ's resolution is 216 dpi. Both types of printers handle both continuous-feed and single-sheet paper.

HOW A DOT MATRIX PRINTER WORKS

Images are transferred to paper by means of a printhead, a matrix of tiny pins. Controlled by the Mac as the printhead moves across the page, the appropriate pins strike the printer's inked ribbon, printing round dots that reproduce the screen image on paper. Because these printers work by impact, they're quite a bit noisier than laser printers and other nonimpact output devices.

The ImageWriter has two ways of printing in color — (1) a page can be fed through the printer several times, each time with a different color ribbon, or (2) the printhead can make multiple passes across the page, using a four-color (black, magenta, yellow, cyan) ribbon, before the paper is advanced a line. Several of the current Mac graphics software packages support dot matrix

Figure 11-1. The ImageWriter II dot matrix impact printer.

TIP

Using Both Kinds of Paper

If you've loaded your ImageWriter or ImageWriter II with continuous-feed paper and need to print a single sheet, turn the platen knob to roll the pin-fed sheet backwards only to the point where it's no longer in contact with the platen but still on the tractor pins. This saves reloading the pin-fed paper later.

TIP

Dot Matrix Color

For best results with dot matrix color printing:

- Use high-quality absorbent paper.
- When they're not in use, keep colored ribbons in airtight containers such as zip-closure plastic bags to keep them from drying out.
- Clean the printhead regularly. Otherwise, ink can build up and cause discoloration of both ribbon and output.

color printing — for example, *ColorPrint* (a program designed exclusively for that purpose), *GraphicWorks*, and *SuperPaint*.

USING A DOT MATRIX PRINTER

In general, dot matrix printer images are too coarse for most graphics applications. And unlike laser printers, the dot matrix printer can't serve as a proofing device for higher-resolution output devices, because its output format doesn't match theirs. But ImageWriter art is an established genre of its own (Figure 11-2), and the ImageWriter II does provide a relatively inexpensive way of generating hard copy. In combination with *ThunderScan* hardware and software (see Chapter 7), it also serves as a scanning system for importing digitized images from printed sheets.

While the LQ's resolution is higher than that of the ImageWriter II, so is its cost, and its niche is probably that of a business document printer rather than a graphic artist's alternative.

Figure 11-2. This illustration, *"Checker Game"* by Nira, was created in *MacPaint*. Color was added with the *ColorPrint* utility and printed on the ImageWriter II. This is a halftone of the color print.

CHAPTER 12

Ink Jet Printers

Like dot matrix machines, ink jet printers provide a relatively low-cost way to produce color output from the Mac II. And like that from dot matrix printers, the output (both graphics and text) is cruder than is useful for most professional applications. But color ink jet printers can produce output to serve as color samples, design comps, position pieces, or artworks of their own particular genre.

The two most popular ink jet printers for the Mac II, both priced under $1500, are the Hewlet-Packard PaintJet and the Xerox 4020. Printer drivers for Mac II color graphics applications should become increasingly available for these two printers. Figure 12-1 shows an HP PaintJet ink jet printer.

HOW INK JET PRINTERS WORK

Ink jet printers use tiny spray nozzles to apply ink to the page as a series of dots to make up type and graphic images. The dots are smaller and more densely packed (typically 120 to 240 dpi) than those produced by dot matrix printers. Ink is stored in cartridges, each of which feeds a number of nozzles. Typically, cyan, magenta, yellow, and black inks are used, and the printer can produce three additional colors (red and green, and either blue or violet, for example) by "mixing" — overlapping colored dots on the printed page. Other colors (thousands by some printers) can be produced by **dithering**, creating the illusion of a single mixed color by interspersing dots of two or more primary colors. Software controls

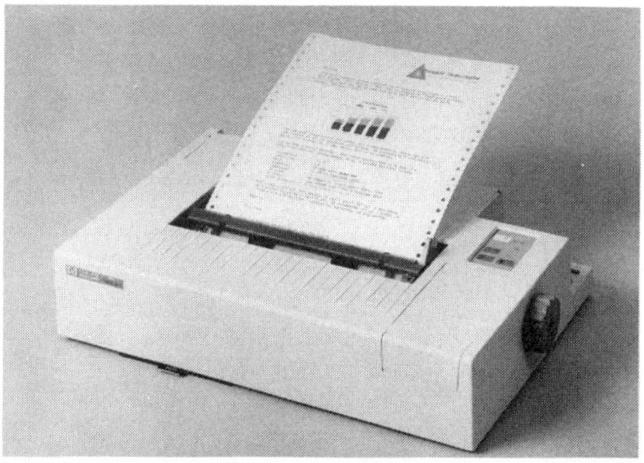

Figure 12-1. The HP PaintJet ink jet printer.

TIP

Printing Transparencies

Because transparency film doesn't absorb ink the way paper does, ink jet–printed transparencies take longer to dry than paper prints. Take extra care in removing them from the printer, touching them only on the edges, so the ink doesn't smear; and don't stack them on top of each other.

TIP

Vacation Maintenance

Letting your ink jet printer sit idle for too long (more than a week or so) can allow ink to dry and clog the nozzles. Exercise it regularly. If you will be away for an extended period, either remove the cartridges and clean the nozzles or have someone come in and run the printer periodically.

color application by telling the printer which ink jets to fire as the printhead moves over the paper.

You can get the best output from ink jet printers by using special clay-coated paper made especially for that purpose. Paper is available as single or pin-fed sheets and as rolls. Ink jet printers can also print on transparency film.

WHAT TO LOOK FOR IN INK JET PRINTERS

Here are some things to check for if you're shopping for an ink jet printer:

- What is the **life cycle** of the printer? That is, how long can you expect it to last?
- What is the **cartridge capacity?** How often will you have to change or refill ink cartridges? And can you refill them yourself if you want to experiment with mixing your own inks?
- How easy is **maintenance**? Some printers have built-in maintenance fluid cartridges to simplify maintenance for the user, as well as plugs to protect ink from drying and clogging the nozzles.
- Does it support **bidirectional printing**? This increases printing speed.
- Is there adequate **software support** for the printer? Print drivers are usually written for only the most popular printers and graphics applications.
- What will it take to **interface** the printer to the Mac II? While ink jet technology has existed for quite a while, not all ink jet manufacturers have been quick to develop hardware connections for the Macintosh.

CHAPTER 13

Thermal Transfer Printers

Thermal transfer printers such as the Tektronix 4693D shown in Figure 13-1 provide a quick and easy way to transfer a color image from the Mac II screen to paper. The output quality is denser, smoother, and more precise than what you get from a dot matrix printer (see Chapter 11) or most ink jet machines (see Chapter 12). The dot density is higher, so the resolution is better. But thermal transfer printer output is not as good as you would get from the digital separation process available from higher-end machines (see Chapter 15), and it isn't currently suitable for most professional printing applications. Thermal transfer printer output is perhaps most appropriate for color proofing and comprehensives. It can also be used effectively to print transparencies on polyester film for overhead projection.

As in printing with the ImageWriter and ink jet printers, color separation is done by graphics program software such as *SuperPaint*, *PixelPaint*, and *GraphicWorks*.

HOW COLOR THERMAL TRANSFER WORKS

Instead of cloth ribbons or ink reservoirs, thermal transfer printers use rolls of transfer sheeting, or "film ribbon,"covered with ink, wax, or plastic coloring media. During the printing process, the sheet unwinds from the roller so that successive page-sized areas of color — cyan, magenta, yellow, and black — come in contact with the printer paper or film. As printing begins, selected pins of a ceramic or metal printhead apply heat and pressure, which applies and fuses dots of one of the four colors to the paper. The transfer sheeting is repositioned, and another color is printed, until all four colors are on the page. When the process is complete, there's a four-color print on the page and four "separation negatives"on the roll of transfer sheeting.

Thermal transfer printers vary in resolution, starting at a low end of 200 dpi, and in the number of colors that can be produced. The lower-end machines, such as the Tektronix 4693D are limited to QuickDraw-based output. Some offer the full 16.7 million color range available from the Mac II screen. Price increases with resolution and with the ability to handle PostScript, which gives users access to high-quality fonts and allows them to output PostScript graphics.

PRINTER DRIVERS

Printer drivers, the programs necessary to make the printer work with the Mac II are available from manufacturers of both printers and desktop publishing and graphics software packages. Some of the drivers from software manufacturers are resolution independent, so that users can take advantage of the highest resolution their output device can provide. In addition to software, or sometimes in place of it, most thermal transfer printers require that a special interface card be installed in one of the Mac II's expansion slots. Video interface cards read the video signal to the monitor screen and convert it into a digital record that is stored in and printed from the printer's image memory.

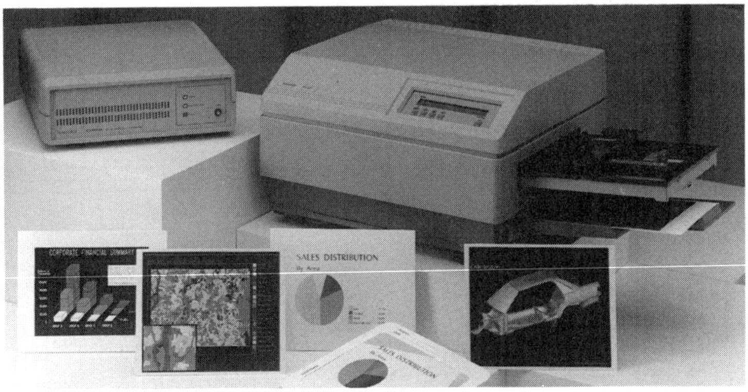

Figure 13-1. The Tektronix Color Image Printer, model 4693D thermal transfer printer.

Using Thermal Transfer Printers

Thermal transfer printers can be expensive enough (approximately $2,000 to $25,000) so they're a considerable investment for a Mac II owner. As Mac-generated color output becomes more common, however, we should see these printers appearing in settings that allow you to bring your art files and an appropriate printer driver on disk and print your color graphics in a shop such as those now operating laser printers.

CHOOSING A THERMAL TRANSFER PRINTER

Unless your thermal transfer printer is also serving as your workhorse printer, speed is probably not an issue. Thermal transfer printers do vary in several important aspects, though. Here are some things to check for:

- Will the printer produce copy that's **consistent in quality,** regardless of environmental conditions or work load?
- Will it produce the range of **output sizes** you need?
- Will it produce **special effects** — modifications of the image performed by printer software rather than on the Mac II? Some of the modifications thermal printers allow are color assignment (enabling color substitution), scaling, image rotation, and print density adjustment.
- Will it allow **multiplexing** (more than one user connected to the printer at once) or **remote starting** (so you can warm up the machine from a switch at your desk and print when you hear the ready signal)?
- Beyond the initial investment in the printer itself, what will be the **cost per output page**? This is a function of cost per print roll (transfer sheeting and paper or polyester film) and number of prints per roll.
- What are the **cost and availability** of service?

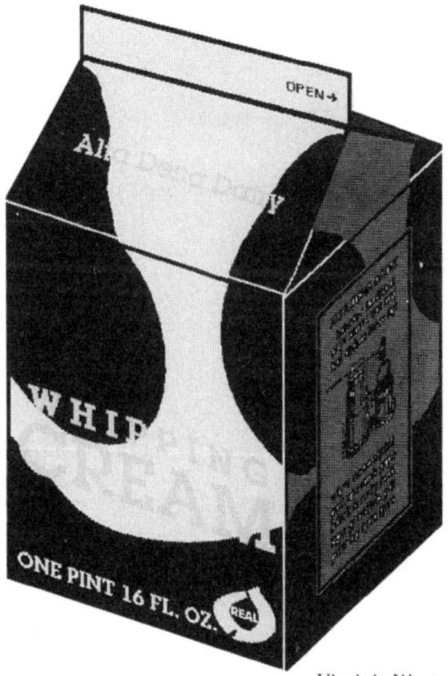

Virginia West

SOME EXAMPLES

Figures 11, 14, 16, 22–24, and 29–31 in the Color Gallery are examples of thermal transfer prints (all reduced from 8–1/2-by–11–inch originals for reproduction).

CHAPTER 14

Image-setting

While the ease-of-use, versatility, and relative affordability of the LaserWriter has been one of the keys to the Macintosh's success in the design world, for most graphic designers the higher-resolution Linotronic imagesetters have been the compelling reason for using the Macintosh. With resolutions of 635, 1270, and 2540 dots per inch (dpi) available from the high-end Linotronic 300, artists and designers can take advantage of the ease and flexibility of the Macintosh without having to sacrifice anything in terms of crisp, high-quality typesetting. Indeed, for many users, the LaserWriter has become the proofing machine, suitable for comps, mock-ups, and drafts, while the final production is done on a Linotronic machine. In addition, the high resolution of the imagesetter has made possible the use of both color separations and halftones produced from the Macintosh, though both of these technologies are still in their infancy.

HOW AN IMAGESETTER WORKS

Basically, the PostScript commands sent to the imagesetter are the same as those sent to the LaserWriter. These commands from the Mac are processed in a device called the Raster Image Processor (RIP). The RIP converts the PostScript (vector) commands into a raster (bitmapped) image that matches the page size and the selected resolution (310, 635, 1270, or — Linotype 300 only — 2540 dpi). The time required to do all this depends on three factors: the speed of the processor, the size and complexity of the image, and the resolution. Recent enhancements to the RIP from Linotype have made this a more efficient process, less likely to result in monstrously long output times.

After conversion, the rasterized image is printed line by line on the target medium. The medium can be one of two materials: high-quality paper in positive mode, or film negative. In addition, 3M has recently developed a photographic plate medium for direct printing of plates from the imagesetter. The Linotronic 100 and 300 can print on 11-inch-wide media with variable length up to 23-1/2 inches; the less common Linotronic 500 prints on an 18-inch-width medium (tabloid width). The time required for printing is dependent on the size, complexity, and resolution.

After printing, the output must then be placed in a film processor for development. If positives are produced, they can be used for paste-up or further corrections, they can be used directly for quick printing plates, or they can be sent to the printer to make a negative and plates. If negatives are used, they go directly for plates (film density in this case may be crucial).

CHOOSING A SERVICE BUREAU

Few graphic designers at the current time have the resources to own and maintain an imagesetter. A number of service bureaus are available that offer imagesetting services, along with other similar work. These bureaus vary in terms of their price structures, expertise, and reliability, so you should spend some time investigating before committing a critical job to the care of a single service bureau. Most designers build up a relationship with a service bureau in which both sides understand the rules of the game and each other's requirements. A good service bureau bends over backwards to maintain high-quality output and to help its users realize that goal.

Unfortunately, the process of printing from Mac to imagesetter is still prone to mysterious failures and quirks. Moving a project from your Mac setup to that of the service bureau is likely to cause problems, most notably inconsistencies in the identification of fonts. Good service bureaus take pains to keep their users aware of these problems and the strategies for avoiding them.

Changes in resolution from LaserWriter proof to imagesetter print can also make big changes in the appearance of a page. In many programs, 20 percent gray fills, for example, look different at different resolutions. What appears fine at 300 dpi

TIP

Page Resolution

If your service bureau has a Linotronic 300, you have a choice between 1270- and 2540-dpi resolutions. You might assume that the higher resolution would be more desirable, but that's not necessarily the case. Here are several factors to consider in choosing resolution:

(1) **The naked eye**. The difference in resolution between 1270 and 2540 dpi is not apparent to the naked eye in line art, but there is a definite difference in halftone screens.

(2) **Time**. Many service bureaus charge overrun costs for pages that take longer than a given time to print — for example, 10 or 12 minutes. A 2540-dpi page may take four times as long, since it has four times as many dots in every square inch as a 1270-dpi page does. This could add significantly to the expense.

(3) **Camera limitations**. If you print in positive and have your printer make the plates or photostats from the output, you will lose much of the gain in resolution simply because most cameras are incapable of taking advantage of the higher resolution. If, on the other hand, you output directly to film negative, you can make direct use of the higher resolution.

(4) **Special work**. For certain special work, like printing halftones or doing color separations, the higher resolution may indeed make a significant difference in the final product.

may be too dark at 1270. Likewise, hairlines have a habit of disappearing at higher resolution with most programs, as exact point sizes are used rather than approximations. Then too, some other programs simply don't output properly on the Linotronic machines. A good service bureau operation will afford you ample warning on what programs and types of output are difficult or impossible to run.

Spotting or blotching on output can be the result of poor upkeep and less-than-vigilant quality control. Similar problems can occur when a service bureau does an inadequate job of checking the output against proof copies to make sure that your job comes out according to your specifications. A good service bureau will phone you when problems occur and help you find ways to get around problems and correct errors.

NEW IMAGESETTERS

While Linotype has ruled the roost as the sole supplier of PostScript compatible imagesetters and has set high prices for its equipment, that situation is already beginning to change. Established companies like AM Varityper are entering the market with high-resolution imagesetters that are fully compatible with PostScript. Smaller companies have announced plans to release moderate-cost, high-performance imagesetters as well.

Each of these new machines will probably have its share of new incompatibilities and difficulties. After all, Linotype has been in this business for four years and is only now delivering a fairly stable and predictable product. But the prospect of competition in price, performance, and features is bound to benefit every imagesetter user.

TIP

Font Problems

When the Macintosh was created, no one envisioned the explosion of fonts that would occur. Apple provided for uniquely identifying no more than 128 fonts beyond its handful of proprietary ones (like Chicago and Geneva). While this limitation is not a serious problem if you print from your own in-house system, it has become a nightmare in dealing with service bureaus. The System identifies fonts by number rather than by name. What you specified as Bodoni Bold in your manuscript might have the same number as New Century Schoolbook Italic on the service bureau's system, for example.

Adobe alone has issued hundreds of distinct fonts, and is releasing more every month. Other companies are releasing fonts even faster, with the ideal object being the thousands of fonts you would expect from a conventional typesetter. It is assumed (fervently hoped) that Apple will soon offer a solution to this problem.

The best service bureaus have developed ways to cope with this problem. You and your service bureau operator should understand what fonts you're using in your document. Supply a copy of your LaserWriter proof so they can check the final result. Advance planning can save time–consuming and expensive mistakes.

Chapter 15

Color Separations

Color separation is a term loosely applied in the desktop publishing world to three distinct processes:

- spot color overlays
- flat color separations
- four-color process separations

While the exact meaning of these terms is applied differently in different programs (and in different circles in the printing industry), they encompass the three principal ways of creating prepress guidelines for color printing. All three processes are still in early stages on the Mac.

SPOT COLOR

Spot color overlays involve the separation of an image into layers of distinct color. These specific colors are traditionally assigned numeric values based on a system called the Pantone Matching System (PMS), and printers can get the inks that correspond to the colors in that system. However, a looser specification is often used if terms like "light blue" or "cherry red" are sufficient descriptions for the designer (if precise color matching is not required). Each color specified involves a separate run through the press. Spot color makes sense particularly for two- or three-color print jobs.

FLAT COLOR

Flat color separations involve the printing of line art illustrations. Flat color separations are used when there are a number of specific colors. For current Macintosh use, flat color involves creating at least four separations using the CYMK color separation model. This separates the colors into percentages of the colors cyan, yellow, magenta, and black, so that a specific green area might be composed of 40 percent cyan and 30 percent yellow, for example. Other specific colors, such as PMS values, as well as a separate black layer for printing type (especially when it's set over color areas) can also be used. Approximate color values can be used for most flat art separations since the color areas do not represent any real colors in nature.

FOUR-COLOR PROCESS

Standard **four-color process separations** are used for photos and other scanned art. Process color uses the same CYMK four-color separations, but usually requires very good color matching. Flesh tones and sky colors, for example, are the tests of color photo reproduction. Even with the most expensive color prepress equipment and most experienced teams, color printing can be problematical.

GETTING GOOD RESULTS

At the present time, you can do all three kinds of separations with the Macintosh, but with varying results. Programs like *Illustrator '88*, *FreeHand*, *LaserPaint*, and *PageMaker* offer software solutions, and color scanners and associated software are being developed and improved all the time.

Color overlays seem to work fine, especially when no two color areas are contiguous. When two areas are close, the stresses of the printing process may misalign the colors and either overprint or (even worse) allow gaps between the color fields. Traditionally, this problem is resolved with a process called trapping, a deliberate slight overprinting to ensure that such gaps do not appear. Adobe's *Separator* program, which accompanies *Illustrator '88*, is a first try at addressing this problem.

While trapping is also a problem with flat color separations, a more serious difficulty comes from moire patterns. The separate color layers are output on the imagesetter as halftone screens, each made up of great numbers of small dots. Each layer is printed at a different angle to allow for overlap of the

TIP

Monitor Color Versus Printed Color

You've probably heard it, but it's easy to forget it. The colors on your Mac II color monitor, if you have one, differ in two major ways from any you'll get in printing.

First, the monitor's colors are produced through light. The opacity, density, and flow characteristics of ink on paper cannot be directly compared to the even, almost insubstantial colored light on your screen. In terms of ink flow, absorbency, and reflectivity, the appearance and interaction of colors on a page differ from anything on a monitor. Remember that the monitor is projecting, not reflecting light.

Second, the monitor uses an RGB (red-green-blue) color model, the converse of the CYMK model of most color printing. The effect of this difference is subtle but pervasive. Again, be aware that colors represented on the screen bear only a kinship to the colors that may be reproduced on paper.

primary colors. If these layers are out of alignment, or if the paper when printed is even slightly off registration, odd-looking patterns can occur on the page. This is a problem particularly with colors like brown that use all four of the component primaries, and with large areas of the same color. The solution is great skill from the printer, designer, and imagesetter operator, and more highly developed software.

Most observers agree that high-quality color photographic reproduction on the Macintosh is still to come. In addition to trapping and moire problems, the user comes directly up against the very high-level demands of professional color processing. Slight color mismatches or mistakes that can be easily forgiven in flat art become very noticeable when the picture is to realistically represent some real-life object. Color photo processing and printing is still somewhat of a black art, and the initial attempts of software companies and even the advent of high-quality color scanners have taken only the first steps in pursuit of this goal.

A word to the wise. Color work on the Mac is still not for the novice. You must have solid relationships with your Lino operator and your printer, and a willingness to experiment. The difficulties, especially for overlays and flat color are not insurmountable, but expect your first few jobs to take longer and cost more than traditional technologies until you get the system down.

GREAT EXPECTATIONS

An exciting development in color processing is the creation of strategic alliances such as one between Quark and Scitex, manufacturer of the deluxe models of high-quality color scanners and prepress systems. Crosfield, another leader in this field, has just bought out Lightspeed, a developer of Mac–to–prepress system connectivity. Expect the impressive early strides in color processing technology to continue, with it a gradual de-escalation of price in color print preparation.

CHAPTER 16

Film Recorders

Art to be presented to a sizable audience or delivered as a reproduction master for publication can be output to a film recorder that produces 35 mm full-color slides. The quality of the image from a film recorder generally exceeds that available from a comparably priced color printer. The reason is simple: printers are mechanical devices that deposit colored dots onto a paper surface, while film recorders write with microscopic points of light onto a high-resolution electronic imaging device, and the composite picture is captured on film with a perfectly focused lens.

HOW FILM RECORDERS WORK

Whereas some printers produce color by dithering, mixing separate dots of different colors to form a rather diffused and coarse-looking image, the film recorder overlays the red, blue, and green light components of a pixel onto a one-dot area. The normal photographic process then combines the color mix into a single dot of the appropriate final color. Typically, 2000 to 4000 such dots are placed along the width of a 35 mm slide.

Some commercially available film recorders render smooth-edged text by using physical font wheels. This method limits the variety and size of text that can be used on a given slide. Newer recorders use software-based outline fonts, which can be downloaded from the Macintosh, freely scaled in size, and mixed on the same slide. Several fonts (those most often used in presentation slides) are bundled along with the film recorder's software, and additional ones can be purchased, individually or in sets, from the manufacturer.

Film recorders go only as far as exposing photographic film to an accurate rendition of the final image. They don't magically turn out developed and mounted slides. That must be done separately, through normal photo-developing techniques.

SOME CHOICES

Film recorders for the Macintosh II come with the appropriate interfacing software. The devices described here use software-based fonts and connect to the SCSI port of the Macintosh II. They accept images saved as PICT or PICT2 (not PostScript), and are capable of rendering 16.7 million colors.

Lasergraphics LFR

The Lasergraphics LFR has a second SCSI port so it can be daisy-chained anywhere in a line of other SCSI devices. Built-in switches can be used to change its SCSI address to the device won't conflict with other peripherals. It's selected via a queuing desk accessory, (as opposed to using a Chooser-selectable printer driver).

The LFR provides resolutions of 2048 or 4096 lines across the 35 mm slide width. The film compartment is external; it accepts 35 mm (via the standard film back) or 3-1/4-by-4-1/4 Polaroid film (via an optional film back). The LFR can drive a color printer through a built-in Centronics parallel port; printers supported are the Hewlett-Packard PaintJet and Lasergraphics CPS color thermal transfer printer. The LFR can use Mac screen fonts, but they appear jagged.

Mirus Digital Film Printer

Like the LFR, the Mirus Digital Film Printer has a second SCSI port so it can be daisy-chained anywhere in a line of other SCSI devices. Although this device connects to the SCSI port, its driving software enables it to be selected via the Chooser desk accessory, so it can be treated as simply another printing device. The Mirus uses a special technique to digitally aim, focus, and modulate the imaging beam with electrostatic fields instead of magnetic fields. It provides resolutions of 547 to 8191 lines across the 35 mm slide width. Its film compartment is internal, and it accepts only 35 mm slide film.

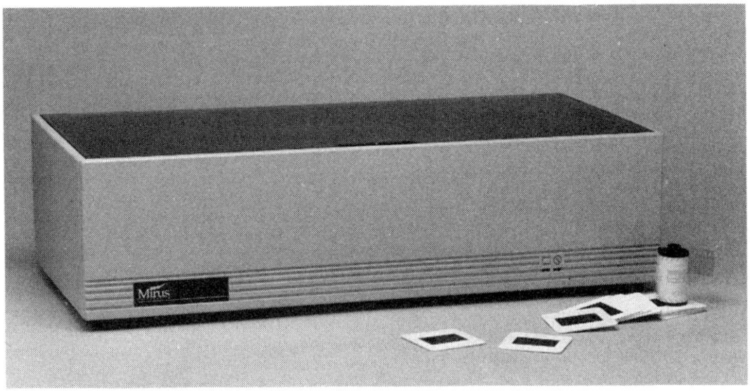

Figure 16-1. The Mirus Digital Film Printer.

SERVICE BUREAUS

It's possible to obtain 35 mm slides of your Mac graphics without owning a film recorder, by sending files via disk or modem to one of several service bureaus. They print the electronic images and return the finished slides, usually overnight. Such services are relatively expensive, but using a service can be helpful if you sometimes need slides in a hurry but you don't need very many slides very often.

CHAPTER 17

Other Output Options

The other chapters in Part III have described technologies typically used to reproduce Mac II creations in hard copy. This chapter covers two other significant output technologies. These are technologies that can be used to fill the gap that can occur if you want a particular kind of output (color on a laser print, for example, or a 35 mm color slide) but don't have access to the relatively expensive equipment needed to produce it in the usual way.

KROY COLOR PLUS

For small projects, the Kroy Color Plus system provides a way to add colors to a laser-printed page — an alternative to buying a color printer or finding a service that will let you run a few color prints. Kroy output can be used to produce color comps, to proof the effect of color before you have thousands of copies printed in color, to add color to just a few pages when you don't need enough copies to make a separate press run worthwhile, or to generate flat color copy for shooting color slides, for example. It's also an excellent system for making signs in small quantities.

Kroy Color Plus is a heat-based process that bonds color from transfer film to the toner on a laser-printed page. The Kroy film comes in an array of 61 colors, including gloss, matte, and several metallic finishes. The process works like this: A laser-printed page and a sheet of transfer film are fed through the Kroy Color Plus machine together. A combination of

Figure 17-1. The Kroy Color Plus system.

heat and pressure bonds the color to the black toner on the page. You can print in more than one color by "piecing" the transfer film, applying partial sheets to the original where you want spot color.

35 MM SLIDES

If you need to create slide presentations, but your budget can't be stretched to include a film recorder (see Chapter 16) and you don't have a nearby service bureau with a film recorder for hire, what can you do? The answer is that you can reproduce your artwork by photographing it in place on the Mac II screen with a 35 mm camera. And once you get the technique down, you may find that you prefer the results to what you get from a film recorder, because, while film recorder output is precisely correct according to the hues specified for your Mac II creation, the final shot-from-the-screen slide is truer to the colors of the image your eye sees on the Mac II. And by shooting your own slides, you can save money, gain creative control of your project, and experiment with the results on your own time.

The techniques described here will give you very good results using a 35 mm camera. As you read the instructions, keep in mind that:

• The clarity and overall quality of your slides will depend on the resolution of your monitor, the quality of your camera lens, and your ability to focus sharply.

• Vertical and horizontal lines extending toward the edges of the computer screen will bow slightly from the curvature of screen if photographed with a 50 mm camera lens.

• If the camera and screen are not absolutely parallel, **pyramiding**, (the tendency for a rectangular image to take on angles other than 90°) can occur.

• Light reflections on the computer screen will degrade the final slide images.

You can achieve satisfactory results by following some rather simple procedures.

Getting the Equipment Together

You'll need a single-lens reflex (SLR) 35 mm camera with a manual mode and a 50 mm (or better yet, an 85 mm or longer telephoto lens — if you set the camera up 10 feet back from the screen, the longer lenses tend to flatten out the curved screen image). You also need a sturdy tripod, filters (Kodak 20 Red or FL Day), and a cable release. With the Polaroid Instant Slide System costing about $70 and the necessary chemicals, you can process your slides yourself in less than a minute (though the results may not approach professional E-6 processing).

Check your film. Kodak Ektachrome 100 Plus Professional Daylight film works well. Fuji films, while okay for geometric images, tend to add contrast to subtle shades of color and to warm up colors. Kodak Ektachrome 100 has a bluish tone, so the addition of color correction filters helps bring slide results closer to screen colors. Choosing the right filter to use is based on your sense of color. Many images (especially with strong blue palettes) require no filter, and most others can be corrected with a 20 Red or an FL Day (fluorescent) filter.

If you have several monitors available, use the one with the highest resolution. Then determine the largest area of the screen that you can use with the least distortion. Try to contain your slide art to that area in the center of the computer screen where the straight lines and rectangles don't appear to bow. For that matter, avoid creating art with straight lines that border the outside edges of the image area of the computer screen.

Setting Up the Shoot

Mount your camera with the telephoto lens installed on a tripod, and aim it squarely at the center of the computer screen. The camera and the screen should be parallel. Use bubble levels to check both the monitor and the camera to make sure they're both level. Load the film. Set brightness on the monitor to full.

Make sure all extraneous light in the room has been turned out or blocked out. Totally darken the room, or shoot at night if necessary.

Your monitor scans and refreshes every 1/30th of a second. To avoid scan lines, set the shutter speed of your camera to 1 second. Connect the shutter release to the camera.

Set the camera meter for the ASA of the film used. To set your exposure, fill the monitor screen with a medium gray field. Set the camera f-stop to this reading. If you have an automatic camera, make sure your flash is turned off.

Bring your graphics up on the screen. If you need to align the image to center it in the camera's field of view, do it by moving the image on the screen, not by moving the camera. Be aware that what you see through the viewfinder will not exactly match the dimensions of the final slide. Most 35 mm cameras only show 95 percent of the picture.

Taking the Pictures

Have a pencil and paper handy. Make a record of each exposure you make. The relevant information you'll want to record for each slide will include: *slide #, f-stop, speed, filter used, image description, date, film type,* and (to be completed after processing) *results.*

As you shoot, "bracket" your photos by making additional shots at 1/2 second and 2 seconds. Additional exposures of 1/4 and 4 seconds would be wise on your first test roll. Bracketing will simply improve your chances of obtaining the best results possible.

Checking the Results

Process your slides, and then view them on the color-corrected light box at the processing lab. If you bracketed your shots, you should see lighter and darker versions of each image . Refer to your notes and check which f-stops worked best for you. This information may come in handy the next time you need to produce slides of your computer graphics.

These procedures offer a good-quality, low-cost alternative to the high price of film recorders.

Painters have special brushes, easels, and thinners. Photographers have light meters, makeup, and lenses. Draftsmen have templates, technical pens, and electric erasers. All artists depend on a variety of support tools.

Traditionally, support tools for visual artists have included T-squares, pica rules, press type, rubylith, templates, phototype-setting systems, waxers, stat cameras, and light tables. While some of these are still useful to the electronic designer, there are many essential new support tools that enhance the primary hardware and software of a Mac II graphic art workstation.

Fonts

Screen fonts, bitmapped fonts, PostScript fonts, outline fonts, design-your-own fonts — more than ever, the graphic artist has control over all aspects of typesetting.

Desk Accessories

From the standard accessories included under the Apple menu to essential miniprograms and utilities, DAs make it easier to get around in the Mac environment and offer many enhancements to productivity. DAs are accessible while you're working within any program.

Clip Art

Years ago, some people in Peoria reportedly invented the clip art industry, providing artists with booklets of illustrations designed for newspaper ad layouts — ready to clip out and paste up. MacPaint *sparked a small industry of digital clip art sold on disk, mostly*

bitmapped images from small start-up software companies. Now there's a flood of art on disk, coming out increasingly as high-resolution EPSF files.

Templates

Although people learned early that a desktop publishing system did not make beautiful design by itself, it also became clear that once a design "template" was completed by a graphically talented human, others could carry on fairly well with the established electronic format. Some of the software companies have taken this process a step further by offering total design package templates.

Stacks

HyperCard *is Apple's "hypertext" software — a multipurpose database engine that's easily customizable, in fact programmable, by users with little or no technical background.* HyperCard *"stacks" are documents created by users, such as a Rolodex stack that consists of individual cards like a real desktop Rolodex, or an instructional desktop "video" on a certain topic.* HyperCard *uses graphic tools, buttons, icons, and text in an amazing interactive format that can include sound and animation.*

Mass Storage

Mass storage systems, the most common of which are hard disk drives, are fundamental *support tools. Your data — your work, your business, your life – is dependent on that whirling disk. Investment in a good, large hard disk drive is essential to a Mac II graphics workstation. And even more massive storage systems are available already.*

Other Input Devices

A graphic tablet with an electronic stylus, a trackball that serves as a stationary mouse, even a sound recording device, all provide additional ways to get information into your Macintosh II.

CHAPTER 18

Fonts

Matching the type you use to the purpose and content of a document is a critical part of good design. In designing with the Mac II, you have a broad spectrum of both bitmapped and PostScript-based type to choose from. To discuss the different kinds of type your Mac II can produce, it's necessary to define some terms:

- A **face**, or **typeface**, is a set of characters (alphabetic, numeric, punctuation, and special symbols) of a particular design (e.g., Helvetica or Times), a particular weight (e.g., light, medium, bold, or extra bold), a particular character width (e.g., condensed or extended), and a particular style (e.g., roman or italic).
- A type **family** is made up of several related faces that share the same design but vary in weight, character width, and style (Figure 18-1).
- A face or a family of faces includes type of many **sizes**.
- Traditionally, a **font** is a character set of a particular face and size.

Other type-related terms are defined in "Type Particulars" on page 252.

Basically, the Mac II uses two kinds of fonts — bitmapped fonts (like most kinds of QuickDraw-based fonts) and outline fonts (like PostScript fonts).

Figure 18-1. A family of type faces.

The Best Sizes

The outlined numbers in the Font menu represent the sizes that look the best when the selected bitmapped typeface is displayed.

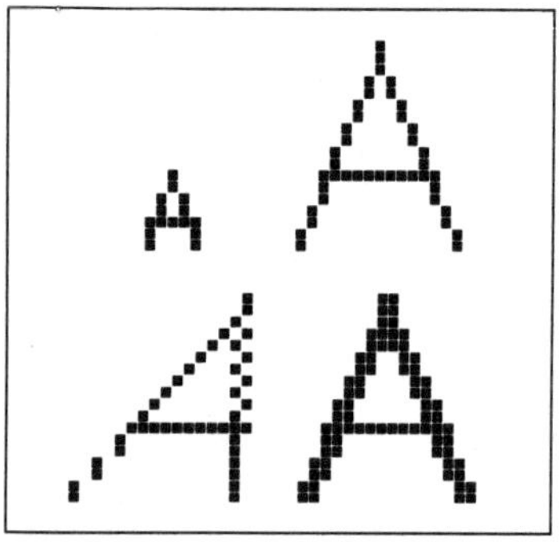

Figure 18-2. A FatBits view of a Geneva "A" in 9- and 12-point sizes as well as 12-point italic and bold.

WHAT IS A BITMAPPED FONT?

A bitmapped character is made up of dots (72 dots per inch [dpi] as displayed on the Mac screen) and stored in memory in that form. A separate dot image is stored for each character. The Geneva "A," for example, requires a separate dot map, stored within the Mac's memory (Figure 18-2). The System fonts provided with the Mac II are bitmapped fonts. To select a type face, we choose a bitmapped type family from the Font menu and then choose the size and style to complete the definition of the bitmapped font we want to use.

Printed on ImageWriter printers in Faster quality, bitmapped characters look very much as they do on screen. Although these printers produce 160 dpi horizontally by 144 dpi vertically, they don't take advantage of the greater dot density to improve type quality. If you select Best quality when you print, the ImageWriter uses a System font twice the size of the one you want to print, scaling this font down to size but using the higher number of bits specified for the bigger size. For example, to print 12-point Geneva, you would need the 24-point font. This reduction gives you smoother-looking characters. (The ImageWriter LQ uses the same principle, but scales down from a triple-size font. On the other hand, laser printers, typically at 300 dpi, use an algorithm to smooth the edges of the 72-dpi image received from the Mac, and this reduction makes the bitmapped font look better.

QuickDraw-based laser printers such as the LaserWriter SC convert the bitmapped Mac System fonts to fonts stored in the printer's system to improve the look of printed type.

Type Particulars

Here are the names type designers use to describe the parts of a typeface:

(1) baseline, (2) x height, (3) serif, (4) descender, (5) ascender

Type size is measured as height in **points**, of which there are approximately 72 per inch. Type size is measured from baseline to baseline, but type faces of the same nominal size might be quite different in actual measure because of the amount of white space above ascenders and below descenders. Often the **x height** conveys the actual visual size of a type face better than the body size does.

An **em** space is the square of any given type size; a 12-point em, for example, measures 12 points wide by 12 points high. An **en** space is half as wide as an em.

WHAT IS AN OUTLINE FONT?

In an outline font (not an outline face as in Figure 18-1), the outlines that define the characters are objects (graphics primitives defined by equations). Sets of equations and anchor points define the lines and curves that outline the characters. The printed characters are resolution independent; that is, the final printed character can take full advantage of the maximum resolution of the printer or other output device. The size and shape of the character can be varied by substituting different numbers into the same set of instructions.

In simple terms, when an outline character is to be printed, any number substitution, or **scaling**, necessary to produce the type size called for is done, the outlined areas of the character are filled in to make the smoothest bit map possible, and this bit map is stored in the printer's RAM for printing.

TIP

Real Fonts in the Menu

An application called *Menu Fonts*, placed in your System folder, helps you choose the face you want by causing the Fonts menu to display the names of the available types in their own faces.

WHAT IS A POSTSCRIPT FONT?

PostScript fonts are outline fonts generated in the PostScript page description language (see Chapter 6). Designed to be printed on laser printers or higher-resolution imagesetters, PostScript-generated (or simply PostScript, or laser) fonts can be manipulated by the graphics operations of the PostScript language to produce many different type effects. For example, fonts can be scaled to virtually any size, characters can be rotated to any angle, character width and line thickness can be manipulated, and character outlines can be filled with patterns to produce shadows or patterned type (Figure 18-3).

Figure 18-3. This type composition by Jack Davis shows several of the PostScript typographic effects available within *Adobe Illustrator*, including Outline, Shadow, Rotation, Skewing, and Neon.

Each PostScript font has two parts — the **printer font** and the **screen font**. The printer font contains the PostScript commands that make up the characters, and the associated screen font contains bitmapped screen representations of all the PostScript characters.

CHOOSING AND USING BITMAPPED FONTS

The fonts you'll use most often for typesetting with the Mac II and a laser printer or higher-resolution output system are PostScript fonts, because they look best in print and can be manipulated so extensively. But there are hundreds of other fonts available commercially and in the public domain that are worth knowing about — specialized character sets (foreign language alphabets, and mathematical, scientific, engineering, and international symbols, for example.)

You may want to use bitmapped **display type** (unusual or decorative fonts) for headings, logos, or initial capital letters. And like any bitmapped graphic image, a character from a bitmapped display font can be imported into an object-oriented application and reduced to make it look sharper when it's printed. Bitmapped characters can also be used as templates in PostScript illustration programs such as *Illustrator '88* to provide the basis of a graphic image.

Installing Bitmapped Fonts

To be able to use a bitmapped font, you have to install it in the System file of your startup disk by using the *Font/DA Mover* utility provided with your Mac II. When you double-click the *Font/DA Mover* icon in your System file, you'll see a dialog box like the one in Figure 18-4. The black dot next to "Font" at the top of the box means that the utility is currently set to move fonts rather than desk accessories (DAs). Notice the Help button. Pressing this button provides clear instructions for using *Font/DA Mover*.

You can import a font from the

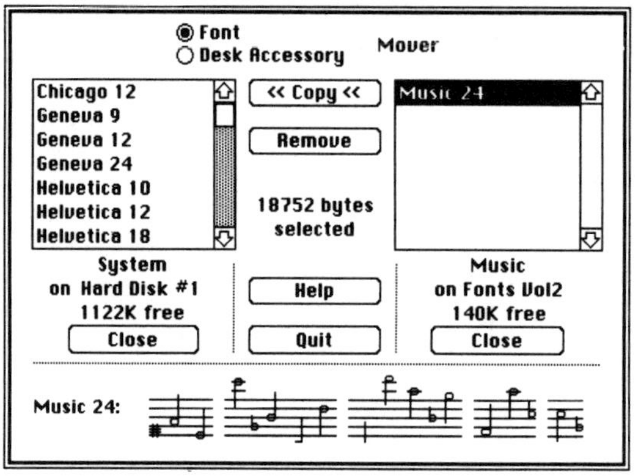

Figure 18-4. The *Font/DA Mover* dialog box.

System of another disk or from a special file that stores only that font. You can also Copy fonts from left to right — that is, from your System to another file. And you can use the Remove button to delete fonts from either file to create free space for new fonts. You can't, however, remove Geneva 9- or 12-point, Chicago 12, or Monaco 9, which are used by the System itself to produce the desktop, window, and dialog box display screens.

TIP

Protecting Fonts

Once you select a font and press the Remove button, it's "Bye-bye, font" — permanently. And for some reason, it seems to be easy to hit Return when you mean to press Copy. So it's a good idea to keep backup files of all your fonts stored safely on locked disks.

Bitmapping Your Own Fonts

Type design is an art. It requires specialized training and much practice to know how to design a well-integrated, readable, pleasing-to-look-at family of typefaces. Creating a family of faces can be considered an artistic accomplishment comparable to writing an epic novel or a symphony. In other words, it's not a task to be undertaken lightly. But you may occasionally want to design a character or character combination for a particular use, or incorporate a special logo or symbol into an existing font so you can use it by pressing a single key. You can create your own bitmapped characters by using Apple's *ResEdit* (resource editor utility), a font-design program such as *Fontastic* by Altsys, or *FontEdit*, which is available in the public domain.

CHOOSING AND USING POSTSCRIPT FONTS

PostScript fonts used with the Mac II can be grouped in two categories: **built-in** (or **resident**) and **downloadable.** Resident fonts have been built into the firmware (ROM) of the typesetting hardware. The LaserWriter Plus and LaserWriter II NT have a total of 35 built-in faces (Figure 18-5). The number of resident fonts of the LaserWriter II NTX can be increased by the addition of a hard disk attached via its SCSI port.

Most of the type for this book was set in resident fonts from Adobe's Palatino family of faces. The faces used, like many of the other resident and built-in fonts manufactured by Adobe Systems, are based on carefully designed, well-established type

Figure 18-5. Samples of the 11 Apple type families built into the LaserWriter Plus and LaserWriter II printers.

Times®
Helvetica®
ITC Zapf Dingbats® ☞✉✗✆✎
Symbol Φ≡π∞
Palatino®
ITC Avant Garde Gothic®
ITC Bookman®
Courier
Helvetica Condensed
New Century Schoolbook
ITC Zapf Chancery® Medium Italic

TIP

More Characters

The "hidden characters" of any font can be accessed by using letter or number keys in combination with the Option or Shift key. The Key Caps desk accessory (see Chapter 19) can help you find them. Here are some useful characters common to many typefaces:

Quotation marks:
- **Opening double "**
  - Option-[
- **Closing double "**
  - Shift-Option-[
- **Opening single '**
  - Option-]
- **Closing single '**
  - Shift-Option-] (apostrophe)

Trademark ™
- Option-2

Copyright ©
- Option-g

Tilde ñ
- Option-n, followed by n.

Accented letter á
- Option-e, followed by the letter to be accented.

Em dash —
- Shift-Option-hyphen; may stand alone or be preceded and followed by a space; used, for example, to separate a word from its definition — or for emphasis, to set off a parenthetical phrase or clause that would otherwise be set off by commas.

En dash –
- Option-hyphen; used between dates (e.g., 1870–1970) or page numbers (e.g., pp. 144–145), for example, to indicate an inclusive span.

families originated by Merganthaler and International Typeface Corporation (ITC).

Several manufacturers in addition to Adobe Systems produce a variety of other typefaces that can be stored on disk and downloaded from the Mac II to the RAM of the typesetting equipment, but Adobe fonts have become the standard for Linotronic imagesetter output, for example. Figure 18-6 shows a few of the downloadable fonts available for PostScript-driven laser printers and typesetting machines.

Installing and Loading PostScript Fonts

Before your Mac II can use a downloadable font, you have to install it. In fact, you have to install both the printer font and the screen font. The icons for screen font files are the same little suitcases used for non-PostScript bitmapped fonts. And you install them in the System file the same way — with the *Font/DA Mover* (see "Installing Bitmapped Fonts" earlier in this chapter). Printer fonts are installed by dragging the printer font icon into the System file or by using an installation utility provided by the font manufacturer.

Once installed, downloadable fonts can be loaded "manually" or automatically. In manual loading, a program specifically designed for that purpose is used to send the PostScript code for the font to the printer's RAM before printing begins. The font remains in RAM until the printer is turned off. In automatic downloading the application used to print the document (*PageMaker* or *Ready,Set,Go!*, for example) downloads the font only when it is needed, and the font leaves the printer's RAM as soon as the text block or file that requires it is "typeset."

If you'll be using a downloadable

Figure 18-6. A variety of downloadable PostScript fonts.

font routinely throughout the day, manual downloading saves printing time, because the font has to be downloaded only once, not each time it's called for. But while the font sits in RAM, it occupies space that therefore can't be used by any other font. So if you typically design documents with a wide variety of fonts, the RAM space may be more valuable to you than the time savings.

The number of fonts you can download for one document is a little unpredictable, because it depends on one constant and several variables. The constant is the amount of memory built into your printer or phototypesetting system. Two of the variables are (a) how much of the memory is occupied by graphics information that has to go on the page you're printing and (b) how the application you're using handles automatic downloading of fonts. For example, *PageMaker* downloads fonts by text block, while *Ready,Set,Go!* downloads all fonts needed to print an entire page. The *PageMaker* method is slower, but it allows you to use more fonts per document.

If you try to use too many fonts in a graphically complex page layout (especially with page–layout applications that download the way *Ready,Set,Go!* does), the page won't print. But your system may spend a long (and, for you, frustrating) time downloading before it runs out of memory and resets itself (at least doubly frustrating).

TIP

Custom Lettering

You can create customized lettering in a page–layout program such as *PageMaker*. This pin-striped font was created by using *PageMaker*'s guidelines to position lines at even intervals over Helvetica lettering and then reversing them with the Reverse line selection from the Line menu:

OVERWEIGHT EXECS

This "invisible" shadowed type was created by placing Helvetica type off center on top of Helvetica bold and then reversing the Helvetica with Reverse type from the Type menu:

GHOST

PostScripting Your Own Fonts

Just as it's possible to design your own bitmapped characters or complete fonts, it's also possible to design PostScript fonts. You can write your own PostScript code — a far greater task than most of us want to tackle. Or you can use one of the application programs such as *Fontographer* that let you create fonts with a typical Macintosh tool set and then convert them to downloadable PostScript files (Figure 18-7).

Figure 18-7. "Gothic Sans" a typeface created by John Odam with *Fontographer*.

Types of Type

Gothic

Gothic faces reflected the local handwriting of Germany, where movable type was developed. Curved forms were kept to a minimum, because it was difficult to produce them by this writing method. This face is ITC Franklin Gothic by Adobe Systems.

Old Style

Lighter and more legible than Gothic, Old Style faces featured triangular serifs. They emphasized the diagonal in their curved strokes, and characters tended to be heavier in their upper left and lower right corners than in their lower left and upper right. This Old Style face is Goudy Old Style by Adobe Systems.

Transitional

Transitional faces emphasized the vertical in their curved strokes rather than the diagonal. Serifs were more horizontal than those of Old Style, and blocks of this type created a lighter "color." This Transitional face is ITC New Baskerville by Adobe Systems.

Modern

Modern faces were developed in the eighteenth century and were influenced by the classical Greek and Roman artistic styles then in vogue. They provide marked contrast between thick and thin strokes and have fine horizontal hairline serifs and long ascenders and descenders. This Modern face is Bodoni by Adobe Systems.

Sans Serif

When the faces couldn't get any fatter without becoming illegible, sans serif faces were developed as something different for advertising. They had no serifs at all, and soon they were being used for text as well. This Sans Serif face is Helvetica, one of the resident LaserWriter fonts.

Script

Script faces were developed to simulate handwritten letterforms. This face is Zapf Chancery by Adobe Systems.

Many kinds of type have evolved to meet the needs of typesetters over the years. The names given to several of these kinds have persisted and have been incorporated into the names of some of today's typefaces.

FONT BASICS

Feeling like the proverbial kid in the candy store? All those fonts available and ready to sample! Here's a gentle caution: Go easy. Use some discretion and restraint. If you use fonts that are too "rich" for your project, or if you try to mix too many fonts in a single document or page layout, the result could be a metaphorical stomach ache. Here are a few pointers for choosing and combining type (Refer to "Types of Type" on page 258 for descriptions of some of the kinds of type available.):

- Any typeface you use should be **legible**. That is, each character should be easy to recognize and distinguish from other characters.
- Type used for blocks of text should be easily **readable**. That is, reading several pages of it shouldn't tire the reader's eyes. Legibility and readability are not the same thing. A sans serif face and a face with serifs may both be very legible, but in general, serif faces are more readable than sans serif. Script faces should generally be restricted to short display lines or to text with addional leading, such as the body copy for an invitation.
- Blocks of type become part of the graphic impression created by a page. Type **color** — that is, the visual impression of a shade of gray created by a block of text — is important to the overall graphic impression created by a document.
- In choosing a typeface, consider any special characters required by the text you'll be setting. Does the copy call for bullets, ligatures (two or more letters joined as a single unit), fractions, or small caps (capital letters that are only as large as the x-height of the face), for example?

TIP

Font Sampler

Would you like a complete look at what's available in PostScript fonts? The *Laser-Sampler* catalog by MacTography, updated several times a year, provides printouts of popular fonts produced by many manufacturers (see the "Publications" appendix at the end of this book).

Chapter 19

Desk Accessories

Sitting on the metaphorical desktop at the far left side of the menu bar is the apple icon, representing the Apple menu of **desk accessories (DAs).** This menu, accessible from the *Finder* and from almost all applications running on the Mac II, presents a list of the DAs, or miniapplications, that have been installed in the System file of the startup disk (Figure 19-1).

DAs can be opened, closed, and moved around the desktop like other Mac windows. How are DAs different from other applications then? Because they're accessible through the Apple menu, they can be used without quitting an application you're currently using and without your working back through the *Finder* to open another application. Working with a DA is like having a second application open on the desktop.

How is using a DA different than using *MultiFinder* with two or more applications running concurrently? Using DAs does not require the memory expansion needed to use *MultiFinder* efficiently. But neither do DAs generally provide as many features as standard application programs.

Using *Font/DA Mover*, you can add DAs to the System file or remove them, as described for fonts in Chapter 18 and in the manual supplied with the Mac II.

Figure 19-1. The apple menu with *Suitcase* accessing more than the standard 15 desk accessories.

TIP

Keeping Track

Pasting the time and date into the header or footer of a word processing document or onto the master page of a page-layout document is a good way to keep track of which is the latest version. This is especially useful if several people are working on the same document. Initials can be added to show not only when the file was last changed, but also who changed it.

THE STANDARD DAs

The Mac II comes with the eight DAs described here, and it allows you to have a total of 15 DAs stored in the System file and displayed under the apple menu. You can add to the ones supplied with the machine and you can remove some of them to make room for still more. You don't need to worry about removing an indispensable DA — some DAs are required by the System, but if you remove them, they'll be replaced automatically. The eight standard DAs are the following:

Figure 19-2. The Alarm Clock, Calculator, and Note Pad DAs.

- **Alarm Clock , Calculator,** and **Note Pad** (Figure 19-2) — These DAs perform functions you would expect from their names. Information produced by any of the three can be cut out and pasted into the documents you create.
- **Chooser** (Figure 19-3) — Any device connected to your Mac II directly (through the printer or modem port) or indirectly (via the AppleTalk network; see Chapter 3) can be accessed through this DA.

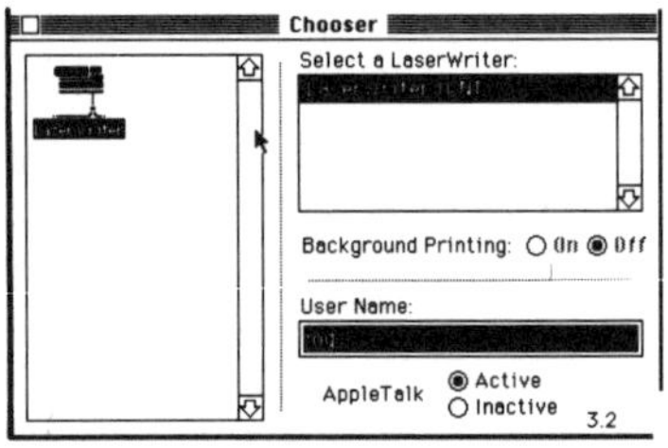

Figure 19-3. The Chooser for a Mac II using the AppleTalk network.

- **Control Panel** (Figure 19-4) — You can use the Control Panel to customize such Mac II characteristics as speaker volume; RAM cache size; rates for repeating keys, menu blinking, and mouse movement; background pattern and color of the desktop; display of time and date; number of colors or grays you want to see on the monitor screen; and relationships between monitors if you have more than one. Chapter 2 provides more information about using the Control Panel.

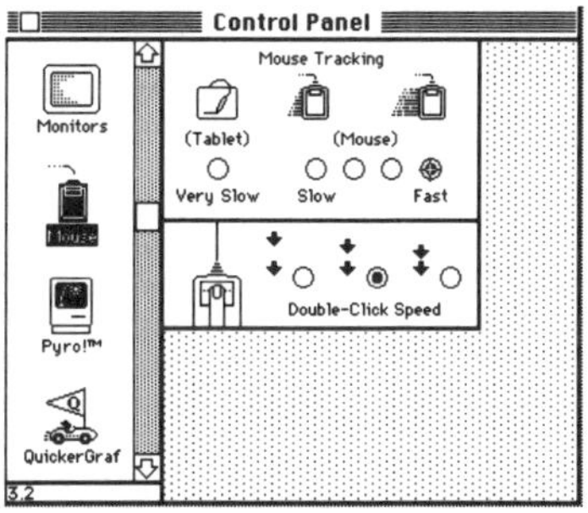

Figure 19-4. Setting the mouse tracking speed in the control panel.

- **Scrapbook** (Figure 19-5)—The Scrapbook DA stores pictures and text in a 256-page Scrapbook file on the startup disk. The Scrapbook can store pictures and text you use often, such as a logo, letterhead, or copyright information. It can also hold a series of selections cut from several documents to paste into a single document you're working on. You can scroll through the Scrapbook page by page to find the selection you want.

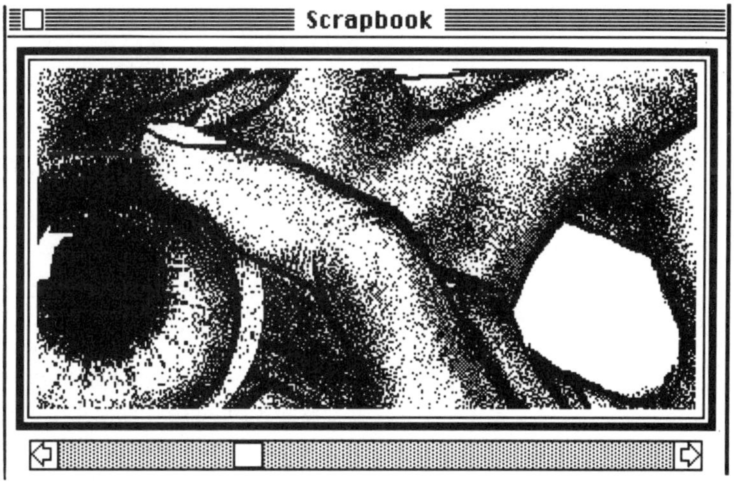

Figure 19-5. A page in the Scrapbook.

- **Find File** (Figure 19-6) — With a hard disk and a hierarchical file system, this DA is invaluable.

Given a keyword or keyword combination, Find File searches your disks to find files and folders whose names include the key. When you choose a name from the list of found files, Find File tells you where it is (in which disk and folder), when it was created and last changed, and how big it is. You can then move the file to the desktop.

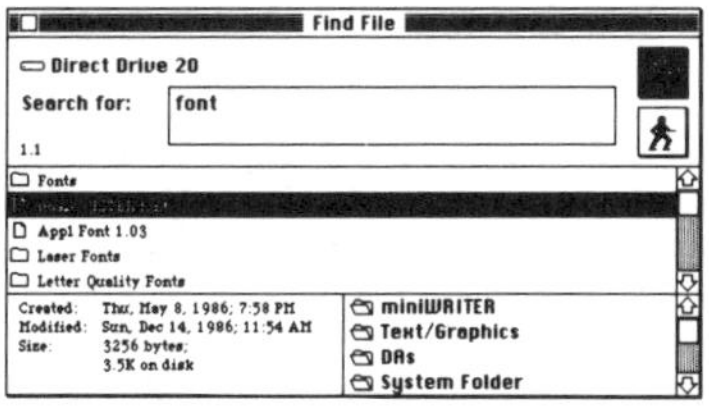

Figure 19-6. Find File at work.

TIP

Scrapbook Organization

The page that appears on the screen when you open the Scrapbook contains the last picture you pasted in, so for best efficiency, store images in the Scrapbook in LIFO (last-in-first-out order). That is, the first picture you paste into the Scrapbook should be the last one you'll place in the document, and so on. That way you won't have to flip through the pages of the Scrapbook looking for the images you need.

- **Key Caps** (Figure 19-7) — Selecting Key Caps and then selecting a font from the Key Caps menu that will appear in the menu bar lets you see the characters from that font that are associated with all the keys. By pressing the Option, Shift, and CapsLock keys, you can change the Key Caps display to show the characters produced by pressing combinations of these along with character keys.

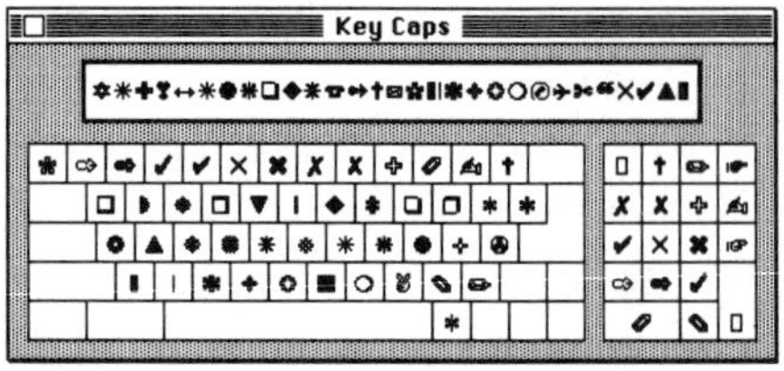

Figure 19-7. Zapf Dingbats font displayed with the Key Caps desk accessory.

(For more complete explanations of the functions of the standard DAs, refer to the *Macintosh II* manual).

DAs FOR MAKING ART

Besides those provided by Apple and supplied with the Mac II, there are many DAs marketed by other software developers. Here are examples of the kinds of DAs that are especially useful for graphic arts tasks:

- ***SmartScrap*** and ***The Clipper*** (sold together)— *SmartScrap* is a replacement for the Scrapbook DA. It has these advantages over the original: (1) It allows you to have as many Scrapbook files as you need; you can make a separate file for each document you're working on, for example. (2) It lets you maintain these multiple Scrapbooks on different disks if you want to. (3) Within a Scrapbook file, it lets you see the whole page, no matter how big it is, by vertical and horizontal scrolling. (4) It provides a pictorial table of contents for each Scrapbook, so that you can make a selection directly instead of scrolling through all of the pages to find it. *The Clipper* lets you make changes (cropping and scaling) to the contents of the Clipboard before you paste the selection into a document.
- ***DeskPaint*** — Providing more features than *MacPaint*, this DA can import, modify, and export paint and TIFF images. It can zoom, rotate, and set gray-scale levels.

- ***Canvas*** — A draw and paint program that comes as both an application and a DA for convenient use with other applications, *Canvas* provides all the features of *MacPaint* and *MacDraw* as well as the ability to edit at several levels of reduction and enlargement and the ability to produce very large (9-foot by 9-foot) drawings (see Chapters 4 and 5 for more information about *Canvas*).
- ***Artisto*** — If you don't have a painting or drawing DA such as *DeskPaint* or *Canvas*, you'll probably want a DA like this one. This shareware DA will open any paint or PICT file and allow you to scroll the entire extent of the file. A scrolling marquee lets you select any part of the file for cutting or copying to the clipboard.
- ***The Curator*** — This DA (also available as an application with more features) provides a table of contents, by name or picture, of all the paint, PICT, TIFF, EPSF, or Glue files in any folder. Double-clicking a picture or name opens its file. Chapter 20 tells more about how to put *The Curator* to work.

TIP

Extra Scrapbooks

You can store extra Scrapbook files on the startup disk by renaming them. For example, you could rename the file that contains clip art assembled for a newsletter "Newsletter Scrapbook." As soon as you rename a Scrapbook file, the System creates a new, empty Scrapbook. When you select Scrapbook from the Apple menu, your Mac II shows you the one currently called "Scrapbook"; so to use a renamed and stored Scrapbook, you first have to rename the current Scrapbook and then change the name of the one you want to use back to "Scrapbook."

DAs FOR DOING CHORES

- ***DiskTop*** and ***DiskTools*** are two competing DAs designed to perform file-handling chores such as renaming, deleting, creating a new folder, and putting files into a folder without your having to leave the application you're working in to return to the *Finder*.
- ***Tempo*** is a DA that lets you program macros, which are series of keyboard or mouse commands that, once programmed, can be accessed by pressing a single key. *Tempo* helps with repetitive chores such as clicking your way through a series of dialog boxes when printing or when formatting characters or paragraphs in a word processor.

MAKING ROOM FOR MORE DAs

Mac users find DAs so useful that many of them want to install more than the 15 they're limited to. Several software developers have come up with ways to do this. For example, ***DA Switcher II*** is a DA that allows you to group the DAs you use with an application into a set for use with that program. There's no limit to the number of sets you can use. *DA Switcher* presents a hierarchical Apple menu that provides a "tree" structure to let you choose the set of DAs you want to implement .

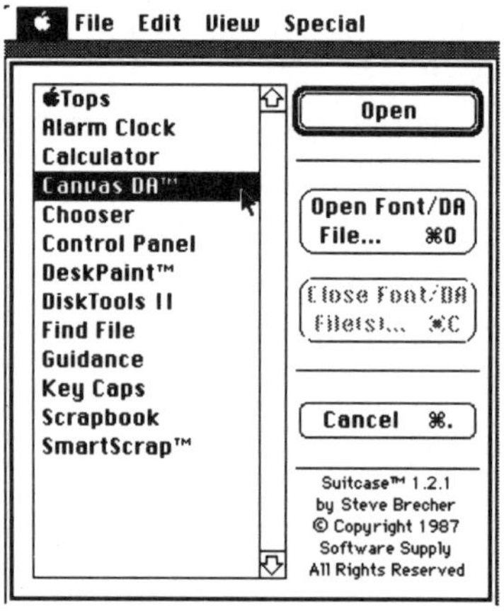

Figure 19-8. *Suitcase* makes it easy to use as many DAs and fonts as you like.

Suitcase itself is not a DA but a program that can be installed in your System folder (Figure 19-8). It automatically opens up fonts and DAs at startup. This provides two advantages. It saves you the time required to install DAs and fonts using *Font/DA Mover*. .And, more important, it circumvents the 15-DA limit, allowing you to use as many DAs (and fonts, too) as you like.

Chapter 20

Clip Art

In the metaphorical Macintosh world the books of clip art traditionally used by commercial artists are represented by disks of images, hand drawn or photographic, ready to clip and incorporate into an original work. Over 30 software developers are now in the business of making and selling clip art on disk and on CD ROM (see Chapter 23, "Mass Storage"). And numerous contributors continue to make clip art available free or as shareware on networks and bulletin boards. Recently, Macintosh clip art by modem is becoming a reality also (see "Mac Clip Art by Subscription" on p. 268).

The first clip art for the Mac was produced in the *MacPaint* (bitmapped) format. *MacPaint*-format clip art consists of original drawings as well as scanned or video-digitized images. These images were created with an inherent resolution of 72 dpi, and without modification they print at that resolution regardless of what printer is used. After bitmapped clip art, came PICT images (which can be produced with *MacDraw* and other QuickDraw-based programs). PICT clip art has the advantage of being resolution (device) independent; that is, the images are printed at the optimal resolution of the printer — 72 dpi for ImageWriter dot matrix printers, 300 dpi for most laser printers, or 2540 dpi for a Linotronic L–300, for example (see Part III). PostScript-based clip art, much of it drawn with *Cricket Draw*, *Adobe Illustrator*, or Aldus *FreeHand*, provides freehand-style images that can be printed at the highest resolution available on any PostScript-driven printer. Gray-scale scanned images and color clip art are becoming available also.

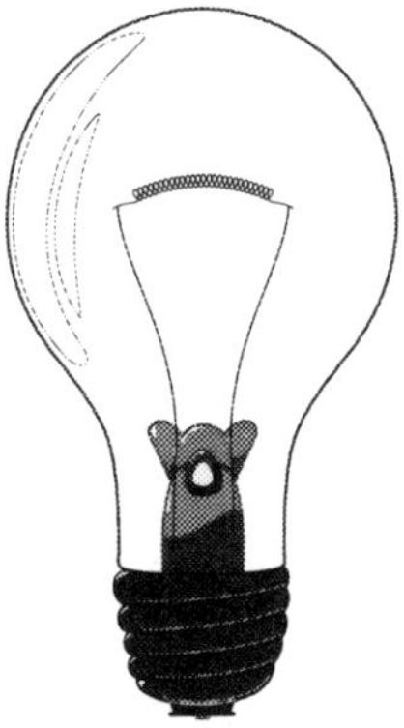

There's more than one way to use electronic clip art on the pages you create with your Mac II. For example, you can import it into the "background" layer of *Adobe Illustrator* to use as a template for an original drawing you create in the

Mac Clip Art by Subscription

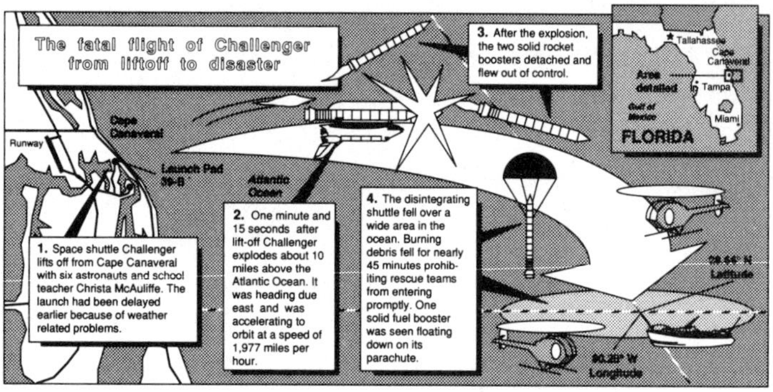

***MacDraw* graphics depicting the Challenger space shuttle disaster, offered by Knight-Ridder through PressLink.**

How do Macintosh users acquire clip art by subscription? Sometimes they use a modem, and sometimes they don't. Individual Mac II users with modems can download public domain and shareware images in all Mac formats (bitmapped, object-oriented, and PostScript, gray-scale and color) from networks such as Compuserve (see Chapter 3). If you don't subscribe to the services of CompuServe or another network, you can still get the best of the public domain clip art, collected and offered on disk at a small cost by public domain distributors (see the "Products" Appendix). Subscription clip art for the Macintosh has also become an important source of graphics for newspapers, through (1) PressLink, Knight-Ridder's network that offers late-breaking news graphics and general-purpose illustrations formatted for newspapers, (2) AP Access, a graphics bulletin board of *MacDraw* art, offered by Associated Press, and (3) Multi-Ad Services' clip art images available by mail. Using AppleLink and a General Electric Information Services telecommunications system, PressLink distributes *MacDraw* diagrams for late-breaking news stories such as the Challenger liftoff disaster in January of 1986 and the Chernobyl nuclear power plant explosion in April of the same year. PressLink users can not only retrieve graphics from the network for their own modification and use, but can also contribute to its development via electronic mail connection. In establishing its similar service, AP has set up the same format and type fonts as PressLink, which will allow graphics from the two systems to be integrated. Multi-Ad Services, originally a publisher of clip art books, advertising art in several sizes delivered to more than half the daily newspapers in the United States, now provides electronic art to subscribers through its Inhouse Graphic Services. A subscription service includes generic and brand-name product art in object-oriented (and therefore scalable) format on CD ROM (see Chapter 23). In addition, subscriber newspapers receive a customized version of Quark's *XPress*, software updates, and a monthly newsletter.

Product clip art supplied to subscribing newspapers with Macs by Multi-Ad Services.

"foreground" (see Chapter 6, "PostScript Illustration"), you can use it in a design comp to indicate the kind of drawing required and its size and position, you can use it in its original form as a part of camera-ready copy, or you can import it into a program such as *PixelPaint* and color it. Figure 20-1 shows several examples of clip art in use. Whichever way you use clip art, you'll find it a far more pleasant experience if you're efficient in organizing, storing, and manipulating the pictures.

Figure 20-1. An example of clip art used to produce final artwork by Steve Brown.

TIP

Protecting Clip Art

Before you modify clip art images, lock the file that contains the original images, making it a "read only" file, so you won't accidentally destroy the commercial image as you experiment with customizing it. Use Get Info from the desktop File menu to bring up the dialog box that lets you lock the file.

After locking the disk or file, use the Save As function from the File menu to make a copy of the file, and do all your customizing in that file.

Locking clip art files protects them from unintentional changes.

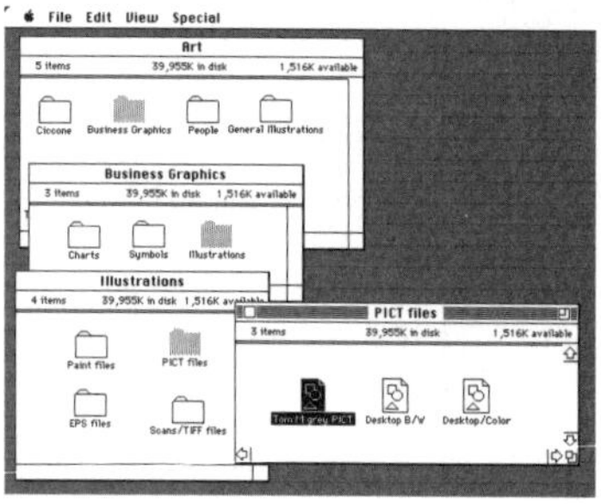

Figure 20-2. Clip art organized in nested folders by subject, type of illustration, and file format.

CLIP ART MANAGEMENT

As it arrives on your desk, commercially produced clip art is, of course, organized according to who manufactured it — the images on a particular disk were all put there by the same developer, though they may span many subject areas. But when you use the clip art pictures, you'll probably be looking for specific subject matter, perhaps in a specific style (silhouette, line drawing, scanned photograph, etc.), and you probably won't care which developer produced which image. Although most manufacturers name their clip art documents to reflect the kinds of images they include and many provide manuals with reduced printouts to show the pictures, it can be difficult to keep mental track of all the images you have (Don't I have a picture of a downhill skier in motion?) and where they're located (I must have three pictures of people sitting at computer consoles, but which disks are they on?). Here are some suggestions for reorganizing your clip art so you can keep track of it easily:

- On your hard disk or on floppies, regroup your clip art images into folders by subject (animals, plants, office implements, etc.) and within folders into files organized by drawing type (silhouettes, line drawings, photographs etc.) or some other criterion you find useful (Figure 20-2). Then print a page of miniature images of all the files in each folder. This can be done for *MacPaint* images with the Print Catalog function, which prints miniatures (at 72 dpi) of all the *MacPaint* documents within the folder or disk you're working in. *Widgets*, a desk accessory, allows you to print miniatures at higher resolution than Print Catalog, providing

Paint pictures from "Human Forms:"

Figure 20-3. A *Widgets* printout of the files in a clip art folder.

a clearer picture of what the art looks like (Figure 20-3). These prints can then be stored in a looseleaf notebook.

- Use a graphics index, a graphics data base, or a *HyperCard* stack to organize and cross-reference your clip art images. Then you can find an appropriate image for a particular project by searching the index, data base, or stack. "Using a Graphics Index or Graphics Data Base" on p. 272 and "Using *HyperCard* as a Graphics Data Base" below describe ways to use such programs with clip art.
- If you don't have graphics indexing software and you don't want to take the time to regroup your clip art by subject, photocopy the image printouts provided in documentation that comes with each clip art package. For those packages without this kind of documentation and for public domain clip art and your own files of images, print out each file (page of images) on an 8-1/2-by-11 sheet. Compile all these sheets in a looseleaf notebook. If a file doesn't include a printed notation of its name or which disk it's from, either add the name and location to the file and Save it before

Using *HyperCard* as a Graphics Data Base

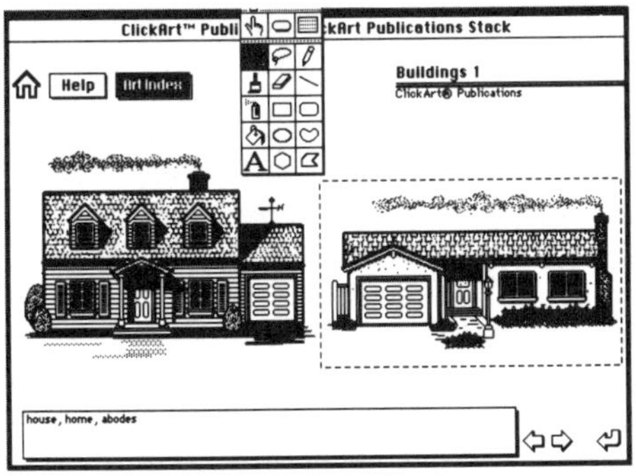

A *HyperCard* stack can be used to store graphic images along with keywords and invisible buttons for cross-referencing to other, related images (see Chapter 22, "Stacks"). *HyperCard* was originally designed to store graphic information in a 72-dpi format only. However, ways have been developed to store PICT and PostScript formats also. Even if 72-dpi paint is the only format you can store, you can track other kinds of clip art images by making cards listing the subject, keywords, and locations (file, folder, and disk) of your nonpaint images and providing access through buttons. Unfortunately, *HyperCard's* index card metaphor limits the size of the images you can store this way. But *HyperCard* offers an advantage over such programs as *Graphidex* and *PictureBase* by providing a full set of graphics editing tools within the graphics data base. Some software developers are now providing clip art in *HyperCard* stack form.

A card from a *HyperCard* clip art stack, *ClickArt Publications* by T/Maker.

Using a Graphics Index or Graphics Data Base

A graphics index or picture data base allows you to find an image easily by appearance, title, or keyword, and copy all or part of it into the document you're working on in a page-layout program, for example. If the index or data base exists in DA form, you can search, copy, and paste without leaving the page-layout application. In general, an

A *Graphidex* graphics index record.

index will be most helpful if your images are stored on several floppy disks, while a data base will help most if you have plenty of hard disk capacity for your clip art.

Graphidex is an example of a picture index. It exists as both an application and a DA. *Graphidex* indexes pictures by name and location. It can index (or convert to fonts) up to 50 *MacPaint* documents or 100 *MacDraw* files at one pass, cataloging images on the fly from any application that supports the clipboard. It searches documents, locating the pictures they contain and reading their file names automatically.

A *PictureBase* graphics data base record.

This saves you time and effort, because you can collect and reorganize your clip art images without having to copy, paste, and save them individually. The font-making capability of *Graphidex* allows you to place images with a single key stroke. This is especially useful for storing symbols used repeatedly in a layout, for example. The program provides a few tools for editing graphics. Unfortunately, *Graphidex* has no keyword feature; it searches by name only.

PictureBase is an example of a graphics data base. It creates a library of images through the File menu. Each library can hold 5500 pictures of up to 32 K each. To each *PictureBase* entry, you can add title, keywords, and up to 32 K of notes. Once a library is formed, you can search for an image by its name, a keyword, or a fraction of a keyword. Or you can use *PictureBase's* Catalog window, which shows the image most recently added to each library and allows you to page through the library like a Scrapbook. You can then use *PictureBase* to copy images into the clipboard. In addition to its own libraries, *PictureBase* can display any paint or PICT files on the disk associated with the active window. The program has proven useful enough so that some clip art developers are offering clip art in *PictureBase* format as an option; the images are already titled, provided with keywords, and collected into *PictureBase* libraries. Perhaps the most useful of the index or data base art managers is ***The Curator,*** also in application and DA form. It combines features of *Graphidex* and *PictureBase,* and it provides cataloging and access to works in more graphics formats: *MacPaint,* PICT (*MacDraw*), TIFF (scanned), EPSF (*Illustrator*), and Glue (*PageMaker, Ready,Set,Go!,* and *Excel*). It can also import IBM PC EPSF files and can extract images from *Picture-Base* libraries.

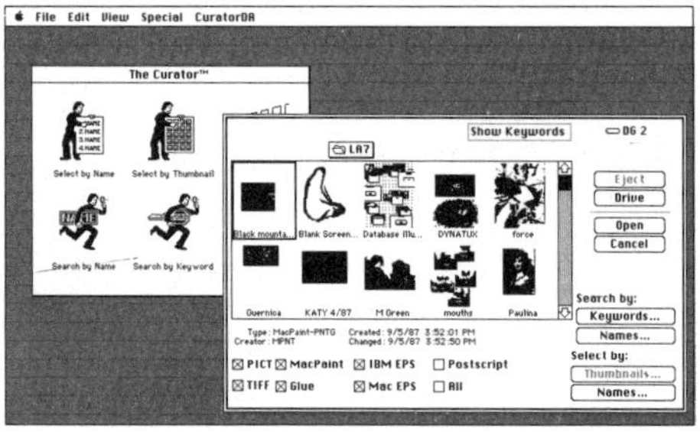

***The Curator* graphics organizer in action.**

printing, or note file and disk names in ink on the printed pages. Within your notebook, group the pages by subject (for example, animals, business activities, sports, etc.), and use tabbed dividers to separate the subjects.

> TIP
>
> **If You Can't Use *MultiFinder***
>
> PostScript-based *Adobe Illustrator* does not support cut and paste into other applications such as *PageMaker*. This means you can't take full advantage of *MultiFinder*'s ability to switch between *Illustrator* and other applications for quick transfer of images. Instead, images can be saved as encapsulated PostScript files, which can then be opened from *PageMaker*.

MANIPULATING AND MOVING

To use clip art you must locate the image, copy it, possibly modify it, and finally paste it onto your page. If you've organized and stored your clip art well, locating the image will be no problem. To copy the image you'll use the clipboard and perhaps the Scrapbook. Modification is done with the appropriate paint, draw, or PostScript-based tools, and the clipboard is used once again to cut the image and paste it into (usually) a page makeup program.

Some programs (*PageMaker 3.0*, for example) allow extended manipulation of certain types of images — changing brightness or contrast or adding line screens or color, for example — even after the art is pasted into the page layout.

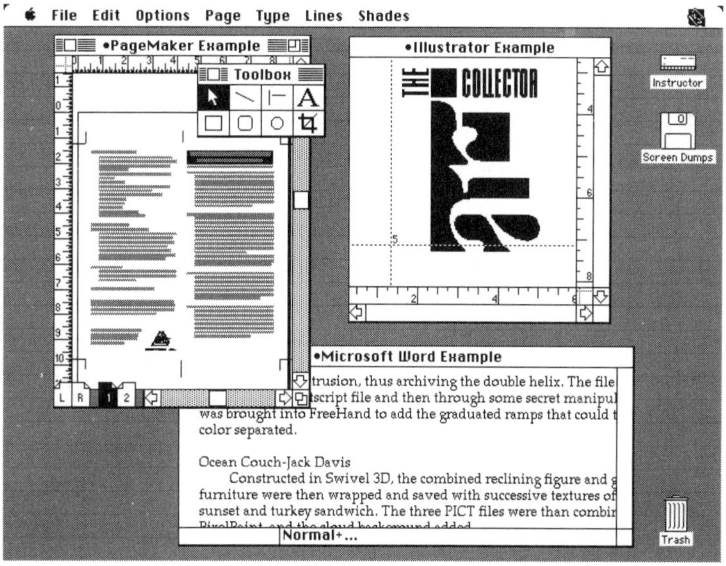

Figure 20-4. *Illustrator, Word 3.0,* and *PageMaker* open on the desktop at the same time, running under *MultiFinder,* Apple's multitasking application.

Moving Clip Art Efficiently

Quitting one application and opening the next as you copy, modify, and finally paste your clip art can get very tiresome. But there are several ways to make these processes more convenient. Here are some examples:

- If you have enough memory to use *MultiFinder* (see "System Software" in Chapter 1), you can open several applications on the desktop at once, so you can easily move from a full-function graphics program (to import and

TIP

Keeping Track of Your Images

If you modify a commercial clip art image, store the modified version in your clip art storage system along with the original. That way it will be easy to find if you need it again.

modify the clip art) to a page makeup program (for final modification and placement). For example, you might open *SuperPaint* for paint or draw images, Microsoft *Word* for word processing, and *PageMaker* for page layout (Figure 20-4). That way you won't have to go through the process of quitting one application and selecting and opening another each time you need to cut or paste an illustration.

- Several graphics programs have desk accessory (DA) versions, usually with fewer features than the full program, but with enough tools to be very functional. By choosing such a DA from the apple menu, you can bypass the process of quitting one application and opening another: the DA is used to copy and modify the image, and to store the modified image on the clipboard or in the Scrapbook. Some DAs that may be especially useful for managing clip art are *DeskPaint*, *Canvas*, *SuperScrap*, *The Curator*, and *FindFile*. Chapter 19, "Desk Accessories," discusses these and other kinds of DAs and how to install and use them.

Using Clipboard and Scrapbook

If you're using a single clip art image in the document you're creating, the clipboard alone, accessed via the Edit menu, can store the image as you move it from clip art file to page-layout program. If you'll be using several clip art images, it makes sense to copy and modify them as needed, and then store

Figure 20-5. **a**. Dove and stained glass window from *Click Art Christian Images* by T/Maker. **b**. A Mac II and some abstract logos from *Click Art Business Images* by T/Maker. **c**. A seashell frpm *SGS Nature Art*. **d**. A bitmapped old-fashioned office scene from *DeskTop Art Graphics*.

them in the Scrapbook. Then they can be cut and pasted from Scrapbook to page-layout program. Chapter 19 tells more about using the Scrapbook and other Scrapbooklike DAs.

MACPAINT-FORMAT CLIP ART

Developers of *MacPaint*-format clip art have produced collections that range from dingbats to full-page mouse-drawn images to video-digitized subjects. Figure 20-5 shows some of the types of images available. Figure 20-6 shows samples from some unique, specialized clip art collections.

Although *MacPaint*-format clip art is to date the most plentiful type and provides some very interesting and applicable images, most graphic artists would agree that the 72-dpi *MacPaint* format does not look sharp enough to use in final copy. Consequently, this kind of clip art is usually reduced before printing. A good way to reduce it is to import the image into a program such as *SuperPaint**that can translate it to a PICT file and then reduce that, producing smoother-looking lines and curves, and with minimal distortion of the image.

Figure 20-6. a. and **d.** Selections from the *WetPaint* clip art collection by Dubl–Click Software. **b.** "The Doctor of Dreams" from *Mac the Knife, Volume 5* by Miles Computing. **c.** A selection from *Japanese Clip Art* by Enzan-Hoshigumi. **e.** Ben Franklin, a scanned illustration in the public domain.

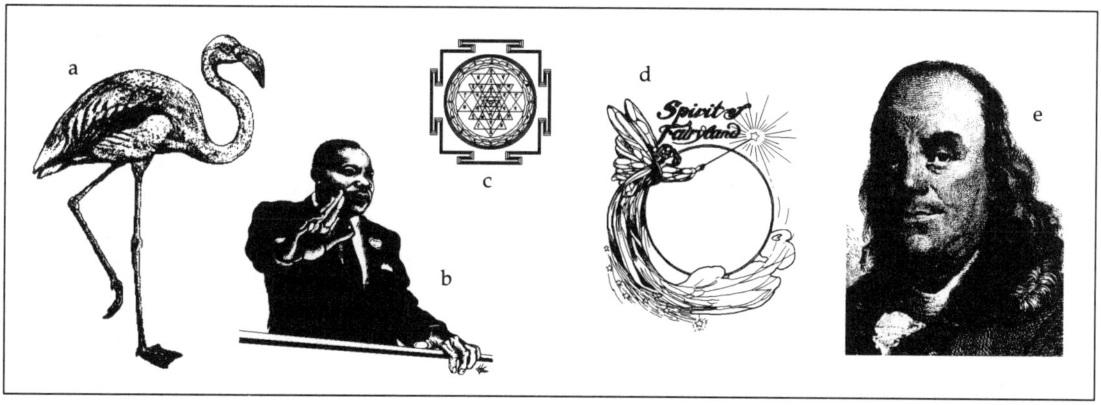

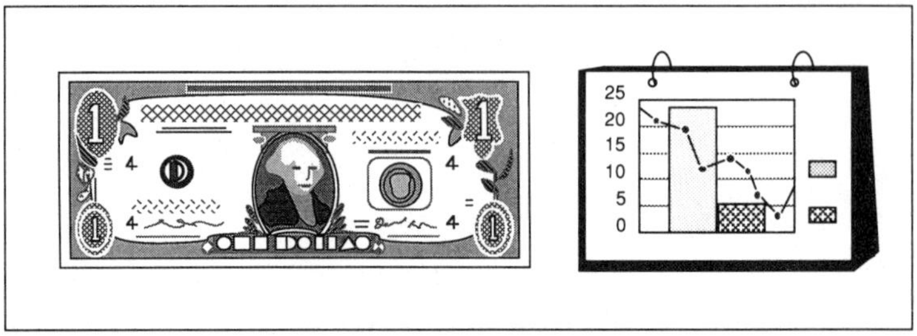

Figure 20-7. PICT clip art: "Money" and "Presentation" from *DrawArt Volume 2* by Desktop Graphics.

When you import MacPaint-format clip art (or your own *MacPaint*-format art for that matter) into a document you plan to print on a printer with higher resolution than 72 dpi, certain reductions give you better results than others. For example, the 300–dpi resolution of the LaserWriter is not an exact multiple of 72 dpi. To get a printed image in which each *MacPaint*-format dot is represented by 16 laser dots (in a 4 x 4 array), the imported image must be reduced to 96 percent of its original size. Reduction to 72 percent results in a 3 x 3 laser dot representation for each original dot, to 48 percent, a 2 x 2 representation, and to 24 percent a 1-dot representation.

Figure 20-8. "Nude," a PICT file, by José Ciccone from *PostArt* by Olduvai Software.

Figure 20-9. Clip art from *Click Art PostScript Images* by T/Maker.

PICT AND POSTSCRIPT FORMATS

Figures 20-7 and 20-8 are examples of PICT clip art. Figure 20-9 shows PostScript clip art. Figure 20-10 is an encapsulated PostScript clip art image before and after modification with *Adobe Illustrator*.

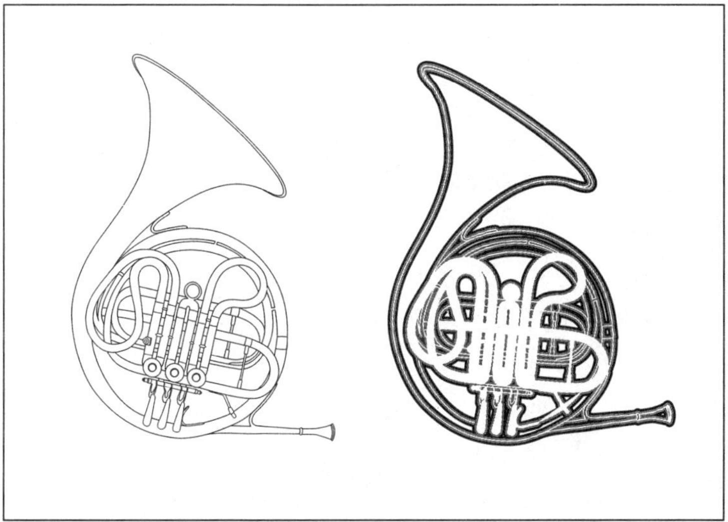

Figure 20-10. A clip art French horn from Adobe, before (left) and after modification by John Odam with *Adobe Illustrator*.

TIP

Perfect Resizing

The *PageMaker* page-layout program provides an easy way to reduce 72-dpi bit maps to the percentages appropriate for your final printout. You simply hold down the Command and Shift keys while resizing, and the graphic image is reduced in the proportional steps best for the printer you've chosen. Even if you're resizing a single image for a logo, for example, and have no need for page-layout features, importing the clip art into *PageMaker* makes sense. If you plan to print your file on a printer other than the kind attached to your Mac II — for example, if your computer is connected to a LaserWriter Plus but you plan to take your disk to an imagesetting service for final output on a Linotronic machine —remember to set the Chooser in your apple menu to the proper Linotronic printer before you resize images this way.

GRAY-SCALE AND COLOR CLIP ART

Scanned and video-digitized images are becoming available as gray-scale and color clip art. Used as is, or modified with an application such as *ImageStudio* or *Digital Darkroom* (see Chapter 7, "Digitizing"), gray-scale images can be pasted into a layout and output at whatever resolution the printer can produce up to the resolution of the image file itself. *MacDraw II* and *PixelPaint* allow modification of color clip art. Figure 20-11 shows an example of gray-scale clip art. 3D clip art, such as Enabling Technologies' *Clip3D*, is also available.

Figure 20-11. Gray-scale clip art from Gold Mine Publishing.

CHAPTER 21

Templates

Engineers, architects, and drafters use metal or plastic templates to generate geometric shapes and symbols they use over and over. Like these traditional tools, templates designed for use with graphic arts software offer speed, convenience, and the benefit of someone else's design and crafting abilities. Templates for use with the Mac are typically forms (for cards of various sizes, stationery, envelopes, newsletters, and so forth) that are designed to be imported into a popular application program so that you can "pour" your own text or artwork into them.

MAC TEMPLATES

Within the Mac graphics realm, templates exist for both graphics and page-layout software. They were developed to help users design greeting cards, business cards, business forms, and other printed products.

Aldus Corporation's *PageMaker Portolio: Designs for Newsletters* was the first set of design models for Macintosh page-layout software. It includes 21 sample newsletter designs on two disks, with a manual that explains (very well) how and why the designs work; how to incorporate copy, headlines, and artwork to make your own newsletters using the templates; and how to customize the templates for your own purposes. Designed for desktop publishers without a lot of graphic design experience, the package also explains

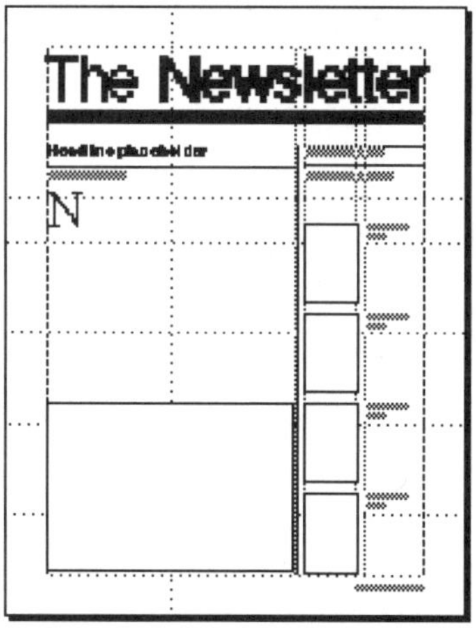

Figure 21-1. A *PageMaker* newsletter template (a sophisticated version).

TIP

Templates for Undersize Sheets

One kind of useful template you can make in *PageMaker* or another page-layout application is a position indicator for an undersized page such as a postcard or even a business card. By experimenting with your laser printer and the page-layout software, you can arrive at a template to hold text and graphics so that the print will be properly positioned on a manually fed undersized sheet.

how to create and use spacing guides, boxes and rules, mastheads, ID lines, deck heads, kickers, captions, picture insets, calendar pages, pull quotes, large initial letters, jumplines, and ragged bottom margins. The manual explains the use of 2-, 3-, 4-, and 5-column grids, and templates are provided for primary, easy, and sophisticated versions of seven basic newsletter layouts.

Today there are more templates for *PageMaker* and other graphics and page-layout programs. Figures 21-1 and 21-2 show some examples.

Figure 21-2. A *GraphicWorks* menu template.

MAKING YOUR OWN TEMPLATES

Making your own templates is partly just a matter of recognizing that the products you generate have potential for future projects also. If you design a piece of a certain size and shape (a business form or postcard, for example) that you like and may want to use again, you can file it as a template.

CHAPTER 22

Stacks

HyperCard, introduced in Chapter 1 and discussed in Chapter 20 as a storage medium for clip art, is an application that allows you to link information in a **nonlinear** manner. To get an idea of nonlinear as opposed to linear treatment of information, think about some of the reading you do. A novel is written to be read in a linear fashion. The reader usually begins at the beginning and proceeds through the book, reading left to right on each line, up to down on each succeeding page, front to back from the first chapter to the last. A magazine, on the other hand, is nonlinear. When you read it, you may read the pages in order, but you're much more likely to look at the story lines on the cover or the listing in the table of contents, find the page number of an article you're particularly interested in, and then turn right to that article, skipping other articles and advertisements to get there. And when you've finished reading that article, you may go back to the table of contents to find another one, or you may browse through the pages or return to something else of interest that you noticed while you were reading the first article. While the chapters of a novel are linked for the reader by a continuing story line, magazine articles are linked by the table of contents and by their physical position on the pages. Usually, the links are not as tight in a magazine as they are in a novel. Now think of one other kind of reading material — the "choose your own adventure" type of novel for children. This kind of story has a plot that branches several times and allows the reader to make a decision at each branch point about which path to follow. Each path through the book results in a different way to get to a final resolution of the story, and there are usually several possible outcomes.

Figure 22-1. A card from the MacRecorder tutorial stack.

Of these three types of reading material, a *HyperCard* stack is more similar to the magazine or the "choose your own adventure" than to the standard novel — but the linking possibilities are even more extensive, and the links are accomplished with lightning speed. With *HyperCard*, as in your mind, any piece of information can be directly connected to any other piece.

HyperCard's basic unit of information is called a **card**. A card fills the screen. It can contain information in the form of text, still or animated pictures, sounds, and communication links to other media. A collection of cards is called a **stack. Buttons** are built-in areas of the screen that can be clicked to call other cards to the screen. The **Home card** of a stack works like the table of contents of a magazine, serving as a place to start and a base to return to. But you can also browse through the stack.

The "writer" of a *HyperCard* stack can make the linking system within a stack very apparent or quite obscure, depending on what the stack is designed to do. At its core *HyperCard* is basically a very powerful and flexible data base program. A stack that's designed as a kind of data base to organize and present information usually has very obvious buttons and logical links, so that the user can easily understand how to get from one piece of infomation to another. The card metaphor is usually also very obvious, with information organized screen by screen. On the other hand, in a stack designed as a poem, a story, or an animated artwork, for example, the stack-of-cards metaphor may not be apparent at all; buttons may be invisible or may be pressed automatically.

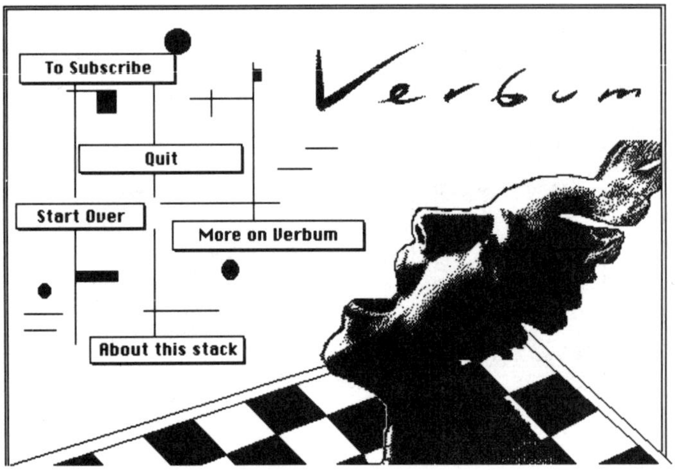

Figure 22-2. A card from the *Verbum* Journal promotional stack.

SAMPLE STACKS

Some of the kinds of stacks that might be of special interest to graphic artists are the following:

- Help and tutorial stacks for some graphics programs are packaged with the software itself (Figure 22-1), and others exist within the public domain.
- Promotional stacks provide information about publications or other products (Figure 22-2).
- Some stacks serve as reference books of general information or of processes and procedures (Figure 22-3).
- As an art form, stacks can provide an animated, soundtracked format for everything from poetry to "light shows" to interactive adventure stories (Figure 22-4).

Figure 22-4. The "title card" from one of the AmandaStories, a series of interactive stacks that can be enjoyed by prereaders as well as readers.

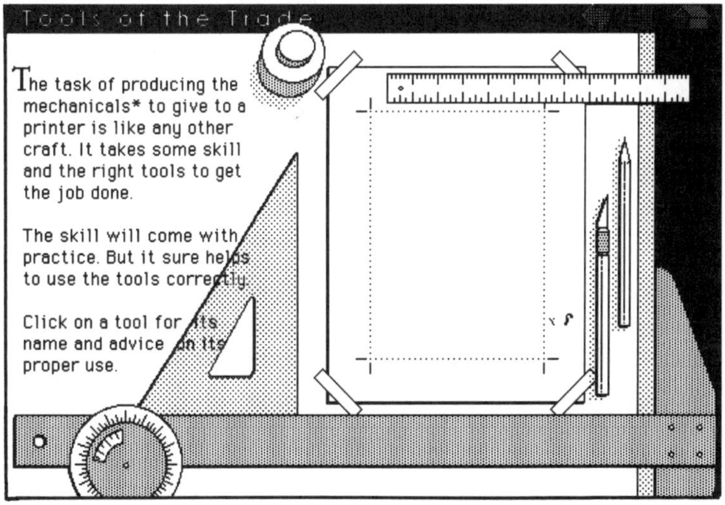

Figure 22-3. A card from the *DTP Advisor* stack, an informative stack about desktop publishing.

MAKING YOUR OWN STACKS

HyperCard is so inexpensive that it's nearly free. It comes with its own artist's tools and prefabbed buttons and an instruction manual that tells how to script your own stacks, invent your own buttons, and so forth. For a complete treatment of programming with *HyperCard*, refer to Danny Goodman's *The Complete HyperCard Handbook* (listed in the "Publications" Appendix).

THE FUTURE OF STACKS

In the future, *HyperCard* is likely to be very useful as a "front end" for CD ROM and other mass storage media that hold hundreds of thousands of megabytes of data. Without a means of linking and quick access to specific bits of stored information, these masses of data would be about as useful as an encyclopedia without table of contents, index, or alphabetization. In addition, *HyperCard* may serve as a controller for interactive video and a way of linking computer, video, music, and other electronic media.

CHAPTER 23

Mass Storage

Ever notice how the amount of paper scattered on your desk expands to match the size of that desk? The same thing is true of computer systems. The more work we do, the more space we need to store that work and the tools we use to do it. Fortunately, the price of such storage has been decreasing, even as the demand increases. This chapter describes the different storage options available, from the most commonly used hard disks to the cutting edge technology of CD ROM, as well as strategies for backing up your work, and finishing up with utilities and tools specific to these large storers of information.

HARD DISKS

Hard disks are simply rigid magnetic disks that can store a large amount of information and get at any of it quickly. The smallest commonly available disk stores about 20 megabytes (Mb) of information. For reference, this is the equivalent of 25 800 K (kilobyte) floppy disks. Most hard disks for the Mac II use the faster SCSI ("scuzzy") port (rather than the serial port) of the computer, and that's the kind you want to get.

The Mac II can use two different types of hard disks: internal and external. Internal disks are usually slightly less expensive and slightly faster at locating files. External drives can be moved from machine to machine easily. (Be aware, though, that some disks that have been optimized to run quickly on a Mac II may not work with other machines.)

Here are a few of the proven and reliable manufacturers of hard disks:

Jasmine sells most of their drives directly through the mail. Jasmine drives are good, reliable, and inexpensive. The company has a history of handling problems well and relatively quickly. Jasmine drives are currently shipped with a large collection of public domain software as well as two useful commercial packages. The external disks have two surge-protected power outlets on the back for other devices. In addition to hard disks, Jasmine sells tape backup units and large floppy drives.

SuperMac makes good drives and ships them with excellent software. Included with each drive is a copy of *SuperLaserSpool*, a print spooler designed to process printing in the background while you continue to work (see Chapter 10). Also included is the *DiskFit* backup software (see "Backup" later in this chapter). The SuperMac drives are sold through dealers and are more expensive then their Jasmine counterparts, but the included software makes them competitive. In the mass storage lines, SuperMac sells hard disks, tape backup units, and software.

Apple drives are good and reliable, but are priced well over the rest of the market.

REMOVABLE MEDIA

The term **removable media** means devices whose recording medium is designed to be removed and replaced. These include removable Winchester drives, Bernoulli drives, and large floppies. These units are useful for both day-to-day use and backup. They all tend to be slower than their fixed-in-place relatives.

Removable Winchesters

Removable Winchester drives have the same type of disk used in normal hard disks, but in a removable case. They're usually large, running 20 to 40 Mb per disk, and they're just as fragile as the fixed disks — perhaps even more so, because of the lack of the protective casing. They're also expensive compared to both of the other removable technologies.

Bernoulli Technology

A Bernoulli disk is basically a large, extremely thin disk in a plastic case that rides on a powerful cushion of air. The disks are relatively inexpensive and usually hold 10 to 20 megabytes apiece. The disadvantages are the relatively short lifespan of the disks (a bit less than a year) and the noise that results from the fan needed to generate the necessary air flow. The technology has been around for several years and is fairly reliable.

Large Floppies

The most recent addition to mass storage technology is the large floppy. These look like, act like, and in fact *are* larger versions of standard Mac floppies. They're about four times the standard size and store 10 Mb of information. The disks cost about $30 a piece and seem to be sturdy. This technology hasn't been in the market long enough to say whether the disks have a longer life than their Bernoulli cousins, but initial experiences have been good.

BACKUP

A few words of warning about hard disks and other mass storage media: They're physically delicate, and can be destroyed or damaged if hit too hard while they're running, or dropped even when they're not. Even with this physical susceptibility as well as the possibility of losing lots of files with a nonphysical accident of some sort, there's a tendency to not back up a hard disk (periodically copy the contents onto floppy disks for safekeeping) because it's perceived as a lot of work. But losing a hard disk that hasn't been backed up can be as devastating as losing your studio or office in a fire.

Backup seems to be the easiest concept in computers to understand and the hardest to learn. The most important part of using a mass storage device is keeping at least one up-to-date backup. The best way to accomplish this seems to be to set up a regularly scheduled backup procedure.

Floppies

The least expensive method of backup is also the most difficult. Maintaining an up-to-date set of floppy disks with the entire contents of your hard disk (or equivalent) takes time. If you figure that an 800 K disk takes about a minute and a half to fill under the best of circumstances, you can imagine how long it could take to back up a 40 or 80 Mb hard disk. There are, fortunately, many programs that make this process a bit easier. Some of them use what's called an **incremental backup**. This means that once the initial backup is made, any subsequent backups will simply reflect the changes that have been made to the disk since the last backup. The second method is called **filtering**. This is basically a method of backing up only files of a certain type. For example, you may choose to back up only documents and not applications. Since most of the applications probably came from floppies in the first place, you essentially already have a backup of those applications, and it makes sense not to back them up again. *HFS Backup* and *DiskFit* are two excellent examples of backup software that's been around long enough to be reliable.

HFS Backup (see Figure 23–1) has been commercially available for several years. It's flexible and reliable, but harder to use than *DiskFit*.

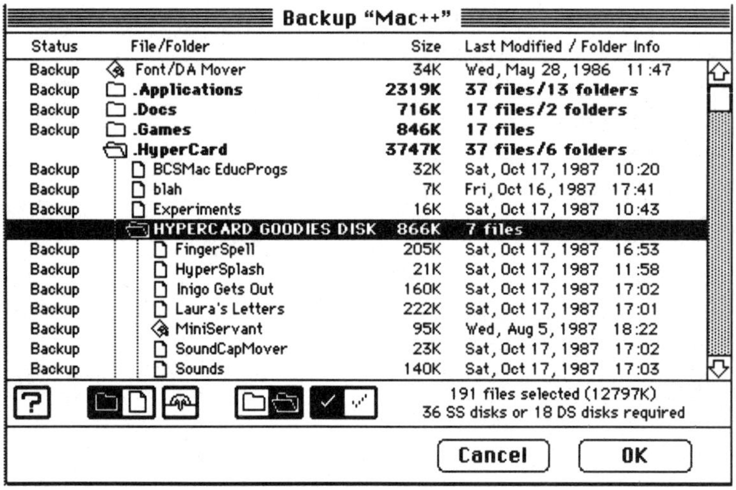

DiskFit is shipped with all SuperMac Dataframe drives and tape units. It's also sold separately in both individual and network versions. *DiskFit*'s main claim to fame is that it's incredibly easy to use. It can be used with floppies, tapes, and large floppies.

Figure 23–1. The *HFS Backup* program at work.

Tape Backup

Tape backup units are essentially tape recorders that archive information from a disk to a compact equivalent of a cassette tape. They are, on the average, not significantly faster than floppies for backing up. Their primary advantage is that they don't need the constant attention it takes to feed multitudes of floppies into the machine. Most tape units are very similar mechanically but very different in the software that runs them. Most tape drives are based on the DC2000 cartridge unit, so if the software were consistent, all these different tape drives could interchange their tapes. But this isn't the case. The software for the current generation of drives is all different and mostly bad. For example, the NuData tape appears on the desktop as if it were just another disk. You can even run a program from the tape itself. (If you ever want to kill a tape, that's a great way to do it.) On the other hand, the Apple tape doesn't appear on the desktop, but instead appears inside a very confusing special-purpose program. Once the software goes through a few generations, tapes could be a good backup alternative.

CD ROM

CD ROM is the mass storage wave of the future, perhaps especially for clip art collections of gray-scale and color pictures and sounds. CD ROM stands for Compact Disk Read Only Memory. CD ROM uses essentially the same technology as musical compact disks. The best way to think of them is as extremely large floppy disks that you can never write to or change. The reason CD ROM is important to the Mac II artist is that mastering and producing such disks is so inexpensive that disk collections of art and sound will become available in ever increasing numbers. Several companies have already started manufacturing and shipping Mac-compatible CD ROM drives.

> **TIP**
>
> **More on Mass Storage**
>
> More information about mass storage systems can be found in *Hard Disk Management for the Macintosh* by Bencion Calica and Charles Rubin. In addition to the topics covered in this chapter, their book covers disk organization and troubleshooting.

WORM DRIVES

WORM drives are one step beyond CD ROM drives. This currently expensive technology allows the user to write to a removable 800+ Mb drive. The hitch is that once something is written to the disk it can never be erased. Hence the name WORM (Write Once Read Many). WORM drives are an interim technology until read/write optical disks are developed. But if you have extremely large amounts of data that you want to archive permanently, a WORM drive is a good solution.

MASS STORAGE UTILITIES

There are several kinds of software utilities that are specifically useful for getting the most from hard disks. ***Finder*** **alternatives** are organizers designed to help you get to the files you use on your hard disk quickly and easily. The most common are *PowerStation* (see Figure 23-2) and *Oasis*.

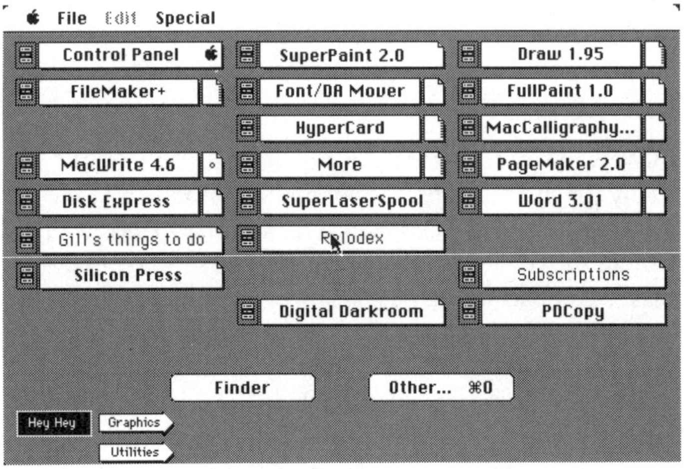

Figure 23-2. *Power Station*, a *Finder* alternative.

Disk optimizers are designed to increase disk performance and reliability. Using a disk optimizer is analogous to tuning up a car. The most popular of the disk optimizers is *Disk Express* (see Figure 23-3).

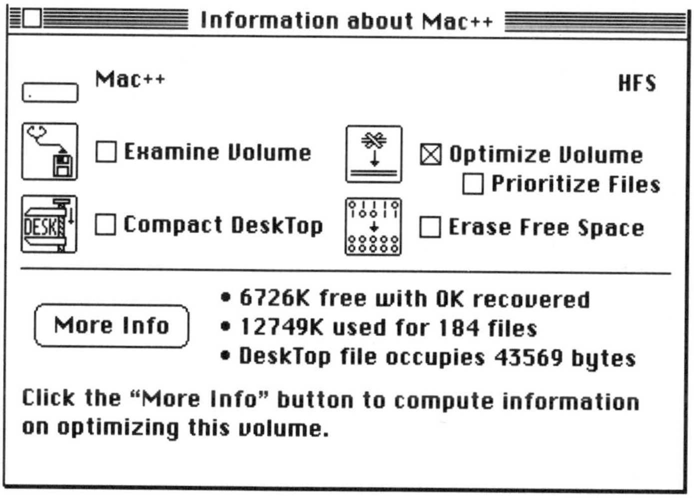

Figure 23-3. *Disk Express,* a disk optimizer program for "tuning up" your hard disk.

Recovery tools can be used when you have a problem such as a disk crash or a file that gets deleted accidentally. Recovery tools have little programs called Inits that you put into your System folder before a problem occurs. It's important to have at least one such Init file installed, as only the files added or changed after these programs are installed can be reliably recovered. The ***MacTools*** recovery tools software is proven and reliable. ***SUM,*** which stands for Symantac Utilities for Macintosh is new, but also very promising.

Chapter 24

Other Input Devices

The Macintosh and the mouse are as conceptually inseparable as painting and brushes. over time, the mouse has proven to be exceptionally popular and versatile, not only as a selecting pointer, but also as an artist's tool. Despite any shortcomings it may have, and despite mouse-doomsday predictions by makers of mouse substitutes, the mouse endures. Other computer manufacturers have adopted it, and whole companies successfully rely on mouse sales for their livelihood.

TABLETS

Electronic tablets have emerged as alternative devices to handle the graphics tasks for which the mouse is indeed cumbersome. A tablet consists of a position-sensing surface and a freely movable hand-held cursor, pen, or see-through puck, whose precise location the tablet surface senses. Tablets offer the capability of absolute positioning, which relates each point on the tablet with a corresponding point on the Mac screen. Instead of rolling to an area, you place the movable pointer on a spot on the tablet to make the on-screen cursor jump to the related spot on the screen.

Tracing drawings originally rendered on paper and simulating the natural motion of an artist's paintbrush are two typically cited reasons for abandoning the reliable rodent for the tablet, at least temporarily. Using a tablet simplifies the tracing of predrawn art. A drawing is fastened onto the tablet's surface, and its contours or key points are traced or touched with a pen or puck. With either tool, it's possible to see precisely where the penpoint is on the paper original. A mouse, which senses only motion and covers only part of the work area, simply can't do that. Tablets are so sensitive and precise that they make it easy to trace art raised as much as half an inch from the sensing surface.

Tablet pens are held like ordinary pens or brushes, and they typically have a side-mounted button used for mouselike clicking. Some artists prefer the pen's familiar feel over that of the mouse or puck. Tablet pucks handle like mice, and most are equipped with several buttons, usually four or more, that can be assigned special time-saving functions. Pens and pucks come in both corded and cordless models.

Software bundled with tablets or purchased separately offers some shortcut alternatives to pull-down menus by setting aside areas of the tablet that act as buttons to trigger programmed actions.

Summagraphics Bit Pad Plus

The Bit Pad Plus tablet has a 12-by-12-inch active area, a one-button penlike stylus, and a clip for holding original art onto the surface. It connects to the Apple Desktop Bus, as do the mouse and keyboard, and it can be used in conjunction with the mouse. It draws all the power it needs from the bus connection. Bundled software allows control of the relative scale between the screen area and tablet area, and customizes several other aspects of the interface.

Kurta I/S ADB Tablets

Kurta I/S ADB tablets are available in three sizes: 8-1/2-by-11, 12-by-12, and 12-by-17 inches. They come with a corded or cordless four-button puck or pen. They connect to the Apple Desktop Bus, drawing all necessary power from the bus connections, and they can be used in conjunction with the mouse. Dedicated spots along the margin of the tablet serve as programmable function keys. Some of these instant functions customize the tablet to the screen size, window size, or whatever working area size is comfortable for the artist.

TRACKBALLS

Trackballs are stationary devices consisting of a stable base with a free-rolling ball seated in a retaining cup. The ball is very smooth and can be as small as a golf ball or as large as a billiard ball. Two clicking buttons are positioned on the top face of the base, within relatively easy reach of the fingers. Using the palm or fingers, the artist can roll the ball in any direction, and the on-screen cursor travels accordingly. Like mice, trackballs are relative pointing devices — that is, they specify how much to move, rather than specifying exactly where to stop. Using accompanying software, the artist can alter the trackball's sensitivity to control how far the cursor moves in response to the ball's rolling.

The primary advantage of trackballs is that they consume very little desktop space. Desktop clutter doesn't stop a trackball from working, because the device doesn't need to go anywhere. Although some users prefer them, many find trackballs unwieldy for fine artwork, especially in drawing freehand paths. Typical, too, is the poor placement of the click buttons — usually they're much tool close to the ball itself, which forces the hand to "bunch up" unnaturally. If you're thinking of buying a trackball, be sure to test it thoroughly for yourself, on the type of work you intend to do with it, before you make any decisions to buy one.

Some commercially available trackballs are the **Turbo Trackball** by Asher, **Pro-Point** by Abaton, and **Turbo Mouse** by Kensington.

Sound and Music with MacRecorder

The Mac II has exciting audio capabilities. Although it takes a lot of memory to record and edit sound, Mac artists are using this medium more and more. MacRecorder from Farallon Computing is the latest advance in sound input for the Mac II. It has a built-in microphone as well as line connections, and it can save pieces as "SND" resources. With the accompanying *SoundEdit* software, the system can record and mix stereo sounds — for use in presentations, for start-up sounds, or for more advanced "desktop video production." The software also includes HyperSound for adding sampled sound to *HyperCard* stacks.

The "Products" appendix of this book lists some of the numerous music (and video) production applications now available for the Mac II.

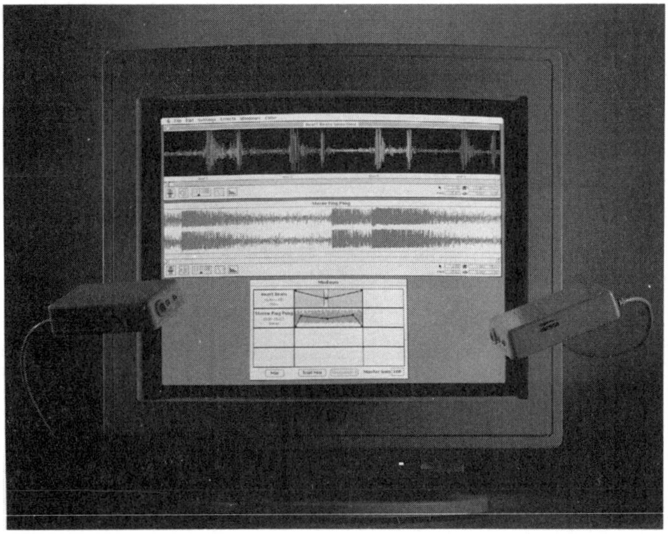

The MacRecorder sound system.

APPENDIX

Products

HARDWARE

Digitizing Systems

Apple Scanner
$1,799
Apple Computer, Inc.
20525 Mariani Avenue
Cupertino, CA 95014
(408) 996-1010
(408) 996-1010

Barneyscan
$8700
Barneyscan Corporation
1198 Tenth Street
Berkeley, CA 94710-9889
(415) 524-6648

ColorCapture Frame Grabber
$2,995
Data Translation, Inc.
100 Locke Drive
Marlboro, MA 01752-1192
(617) 481-3700

ColorFreeze 24
$1,999
Computer Friends
14250 N.W. Science Park Dr.
Portland, OR 92229
(503) 626-2291

Genlock Converter NTSC Video Board
$999
Julian Systems Inc.
2280 Bates Ave., Suite J
Concord, CA 94520
(415) 686-4400
(415) 686-4244

Imagizer System
$2,995
Comtrex Limited
PO Box 1450
El Toro, CA 92630
(714) 855-6600

Imapro Color Scanner
$13,895
Imapro US Inc.
PO Box 67
Suffern, NY 10901
(914) 368-2789

JetReader & MacImage
$1,300
Datacopy Corp.
1215 Terra Bella Ave
Mountain View, CA 94043
(800) 821-2898
(415) 965-7900

LoDOWN Image Scanner
$1,785
LoDOWN
10 Victor, Suite 600
Scotts Valley, CA 95066
(408) 438-7400

MacIntizer
$399
GTCO Corp.
7125 Riverwood Dr.
Columbia, MD 21046
(301) 381-6688

MacRecorder Sound Digitizer
$149
Farallon Computing, Inc.
2150 Kittredge Street
Berkeley, CA 94704
(415) 849-2331

MacScanPro-Panasonic Flatbed
$1,547
New Image Technology, Inc.
9701 Philidelphia Ct.
Lanham, MD 20706
(301) 731-2000

MacVision
$399
Koala Technologies
269 Mount Herman Road
Scotts Valley, CA 95066-4029
(408) 438-0946

Microtek MSF-300G/MSF-400G
$1,995/$3995
Microtek
16901 S. Western Avenue
Gardena, CA 90247
(213) 321-2121

ProViz Grey Scale/Color Video Digitizers
$1,095/1,695
Pixelogic, Inc.
800 W. Cummings Pk., Ste. 2900
(617) 938-7711

QuickCapture DT2255
$1,140
Data Translation, Inc.
100 Locke Drive
Marlboro, MA 01752-1192
(617) 481-3700

Sharp JX-300/JX-450 Color Scanners
$4995/$6,995
Sharp Electronics Corporation
Sharp Plaza
Mahwah, NJ 07430-2135
(800) 223-2121

ThunderScan
$249
Thunderware Inc.
21 Orinda Way
Orinda, CA 94563
(415) 254-6581

TrueCapture 324
$2,495
Raster Ops Corp.
10161 Bubb Road
Cupertino, CA 95014
(408) 446-4090
(408) 446-4168

TV Producer RGB-Pro
$1,500
Computer Friends
14250 N.W. Science Park Dr.
Portland, OR 92229
(503) 626-2291

TZ-3BWC Scanner
Truvel Corporation
8943 Fullbright Ave
Chatsworth, CA 91311
(818) 407-1031
(818) 407-0189

Film Recorders

Mirus Film Printer
$6,000
Mirus Corporation
445 S. San Antonio Road
Los Altos, CA 94022
(415) 949-5544

Montage FR1 Film Recorder
$5,995
Presentation Technologies, Inc.
743 N. Pastoria Avenue
Sunnyvale, CA 94086
(408) 749-1959

ProColor
$6,495
Matrix Instruments, inc.
1 Ramland Rd.
Orangeburg, NY 10962
(914) 365-0190

Lasergraphics Film Recorder (LFR)
$9,750
Lasergraphics
17671 Cowan Ave.
Irvine, CA 92714
(714) 660-9497
(714) 660-8042

Input Devices

Bit Pad Plus
$495
Summagraphics Corp
777 State St. Extension
Fairfield , CT 06430
(212) 751-9005

Kurta Graphics Tablet
$295
Kurta Corp.
4610 South 35th Street
Phoenix, AZ 85040
(602) 276-5533

Kurta Series One Graphics Tablets
$495-795-995
Kurta Corp.
4610 South 35th Street
Phoenix, AZ 85040
(602) 276-5533

NuVista VideoGraphics Adapter
$4,250
Truvision, Inc.
7351 Shadeland Station, Ste 100
Iniianapolis, IN 46256-3921
(317) 841-0332

ProPoint
$159.95
Abaton Technology Corp
48431 Milmount Drive
Fremont, CA 94538
(415) 683-2226

QuadLYNX Trackball and Turbo Trackball
$119.95
Asher Engineering
15115 Ramona Blvd.
Baldwin Park, CA 91706
(800) 824-3522
(818) 960-4893

Turbo Mouse
$169.95
Kensington Microware Ltd.
251 Park Ave. S.
New York, NY 10010
(800) 535-4242
(212) 475-5200

Mass Storage

AppleCD SC Drive
$1,199
Apple Computer, Inc.
20525 Mariani Avenue
Cupertino, CA 95014
(408) 996-1010

AppleShare File Server
$799
Apple Computer, Inc.
20525 Mariani Avenue
Cupertino, CA 95041
(408) 996-1010

Bernoulli Box II
$1,299-2,299
Iomega Corp.
1821 W. 4000 South
Roy, UT 84067
(800) 446-6342
(801) 778-3170

DataFrame Hard Disk Drives
SuperMac Technology
P.O. Box39075
Moutain View, CA 94039
(415) 964-8884

DataPak Drives
$1,775
Mass Micro Systems
550 Del Rey Avenue
Sunnyvale, CA 94086
(408) 522-1200

DirectDrives & MegaDrives
$549-1,499
Jasmine Technologies, Inc.
555 De Haro St.
San Francisco, CA 94107
(800) 347-3228

MacStack and PRO-Series Hard Drives
$695-4,095
CMS Enhancements, Inc.
1372 Valencia Ave.
Tustin, CA 92680
(714) 259-9555

Miscellaneous

Copy FX Color Effect Laser Paper
$12.95-25
Letraset, USA
40 Eisenhower Dr.
Paramus, NJ 07653
(201) 845-6100

Font/DA Juggler
$59.95
ALSoft, Inc.
PO Box 927
Spring, TX 77383-0927
(713) 353-4090

Monitors/Graphics Boards

Laserview Display Systems
$1,995-2,395
Sigma Designs, Inc.
46501 Landing Parkway
Fremont, CA 94538
(415) 770-0100

MegaScreen
$1,995
Micrographic Images Corp.
20954 Osborne Street
Canoga Park, CA 91304
(415) 770-0100

Mitsubishi XC-3310 33" Color Monitor
$5,900
Mitsubishi Electronics America
991 Knox Terrace
Torrance, CA 90502
(213) 515-3993

Mitsubishi XC-3710 37" Color Monitor
$7,599
Mitsubishi Electronics America
991 Knox Terrace
Torrance, CA 90502
(213) 515-3993

PCPC II
$4,995
Personal Computer Peripherals Corp.
6204 Benjamin Road
Tampa, FL 33634
(800) 622-2888
(813) 884-3092

Radius Full Page Display and Color Monitors
$1,995-2,395-4,295
Radius Incorporated
404 E. Plumeria Dr.
San Jose, CA 95134
(408) 434-1010

RasterOps Trinitron Color Monitors
$2,995-4,195
Raster Ops Corp.
10161 Bubb Road
Cupertino, CA 95014
(408) 446-4090
(408) 446-4168

Supermac Monitors
$1,495-2,495-3,695-4,995
Supermac Technology
295 N. Bernardo Ave.
Mountain View, CA 94043
(415) 964-8884

The Big Picture Z21/Z21 IQ
$2,495/$3,495
E-Machines, Inc.
9305 S. W. Gemini Dr.
Beaverton, OR 97005
(503) 646-6699

V-Screen
$1,150
New Image Technology, Inc.
9701 Philidelphia Ct.
Lanham, MD 20706
(301) 731-2000

Viking I/Viking 10
$1,995/$4,795
Moniterm Corp.
5740 Green Circle Dr.
Minnetonka, MN 55343
(612) 935-4151

ColorBoard 100
$1,795
Raster Ops Corp.
10161 Bubb Road
Cupertino, CA 95014
(408) 446-4090
(408) 446-4168

ColorBoard 104 & ColorDraw 24
$3,495
Raster Ops Corp.
10161 Bubb Road
Cupertino, CA 95014
(408) 446-4090
(408) 446-4168

Printers

4693D Color Image Printer
$8,490-11,500
Tektronics Inc.
P.O. Box 1000 MS 63-447
Wilsonville, OR 97070
(800) 224-5434
(503) 235-7202

Color Script 100 Color PostScript Thermal Transfer Printer
$24,995
QMS Incorporated
P.O. Box 81250
Mobile, AL 36689
(205) 633-4300

ImageWriter II
$595
Apple Computer, Inc.
20525 Mariani Ave.
Cupertino, CA 95014
(408) 996-1010

Kroy Design Studio
Kroy Sign Systems
14555 N. Hayden Rd.
Scottsdale, AZ 85260
(800) 521-4997
(602) 948-2222

Kroy Kolor Plus
$875
Kroy Sign Systems
14555 N. Hayden Road
Scottsdale, AZ 85260
(800) 521-4997
(602) 948-2222

LaserWriter Accelerator and Memory Expansion
$2,600
Olduvai Corporation
7520 Red Road, Suite A
South Miami, FL 33143
(305) 665-4665

LaserWriter II Laser Printers
$2,799-6,599
Apple Computer, Inc.
20525 Mariani Avenue
Cupertino, CA 95041
(408) 996-1010

Linotronic Imagesetters
Linotype Company
425 Oser Avenue
Hauppauge, NY 11788
(516) 434-2016

Paint Jet-Graphics Printer
$1,395
Hewlett-Packard Inc
P.O. Box 10301
Palo Alto, CA 94303-0890
(415) 857-1501

Personal LaserPrinter
$2,600
General Computer
215 First Street
Cambridge, MA 02142
(617) 492-5500

ScripTen
$4,795-5,295
Qume Corporation
2350 Qume Drive
San Jose, CA 95131
(800) 223-2479

Seiko CH-5312 Thermal Transfer
$12,495
Seiko Instruments USA, Inc. Graphic Devices and Systems Div.
1130 Ringwood Court
San Jose, CA 95131
(408) 943-9100

Shinko CHC-335 Thermal Transfer
$4,500
Computer Friends, Inc.
14250 N. W. Science Dr.
Portland, OR 97229
(503) 626-2291

VT600W 600 dpi Laser Printer
$13,500
Varityper
11 Mt. Pleasant Ave.
E. Hanover, NJ 07936
(201) 887-8000

Xerox 4020 Color Ink Jet Printer
$1,495
Xerox Corporation
101 Continental Blvd.
El Segundo, CA
(818) 351-2351

SOFTWARE

Clip Art

ClickArt Christian Images
$59.95
T/Maker Company
1973 Landings Drive
Mountain View, CA 94043
(415) 962-0195

ClickArt EPS Images
$129.95
T/Maker Company
1973 Landings Drive
Mountain View, CA 94043
(415) 962-0195

ClickArt Image Portfolios
$49.95
T/Maker Company
1973 Landings Drive
Mountain View, CA 94043
(415) 962-0195

Clip 3D
$99.99
Enabling Technologies, Inc.
600 S. Dearborn
Chicago, IL 60605
(312) 427-0386

DeskTop Art Designers Club - EPS Clip Art
$49.50 month
Dynamic Graphics, Inc.
6000 N. Forest Park Dr.
Peoria, IL 61614
(800) 255-8800
(309) 688-8800

Digit-Art, HotType, Art Room CD ROM, Dark Room CD ROM
Image Club Graphics
206, 2915-19th St. N.E.
Calgary, Alberta Canada
00272
(403) 250-1969

DrawArt Vol. 2
$79.95
Desktop Graphics
400 Country Drive, Suite H
Dover, DL 19901
(302) 736-9098

Gutenberg Set
$130
ImageWorld, Inc.
PO Box 10415
Eugene, OR 97440
(503) 485-0395

Images with Impact
$75
3G Graphics
11410 N.E. 124th Street, Suite 6155
Kirkland, WA 98034
(206) 823-8198

Japanese Clip Art
$79.95-149.95
Qualitas Trading Co./ Enzan-Hoshigumi
6907 Norfolk Road
Berkeley, CA 94705
(415) 848-8080

MacAtlas Pro Version
$199
MicroMaps
PO Box 757
Lambertville, NJ 08530
(609) 397-1611

MacGraphics Clip Art Collections
$125-325
GoldMind Publishing
12155 Magnolia Avenue, Suite #3-B
Riverside, CA 92503
(714) 785-8685

Post-Art
$49.95
Olduvai Corporation
7520 Red Road, Suite A
South Miami, FL 33143
(305) 665-4665

WetPaint
$3,959
Dubl-Click Software, Inc.
18201 Gresham St.
Northridge, CA 91325
(818) 349-2758

Clip Art CD ROM-Desktop
Photography Disc
$500 Comstock
30 Irving Place
New York, NY 10003
(212) 353-8600

Communications

MicroPhone II
$295
Software Ventures Corporation
2907 Claremont Ave., Ste. 220
Berkeley, CA 94705
(415) 644-3232

Red Ryder
$80
FreeSoft
150 Hickory Dr.
Beaver Falls, PA 15010
(412) 846-2700

MacLink Plus
$195 Dataviz, Inc.
16 Winfield St.
Norwalk, CT 06855
(203) 866-4944

TOPS Local Area Network
$249
Tops, A Sun Microsystems Co.
950 Marina Village Pkwy
Alameda, CA 94501
(800) 445-8677
(415) 769-8700

InBox
$125
Symantec Corp.
135 South Road
Bedford, MA 01730
(800) 808-6306
(617) 275-4800

Desk Accessories

Adobe Separator
Included with Illustrator 88
Adobe Systems, Inc.
1785 Charleston Road, P.O. Box 7900
Mountain View, CA 94039-7900
(415) 961-4400

Disk Tools Plus
$49.95
Electronic Arts
1820 Gaterway Dr.
San Mateo, CA 94404
(415) 571-7171

DiskTop
$49.95
CE Software
801 73rd St.
Des Moines, IA 50312
(515) 224-1995

QuickMail
$300
CE Software
801 73rd St.
Des Moines, IA 50312
(515) 224-1995

SmartScrap & The Clipper
$59.95
Solutions International
P.O. Box 989, 29 Main St.
Montpelier, VT 05662
(802) 229-0368

Tempo II
$99
Affinity Micro Systems
1050 Walnut St.
Boulder, CO 80302
(303) 442-4840

Desktop Publishing

Lighspeed Color Page Layout
System
$6,000
Lightspeed
47 Farnsworth Street
Boston, MA 02210
(617) 338-2173

MacTEX
$750
FTL Systems, Inc.
234 Elington Ave.
East Toronto, Ontario Canada 00415
(416) 487-2142

PageMaker 3.0
$495
Aldus Corporation
411 First Ave. South
Seattle, WA 98104
(206) 622-5500

Portfolio: Designs for Newsletters
$79.95
Aldus Corporation
411 First Ave. S., Suite 200
Seattle, WA 98104
(206) 622-5500

Quark XPress
$795
Quark, Inc.
2525 West Evans
Denver, CO 80219
(800) 543-7711
(303) 934-2211

Ready,Set,Go! 4.0
$495
Letraset, USA
40 Eisenhower Dr.
Paramus, NJ 07653
(201) 845-6100

Textures
$495
Addison-Wesley, Inc.
Route 128
Reading, MA 01867
(617) 944-3700

Fonts

Adobe Collector's Edition 1
$125
Adobe Systems, Inc.
1785 Charleston Road, P.O. Box 7900
Mountain View, CA 94039-7900
(415) 961-4400

Adobe Collector's Edition 2
$125
Adobe Systems, Inc.
1785 Charleston Road, P.O. Box 7900
Mountain View, CA 94039-7900
(415) 961-4400

ArtFonts
$99
Olduvai Corporation
7520 Red Road, Suite A
South Miami, FL 33143
(305) 665-4665

CG Type for the Macintosh
$149
Compugraphic Corporation
200 Ballardvalle St. MS 200-4-5H
Wilmington, MA 01887
(508) 658-5600

Fluent Laser Fonts
$69.95
CasadyWare, Inc.
P.O. Box 223779
Carmel, CA 93922
(408) 646-4660

LaserFonts
$34.95-44.95
Century Software, Inc.
2483 Hearst #175
Berkeley, CA 94709
(213) 829-4436

LaserPerfect Fonts
$295
Adobe Systems, Inc.
1870 Embarcadero Road
Palo Alto, CA 94303
(415) 961-4400

Logos On-Line
Software Complement 8
Pennsylvania Avenue
Matamoras, PA 18336
(717) 491-2492

PostScript Type Sampler
$53.95
MacTography
702 Twinbrook Parkway
Rockville, MD 20851
(301) 424-1357

Type Library Publishing Packs
$475
Adobe Systems, Inc.
1870 Embarcadero Road
Palo Alto, CA 94303
(415) 961-4400

World-Class Fonts
$3,959
Dubl-Click Software, Inc.
18201 Gresham St.
Northridge, CA 91325
(818) 349-2758

Fonts Music-MIDI
MidiCom MIDI Fonts
Coda Music Software
1401 E. 79th St
Bloomington, MN 55425-1126
(612) 854-1288
(612) 854-4631

Graphics - General

CalendarMaker
$49.95
CE Software
801 73rd St.
Des Moines, IA 50312
(515) 224-1995

Comic Strip Factory
$89.95
Foundation Publishing, Inc.
10301 Yellow Circle Dr.
Minneapolis, MN 55343

Easy Trace
$39.95
Heizer Software, Inc.
5120 Canal Court
Concord, CA 94521
(415) 943-7667

Innovative Design Templates
Letraset, USA
40 Eisenhower Dr.
Paramus, NJ 07653
(201) 845-6100

Pict-O-Graph
$175
Cricket Software
30 Valley Stream Parkway
Malvern, PA 19355
(215) 251-9890

Graphics - Animation

VideoWorks II
$295
MacroMind, Inc.
1028 W. Wolfram Street
Chicago, IL 60657
(312) 871-0987

Showcase F/X
$395
Aegis Development, Inc,
2115 Pico Boulevard
Santa Monica, CA 90405
(213) 392-9972

Graphics - 3D

Design Dimensions II
$1,595
Visual Information Inc.
16309 Doublegrove St.
La Puente, CA 91744
(818) 918-8834

Mac3D
$249
Challenger Software, Inc.
18340 Kedzie Ave
Homewood, IL 60430
(800) 858-9565
(312) 957-3475

MacTracer
$895
Ray Tracing Research Corporation
2516 Via Tejon, Suite 316
Palos Verdes Estates, CA 90274
(213) 373-2998

ModelShop
$495
Paracomp
123 Townsend Street, Suite 310
San Francisco, CA94107
(415) 543-3848

Pro 3D
Enabling Technologies, Inc.
600 S. Dearborn
Chicago, IL 60605
(312) 427-0386

Space Edit
$625
Abvent, Inc.
9903 Santa Monica Blvd.
Beverly Hills, CA 90212
(213) 659-5157

Super 3D/Super 3D enhanced
$295/$495
Silicon Beach Software, Inc.
9770 Carroll Center Rd, Suite J
San Diego, Ca 92126
(619) 695-6956

Swivel 3D
$395
Paracomp
123 Townsend Street, Suite 310
San Francisco, CA 94107
(415) 543-3848

VideoWorks 3D
MacroMind, Inc.
1028 W. Wolfram Street
Chicago, IL 60657
(312) 871-0987

Graphics - CAD

AutoCAD Reference Library
$197
Ventana Press
PO Box 2468
Chapel Hill, NC 27515
(919) 942-0220

EZ Draft
$1,995
Bridgeport Machines, Inc.
500 Lindley Street
Bridgeport, CT 06606
(617) 642-7200

MacDraft
$239
IDD, Inc.
2280 Bates Ave.
Concord, CA 94520
(415) 680-6818

MGMS: Professional CAD for Macintosh
$799
Micro CAD/CAM, Inc.
3230 Overland Ave.
Los Angeles, CA 90034
(818) 376-0008

MGMStation CAD and CAD/CAM
Micro CAD/CAM Inc.
5900 Sepulveda Boulevard
Van Nuys, CA 91411
(818) 376-0008

MiniCad
$495
Diehl Graphshot, Inc.
8370 Court Ave., Suite 202
Elliot City, MD 21043
(301) 461-9488

Versacad/Macintosh Edition
$1,995
Versacad Corp.
7372 Prince Drive
Huntington Beach, CA 92647
(714) 960-5826

Graphics - Drawing

Cricket Graph
$195
Cricket Software, Inc.
30 Valley Stream Parkway
Malvern, PA 19355
(215) 251-9890

Canvas 2.0
$299.95
Deneba Systems Inc.
7855 N.W. 12th St., Suite 202
Miami, FL 33126
(305) 594-6965

Cricket Draw
$295
Cricket Software, Inc.
30 Valley Stream Parkway
Malvern, PA 19355
(215) 251-9890

Draw It Again, Sam
$150
ABA Software, Inc.
P.O. Box 850
Frazer, PA 19355
(215) 644-3580

Drawing Table
$129.95
Broderbund Software Inc.
17 Paul Drive
San Rafael, CA 94903-2101
(800) 527-6263
(415) 492-3200

Dreams
$500
Innovative Data Design, Inc.
2280 Bates Avenue, Suite A
Concord, CA 94520
(415) 680-6818

FastForms! Construction Kit
$149
Shana Enterprises, Inc.
9704 54th Ave., Suite 200
Edmonton, Alberta Canada 00069
(403) 463-3330

MacDraw II
$395
Claris, Inc.
440 Clyde Ave.
Mountain View, CA 94043
(415) 962-8946

MapMaker
$295
Select Micro Systems, Inc.
40 Triangle Ctr.
Yorktown Heights, NY 10598
(914) 245-4670

Microsoft Chart
$125
Microsoft Corp.
16011 NE 36th Way P.O. Box 97017
Redmond, WA 98073
(206) 882-8088

DeskDraw
$129.95
Zedcor, Inc
4500 E. Speedway Tucson
Tucson, AZ 85712
(800) 482-4567
(602) 881-8101

Graphics - Paint

Cricket Paint
$149
Cricket Software, Inc.
40 Valley Stream Parkway
Malvern, PA 19355
(215) 251-9890

Crystal Paint
$49.95
Great Wave Software, Inc.
5353 Scotts Valley Dr.
Scotts Valley, CA 95066
(408) 438-1990

Desk Paint 2.0
$129.29
Zedcor, Inc
4500 E. Speedway Tuscon
Tucson, AZ 85712
(800) 482-4567
(602) 881-8101

FullPaint
$99.95
Ashton-Tate
20101 Hamilton Ave.
Torrance, CA 90502
(213) 329-8000

GraphicWorks
$149.95
Mindscape, Inc.
3444 Dundee Road
Northbrook, IL 60062
(800) 221-9884
(312) 480-7667

GraphistPaint II
$495
Aba Software
41 Great Valley Pkwy.
Malvern, PA 19355
(800) 234-0230
(215) 644-3580

MacCalligraphy
$175
Qualitas Trading Co
(made Enzan-Hoshigumi
6907 Norfolk Road
Berkeley, CA 94705
(415) 848-8080

MacPaint 2.0
$125
Claris, Inc.
440 Clyde Ave.
Mountain View, CA 94043
(415) 962-8946

Modern Artist 2.0
$199
Computer Friends, Inc.
14250 N.W. Science Park Dr.
Portland, OR 92229
(503) 626-2291

Pixel Paint/Pixel Paint Professional
$495-595
Supermac Software
P.O. Box 390725
Mountain View, CA 94039
(415) 964-8884

Photon Paint by MicroIllusions
$299.95
MicroIllusions
3885 Bohannon Dr.
Menlo Park, CA 94025-1001
(415) 329-0800

Studio/8
Electronic Arts
1820 Gateway Drive
San Mateo , CA 94404
(415) 571-7171

SuperPaint 2.0
$199.95
Silicon Beach Software, Inc.
9770 Carroll Center Rd, Suite J
San Diego, CA 92126
(619) 695-6956]

Graphics - PostScript

Adobe Illustrator 88
$495
Adobe Systems, Inc.
1870 Embarcadero Road
Palo Alto, CA 94303
(415) 961-4400

Freehand 2.0
$495
Aldus Corporation
411 First Ave. S., #200
Seattle, WA 98104
(206) 622-5500

LaserPaint/LaserPaint Color II
$495-595
LaserWare, Inc.
P.O. Box 668
San Rafael, CA 94915
(800) 453-9500
(415) 453-9500

Image Processing

Digital Darkroom
$395
Silicon Beach Software, Inc.
9770 Carroll Center Rd, Suite J
San Diego, CA 92126
(619) 695-6956

Image Studio
$495
Letraset, USA
40 Eisenhower Dr.
Paramus, NJ 07653
(201) 845-6100

PhotoMac
Avalon Development Group
1000 Massachusetts Ave.
Cambridge, MA 02138
(617) 868-3608
(617) 661-1405

Music - MIDI

Finale
$1,000
Coda Music Software
1401 E. 79th St
Bloomington, MN 55425-1126
(612) 854-1288
(612) 854-4631

Perceive - Music Training Course
$99.00
Coda Music Software
1401 E. 79th St
Bloomington, MN 55425-1126
(612) 854-1288
(612) 854-4631

Presentation Graphics

Aldus Persuasion
$495
Aldus Corp.
411 First Ave. South, Ste 200
Seattle, WA 98104
(206) 628 6671

Cricket Presents
$495
Cricket Software
30 Valley Stream Parkway
Malvern, PA 19355
(215) 251-9890

PowerPoint 2.0
$395
Forethought, Inc.
250 Sorbrante Way
Sunnyvale, CA 94086
(800) 622-9273

StandOut!
$495
Letraset, USA
40 Eisenhower Dr.
Paramus, NJ 07653
(201) 845-6100
(201) 845-7539

Specialty

ClipShare
$195
Olduvai Corporation
7520 Red Road, Suite A
South Miami, FL 33143
(305) 665-4665

ColorPrint
$29.95
I/O Design Corporation
P.O. Box 156
Exton, PA 19241
(800) 241-2122

DA Switcher
$39.95
Olduvai Corporation
7520 Red Road, Suite A
South Miami, FL 33143
(305) 665-4665

HFS Back-up
Personal Computer Peripherials Corp.
6204 Benjamin Rd.
Tampa, FL 33634
(800) 622-2888

Icon-it!
$39.95
Olduvai Corporation
7520 Red Road, Suite A
South Miami, FL 33143
(305) 665-4665

MCS
Yves Lempurer
2861 1B Canwood St.
Agoura Hills, CA 91301
(818) 991-6540

MenuFonts 2
$49
Beyond Inc.
6069 E. Grant Rd.
Tucson, AZ 85712
(602) 290-9790

MultiClip
$69
Olduvai Corporation
7520 Red Road, Suite A
South Miami, FL 33143
(305) 665-4665

SuperGlue
$89.95
Solutions International
29 Main Street P.O. Box 989
Montpelier, VT 05602
(802) 229-0368

Utilities

Copy II Mac
$39.95
Central Point Software
9700 SW Capital Hwy.
Portland, OR 97219
(503) 244-5782

Disk Express
$49.95
Alsoft, Inc P.O. Box 927
Springs, TX 77383
(713) 353-4090

HFS Navigator
$59.95
Symantec Corp., Think Technologies Division
135 South Rd.
Bedford, MA 01730
(800) 648-4465

MacTools
$39.95
Central Point Software
9700 SW Capital Hwy.
Portland, OR 97219
(503) 244-5782

DiskFit
$99.95
Supermac Technology, Inc.
295 N. Bernardo Ave.
Mountain View, CA 94043
(415) 964-8884

PictureBase
$69.95
Symmetry, Inc.
761 E. University Drive
Mesa, AZ 85203
(800) 624-2485
(602) 844-2199

SuperLaserSpool
$149.95
Supermac Technology, Inc.
295 N. Bernardo Ave.
Mountain View, CA 94043
(415) 964-8884

Graphidex
$124.95
BrainPower, Inc.
24009 Ventura Blvd.
Calabasas, CA 91302
(800) 345-0519
(818) 884-6911

The Curator
$139.95
Solutions International
29 Main Street , P.O. Box 989
Montpelier, VT 05602
(802) 229-0368

Stackware

AmandaStories
Voyager Company
2139 Manning Ave.
Los Angeles, CA 90025
(213) 474-0032

DTP Advisor
$89
Broderbund Software
17 Paul St.
San Rafael, CA 94903
(415) 492-3200

Focal Point II by TENpointO
$199.95
Mediagenic
3885 Bohannon Dr.
Menlo Park, CA 94025-1001
(415) 329-0800

HyperANIM
$150
Aegis Development, Inc.
2115 Pico Boulevard
Santa Monica, CA 90405
(213) 392-9972

HyperCard
$49.95
Apple Computer, Inc.
20525 Mariani Ave.
Cupertino , CA 95014
(408) 996-1010

The Louvre
Voyager Company
2139 Manning Ave.
Los Angeles, CA 90025
(213) 474-0032

The Macintosh Bible: Stax Edition!
$69.95
STAX!
8008 Shoal Creek Blvd.
Austin, TX 78758
(512) 467-4563
(512) 467-4564

The Verbum Stack
$15
Verbum, Inc
P.O. Box 15439
San Diego, CA 92041
(619) 463-9977

The Voyager VideoStack
Voyager Company
2139 Manning Ave.
Los Angeles, CA 90025
(213) 474-0032

Typography

Fontographer
$395
Altsys Corporation
P.O. Box 865410
Plano, TX 75086
(214) 424-4888

LetraStudio
$495
Letraset, USA
40 Eisenhower Dr.
Paramus, NJ 07653
(201) 845-6100

PosterMaker Plus with SmoothFonts
$59.95
Broderbund Software Inc.
17 Paul Drive
San Rafael, CA 94903-2101
(800) 527-6263
(415) 492-3200

Word Processing

Fullwrite Professional
$395
Ashton-Tate
20101 Hamilton Ave.
Torrance, CA 90502
(213) 329-8000

FullWrite Professional
$395
Ashton-Tate
20101 Hamilton Ave.
Torrance, CA 90502
(213) 329-8000

MacWrite
$125
Claris
4440 Clide Ave.
Mountain View, CA 94043
(415) 962-8946

Word
$395
Microsoft
16011 NE 36th Way
Redmond, WA 98073
(206) 882-8088

WordPerfect
$395
WordPerfect Corp.
1555 North Technology Way
Orem, UT 84057
(801) 225-5000

WriteNow 2.0
$195
T/Maker Co.
1973 Landings Dr.
Mountain View, CA 94043
(415) 962-0195

Appendix

Publications

Books - General

Adobe Illustrator: The Official Handbook for Designers
Tony Bove, Fred Davis & Cheryl Rhodes
$21.95
Bantam Electronic Publishing/ Bantam Books
666 Fifth Ave.
New York, NY 02742
212-765-6500

Design Principles for Desktop Publishers
Tom Lichty
$19.95
Scott, Foresman and Co
1900 E. Lake Ave
Glenview, Ill. 60025
(312) 729-3000

Desktop Publishing Type & Graphics
Deke McClelland & Danuloff
$29.95
Publishing Resources, Inc. HBJ
111 5th Ave
New York, NY 10103
(303) 442-1100

Desktop Publishing With Pagemaker
Fred Davis & John Barry with Martin Hall Dow Jones & Company
1818 Ridge Road
Homewood, Ill 60430
(800) 323-4560

Desktop Publishing with Pagemaker
Tony Bove & Cheryl Rhodes
$19.95
John Wiley & Sons
605 3rd Ave
New York, NY 10158

Edwards Brothers Graphic Arts Glossary
The Edwards Bros
P.O. Box 1007
Ann Arbor, MI 48106

Graphic Designers Production Handbook
Norman Sanders
$9.95
Hastings House Publishers

GraphicsMaster, Third Edition
Dean Phillip Lem
$57.50
Dean Lem Associates
P.O. Box 25920
Los Angeles, CA 90025

Hard Disk Management for the Macintosh
Bencion Calica & Charles Rubin
Hayden Books
P.O. Box PPI 10 Mulholland Dr.
Hasbrouck Heights, NJ 07604
(800) 428-7267

ImageWriter LQ Reference
$22.95
Addison-Wesley Publishing Co.
Route 128
Reading, MA 01867
(617) 944-3700

Inside Macintosh
$19.95-25.95
Addison-Wesley Publishing Co.
Route 128
Reading, MA 01867
(617) 944-3700

Looking Good in Print: A Guide to Basic Design for Desktop Publishing
Roger C. Parker
$26.45
Ventana Press
P.O. Box 2468
Chapel Hill, NC 27515
(919) 490-0062

Mac Insights
Lon Poole
$18.95
Microsoft Press
16011 N.E. 36th Way , P.O. Box 97017
Redmond, WA 98073-9717
(206) 882-8080

MacCats: 99 ways to paint a cat with MacPaint
$5.95
Scott Foresman and Co.
1900 E. Lake Ave. Glenview, IL 60025
(312) 729-3000

Macintosh Desktop Design; Macintosh Desktop Production
John Baxter
$18 each
The Baxter Group
P.O. Box 61672
Sunnyvale, CA 94086

Macintosh Desktop Typography
John Baxter
$20
The Baxter Group
P.O. Box 61672
Sunnyvale, CA 94086

Mastering Aldus Freehand
Deke McClelland & Craig Danuloff
$24.95
Dow Jones/Irwin
1818 Ridge Road
Homewood, Ill. 60430
(800) 323-4560

Mastering MacDraw
Gordon McComb
$18.95
Compute Publications
324 W. Wendover Ave. #200
Greensboro, NC 27408

Mastering Ready, Set, Go!
David Kater
$22.95
Sybex, Inc.
2021 Challenger Dr. #100
Alameda, CA 94501

Newsletter Publishing With Pagemaker
Fred Davis & John Barry with Martin Hall
Dow Jones/Irwin
1818 Ridge Road
Homewood, Ill. 60430
(800) 323-4560

PageMaker: Desktop Publishing on the Macintosh
$21.95
Scott, Foresman and Co.
1900 E. Lake Avenue
Glenview, Ill. 60025
(312) 729-3000

Pocket Pal: a Graphic Arts Production Handbook
Edited by Michael H. Bruno
$6.95
International Paper Company
77 West 45th St
International Paper Plaza
New York, NY 10036

PostScript Language Reference Manual
Adobe Systems Inc.
Addison-Wesley Publishing
Route 128
Reading, MA 01867
(617) 944-3700

PostScript Language Tutorial and Cookbook
Adobe Systems Inc.
Addison-Wesley Publishing
Route 128
Reading, MA 01867
(617) 944-3700

The Adobe Type Catalog
Adobe Systems, Inc.
$15
Adobe Systems, Inc.
P.O. Box 7900
Mountain View, CA 94039
(415) 961-4400

The Art of Desktop Publishing
Tony Bove & Cheryl Rhodes
Bantam Electronic Publishing/
Bantam Books
666 5th Ave
New York, NY 10103
(212) 765-6500

The Book of Fax
Ventana Press
PO Box 2468
Chapel Hill, NC 27515
(919) 942-0220

The Copy to Press Handbook: Preparing Words and Art for Print
Judy E. Pickens
$45
John Wiley & Sons
605 3rd Ave
New York, NY 10158

The Graphic Designer's Handbook, New Revised Edition
Alastair Campbell
$14.95
Running Press Book Publishers
125 South 22nd Street
Philadelphia, PA 19103
(800) 428-1111

The Macintosh Bible
Dale Coleman & Arthur Naiman
$21
Goldstein & Blair
Box 7635
Berkeley, CA 94707
(415) 524-4000

The MacTimes Clip-Art Directory and Guide
$49.95
MacTimes Press
P.O. Box 40-P
Franklin Square NY11010-0040
(516) 775-8841 EX.210

The Print Production Handbook
David Bann
$14.95
North Light/Writer's Digest Books
Cincinati, OH

The Well Connected Macintosh
Harcourt Brace Jovanovich, Publishers
Orlando, FL 32887
(303) 442-1100

Whale Song
$19.95
Beyond Words Publishing Company
112 Meleana Place
Honolulu, HA 96917

Zen And the Art of the Macintosh
Michael Green
$16.95
Running Press Book Publishers
125 South 22nd Street
Philadelphia, PA 19103
(800) 428-1111

Concise Guide to HyperTalk
Barry Shell
$9.95
Management Information Scource, Inc.
1107 N. W. 14th St., P.O. Box 5277
Portland OR 97209
(800) 626-8257

Books - HyperCard

HyperCard Developers Toolkit
APDA
$10.00
Apple Programmers and Developers Assn
290 S.W. 43rd St.
Renton, WA 98055
(206) 251-6548

HyperCard Script Language Guide
APDA
$18.50
Apple Programmers and Developers Assn
290 S.W. 43rd St.
Renton, WA 98055
(206) 251-6548

HyperCard Scripting
Jeff Stoddard
$16.95
Walking Shadow Library
P.O. Box 2092
Saratoga, CA 95071
(408) 534-7833

HyperCard Stack Design Guidelines
APDA
$16.75
Apple Programmers and Developers Assn
290 S.W. 43rd St.
Renton, WA 98055
(206) 251-6548

HyperCard VideoDisc Toolkit
APDA
$16.75
Apple Programmers and Developers Assn
290 S.W. 43rd St.
Renton, WA 98055
(206) 251-6548

HyperTalk Programming
Dan Schafer
$24.95
Hayden Books
P.O. Box PPI 10 Mulholland Dr.
Hasbrouck Heights, NJ 07604
(800) 428-7267

The Complete HyperCard Handbook
Danny Goodman
$29.95
Bantam Electronic Publishing/ Bantam Books
666 Fifth Ave.
New York, NY 02742
(212) 765-6500

Magazines

Desktop Presenter Magazine
$18 subscription
1032 Irving St. #442
San Francisco, CA 94122
(415) 566-4311
FAX (415) 566-4311

How (Ideas & Techniques in Graphic Design)
$33 subscription
RC Publications
6400 Goldsboro Rd.
Bethesda, MD 20817
(301) 229-6700

HyperMedia - The Guide to Interactive Media Production
Mix Publications
$5 per issue
Mix Publications Inc
6400 Hollis St. #12
Emeryville, CA 94608
(415) 653-3307

Personal Publishing
$30 subscription
The Renegade Co.
P.O. Box 390
Itasca, IL 60143
(212) 505-1641

Publish!
$39.90 subscription
PCW Communications
P.O. Box 55400
Boulder, CO 80322
(800) 525-0643

Reality Hackers
$30 subscription
High Frontiers
P.O. Box 40271, Dept. RH5
Berkeley, CA 94704
(415) 995-2606

Step-By-Step Graphics
$42 subscription
Dynamic Graphics
6000 N. Forest Park Dr.
P.O. Box 1901
Peoria, IL 61656-1901
(800) 255-8800

Verbum - Journal of Personal Computer Aesthetics
$28 subscription
Verbum, Inc.
P.O. Box 15439
San Diego, CA 92115
(619) 463-9977

Newsletters

Computer Publishing & Advertising Report
Communications Trends, Inc.
$312 Subscription
Communications Trends, Inc.
2 East Ave.
Larchmont, NY 10538
(914) 833-0600

Corporate Publishing: The Newsletter of Electronic Publishing Products and Management
InterConsult, Inc.
$195 Subscription
InterConsult Inc.
P.O. Box 1774
Cambridge, MA 02238
(800) 424-2377

Desktop Publishing
$195 Subscription
PCW Communications
501 Second St.
San Francisco, CA 94107
(415) 546-7722

MiSS ng PiEC s (Missing Pieces)
$25 Subscription
Robert Morgan
Box 2380
Julian, CA 92036

Seybold Report on Desktop Publishing
$192 Subscription
Seybold Publications, Inc.
428 E. Baltimore Pike, PO Box 644
Media, PA 19063
(215) 565-2480

Step-By-Step Electronic Design
$45 Subscription
Dynamic Graphics
6000 N. Forest Park Dr., P.O. Box 1901
Peoria, IL 61656-1901
(800) 255-8800

The Macintosh Business Letter
Robert R. Wiggins
$295 Subscription
MBL Publications
153 California Ave., Suite F213
Palo Alto, CA 94306-1926
(415) 322-0600

The Page
$49 Subscription
The Page
P.O. Box 14493
Chicago, Il 60614
(312) 549-4219

Training Programs - Video

Design Sense
$49.95
Invision, Inc.
60 Dedham Ave
Neeham , MA 02192
(617) 444-4060

On Becoming a Desktop Publisher
$54.45
The Computer Show Network
1641 N. First St., Suite 160
San Jose, CA 95122
(408) 437-8990

Step-By-Step Videos
Dynamic Graphics, Inc.
6000 N. Forest Park Dr.
Peoria, IL 61614-3592
(800) 255-8800

Think Like an Artist
$49.95
Invision, Inc.
60 Dedham Ave
Neeham, MA 02192
(617) 444-4060

State of the Art of Computer Animation
Odyssey Visual Design
$39.95
Pacific Arts Video
50 N. La Cienega
Beverly Hills, CA 90211
(800) 538-5856

Training Programs - Audio

MacTeach, HyperEasy, LearnMORE,
LearnWord, PageTutor, Learn 88,
LearnWorks, and Excellerate
$39.95-49.95
Personal Training Systems
PO Box 54240
San Jose, CA 95154
(408) 559-8635
FAX (408) 977-1166

Appendix

Organizations

Associations

National Association of Desktop Publishers
P.O. Box 508, Kenmore Station
Boston , MA 02215-9998
(617) 437-6472

Newsletter Association
1401 Wilson Blvd., Suite 403
Arlington, VA 22209

The American Institute of Graphic Artists
1706 Fifth Ave, Suite 202
San Diego, CA 92101
(619) 232-2888

The Newsletter Clearinghouse
44 West Market Street
Rhinebeck, NY 12572

Network Services

CompuServe
5000 Arlington Centre Blvd., P.O. Box 20212
Colombus, OH 43220
(800) 848-8199
(614) 457-0802
$39.95 Sign-Up

Delphi-General Videotex Corporation
3 Blackstone St.
Cambridge, MA 02139
(800) 544-4005
(617) 491-3393
$29.95 Sign-Up

MacNET-Connect Inc.
10101 Bubb Rd.
Cupertino, CA 95014
(800) 262-2638
$49.95 Sign-Up

MCI Mail
2000 M Street, NW
Washington, DC 20036
(800) 624-2255
$25.00 Sign-Up

The WELL -
Whole Earth Electronic Link
27 Gate Five Road
Sausalito, CA 94965
(415) 332-4335
(415) 332-6106
$8.00 Sign-Up

Education

Desktop Publishing Education Center
848 W. Eastman-Suite 205
Chicago, IL 60622

Dynamic Graphics Educational Foundation
6000 North Forest Park Dr.,
P.O. Box 1901
Peoria, IL 61656-1901

Electronic Directions
21 East Fourth St
New York, NY 10003

Services

Autographix
100 Fifth Avenue
Waltham, NY 02154
(800) 548-8558

Data Plot: Mac Graphics Plotting/ CAD Service
Data Plot, Inc.
911 Western Ave., #414
Seattle, WA 98104
(206) 624-9443

Aesthetics Technology – Macintosh Painting Service
Aesthetics Technology
365 Forest Suite 4E
Palo Alto, CA 94301
(415) 326-3936

User Groups

Berkeley MUG
1442-A Walnut St. #62
Berkeley, CA 94709
(415) 849-9114

Boston Computer Society
One Center Plaza
Boston, MA 02108
(617) 367-8080

MS Word User's Group
16011 NE 36th Way Box 9707
Redmond, VA 98073-9717

PageMaker Users Groups
411 First Avenue South, Suite 200
Seattle, WA 98104

Index

Italicized page numbers indicate gallery art.

Notes